Recollecting the Future

A View of Business, Technology, and Innovation in the Next 30 Years

Recollecting the Future

A View of Business, Technology, and Innovation in the Next 30 Years

Hugh B. Stewart

DOW JONES-IRWIN
Homewood, Illinois 60430

© RICHARD D. IRWIN, INC., 1989

Dow Jones-Irwin is a trademark of Dow Jones & Company.

Acquisitions editor: Susan Glinert Stevens, Ph.D.
Project editor: Karen Smith
Production manager: Carma W. Fazio
Jacket Design: Tim Kaage
Compositor: TCSystems, Inc.
Typeface: 11/13 Times Roman
Printer: Arcata Graphics/Kingsport

Library of Congress Cataloging-in-Publication Data

Stewart, Hugh B., 1916
    Recollecting the future.

  Bibliography: p.
    Includes index.
    1. Economic forecasting. 2. Business cycles.
3. Technological innovations   Economic aspects.
I. Title.
HB3730.S75 1989   338.5'443   88 16232
ISBN 1-55623-143-1

Printed in the United States of America

2 3 4 5 6 7 8 9 0 K 5 4 3 2 1 0 9 8

To Jean

PREFACE

"Stocks Plunge 508"
"Wall Street Panic"
"Stock Nose Dive"
"Market Meltdown"

Headlines following "Black Monday" echoed the same theme. But did Black Monday suggest another Great Depression? Did October 19, 1987, mark the end of an economically prosperous era?

For reasons to be explained in *Recollecting the Future*, we should indeed expect an economic growth "bust" lasting from 1988 to approximately 1995. Even the *average* GNP growth for that period can already be "recollected" within reasonable precise limits of uncertainty. Reasons for the growth bust can also be indicated—but not the more familiar ones.

Most significantly, 1987 should not be regarded only as the end of an era. That is not the theme of this book. Instead, equal emphasis is placed here on the emergence of a new growth boom—a boom that will have its genesis in the late 1990s. That boom will begin slowly but will gain momentum over the next two to three decades. It will be rooted in a burst of technology innovations and revolutionary new industries.

Why should *Recollecting the Future* be of interest to you? It focuses on business growths, not business busts. It discusses the ingredients of the long business-growth cycle. It indicates why and when the next boom will occur. And it identifies business- and career-growth opportunities we can expect in that boom. All of this is based on simple growth laws—growth laws that control our industry, our national economy, our national energy consumption, and our work force. It is an exciting story of the future based on nature's growth formulas.

But why "Recollecting the Future?"

Surprisingly enough, in many cases we *can* recollect the future—where it involves growth. We know, for example, that the weight of a new-born child will approximately quintuple in its first five years. Or, as a longer-range recollection, we can be quite confident that a two-fold weight increase will occur between ages 10 and 20—an average growth increase of 7 percent per year (actually, somewhat different for boys and girls). These examples of "recollecting the future" are based on well-established "trends" of growth patterns for children. They are reliable because we know that nature has ordained a child's weight to follow certain patterns. Nature has been equally unbending relative to other organic growth behaviors such as animal growths, vegetable growths, population growths in resource-limited environments, and even certain chemical reaction growths. Projections of growth behaviors for these cases, then, are not really *predictions*. Rather, we are remembering the past and are using that historical knowledge and data to know, relatively confidently, what will happen in the future.

Let's suppose for a moment that various industrial growths or our nation's economic growth could be found to follow well-defined growth patterns. Those growths, then, might also be amenable to recollections of the future. But if we are going to recollect, for example, the economic future, we will certainly be challenged to support those projections with sound reasons for our theories. Doing so is a goal of *Recollecting the Future*.

Recollecting the Future is essentially an application of trend analysis, just as projecting a child's weight growth is based on actuarial trend analyses. Let's draw an important distinction, though, between "trend analysis" as used here and the currently fashionable "trend spotting" used by a number of prestigious consulting firms. Trend analysis is firmly based on certain immutable growth laws of nature—growth laws that, for good reasons, might apply to a variety of industrial, societal, and economic growths as well as biological growths. Admittedly, growth behaviors are not always *precisely* repetitive. For example, the annual growth rate for children between ages 10 and 20 might be 7 percent on the average but vary between 6 and 8 percent for individual cases. Business and economic growths will also be found to show well-defined deviation limits about a mean expected growth. Those well-defined limits only lend greater confidence to our ability to recollect growth patterns of the future.

In contrast to trend analysis, trend spotting is simply a judgment of societal directions based on public opinion polls, newspaper research, or personal observations. Hence, trend *spotting* is subjective. The trend is only as reliable as the judgment of the spotter. That is not to demean the practice of trend spotting. At best, though, trend spotting involves the careful sifting and interpreting of news information by experts, or presumed experts. Trend *analysis*, on the other hand, is objective. It depends on natural growth laws. The uncompromising behavior of growth allows us to avoid the necessity of sifting and interpreting data.

Growth laws generally depend on factors outside our judgment.

As will be seen in the following chapters, a surprisingly large number of societal trends are subject to simple growth laws—or in some cases, growth laws with well-defined idiosyncrasies. Possibly the most interesting and useful societal growth trend is that of our economy. Indeed, you might be more than a little curious to know, for example, the economic trends you can expect in the next 10, 20, or 30 years. What average annual GNP growth rate should you expect between 1988 and 1998? What growth rate should you expect between 2000 and 2020?

Your curiosity might even extend to probable technology, business, or career directions that will be important to you, whether you are a business manager, a business merchant, a career planner, or just a thoughtful person. What dramatic new technology directions should you expect in the next 10 or 20 years? How can your business prepare for these directions? What career planning should you be doing?

Recollecting the Future is unique, though, in at least three respects:

- It uses over 130 years of historical data on *gross national energy consumption* (GNEC), not just gross national product (GNP), to establish patterns of growth for "societal industry" and "economic prosperity" in the U.S. (and the world).

- It uses the GNEC (and related GNP) historical growths to affirm the existence of a long economic wave which has an average period of about 55 years and a well-defined amplitude of variation, economic boom and bust periods are easily inferred.
- It directly relates technology-innovation surges, new-business growths, capital-equipment overexpansions, GNEC growth, and GNP growth in describing causes and effects of the long wave.

A primary goal of *Recollecting the Future* is to provide business people and general readers with a nontechnical digest of forecasting methods and conclusions that have frequently appeared only in technical journals and book. The concepts, methods and conclusions to be described include:

- technology innovation clustering
- S-growth adoption curves for new technologies
- energy/economic relationships
- capital overexpansion concepts
- the long economic wave

If you are not familiar with the terms, relax! *Recollecting the Future* will explain them for you, give concrete examples you can understand, and relate the concepts to situations you face in your own business and personal life.

The sometimes dry economic and mathematical background behind the subjects is omitted here, except for some information in the appendixes to satisfy the more mathematically curious readers. Your understanding of how you might be affected by the long economic wave should not be impaired by that omission.

To paraphrase the famous philosopher-scientist C. P. Snow, our society is evolving more and more into two cultures. In this case, one culture embraces the scholars and teachers who develop the theoretical background and models used in understanding our complicated industrial society. The other culture consists of business pragmatists who, unfortunately, are all too often unfamiliar with much of the interesting and potentially useful work coming from the other community. *Recollecting the Future* will allow you, the business pragmatist, to recognize, appreciate, and utilize more effectively the important contributions coming from the intellectual culture.

Briefly, then, this book is written to help you in your business and personal life. It explains, in layperson terms, how basic technology innovations come in clusters, how these innovation clusters lead to a swarming of business growths, how that growth swarming creates a long economic wave, and how you can recognize and use the long wave in your own personal planning.

Are your ready to recollect the future? Chapter 1, "The Future as It Was," will first review how this sequence of events unfolded in the last 100 years.

Hugh B. Stewart

ACKNOWLEDGMENTS

The attempt to write a reader-friendly and informative book on the projectability of technology, business, and economic growths has been a formidable challenge. In that endeavor I am deeply appreciative of the excellent help I have had.

Most notably, I am indebted to Bettie Youngs, a very successful author, counselor, and former univerity professor who has patiently guided me throughout my final version of *Recollecting the Future*. Dr. Youngs' sound advice on writing style, material reorganization, and even improved logic has gone far beyond just the contributions of an editor.

I am also indebted to John P. Howe, a materials and chemistry scientist and director previously associated with General Electric, Rockwell Inernational, General Atomic, and University of California at San Diego (UCSD). Dr. Howe offered many organizational recommendations on an earlier draft of the book, most of which were adopted.

Very helpful comments were also received from L. D. Mears, managing director of an electric utility development organization; Harry L. Munsinger, former UCSD professor and now an investment counselor; Robert H. Simon, former chemical engineer with General Electric and General Atomic; and Donald S. Frederick, former executive of Rohm and Haas.

At an earlier stage of the book, I imposed on Professor Gerhardt Mensch of Case Western Reserve University for his comments, which were most useful and were generally included in later versions of the book.

I am particularly indebted to my wife, Jean H. Stewart, who read the manuscript more times than I care to admit and offered many helpful suggestions from the point of view of a successful businesswoman in real estate.

The help and cooperation of Susan Glinert Stephens and Karen Smith of Dow Jones-Irwin and copyeditor Terry Brandau are also greatly appreciated. Their suggestions and editing comments have surely made the book more professional and readable.

Last, but certainly not least, Mary Jane McAndrew struggled through many changes in the manuscript with remarkable patience and dedication. Beyond her skills in word processing, she contributed through her preparation of data and graphics.

I hope my own contributions will reflect the excellent assistance I have had throughout this project.

H. B. S.

CONTENTS

PART 4

The Lessons from RECALL

Appendixes

PART 1

THE PATTERNS OF GROWTH

CHAPTER 1

THE FUTURE AS IT WAS

In 10 years, one of the most remarkable revolutions this country has ever seen will begin. It will *not* be a political revolution. It will be a revolution in technology, in economic growth, and in our social system.

What can we expect from this revolution in technology? In only 40 or 50 years, you or your children will think no more of taking a trip across the country than of traveling to a neighboring city. You will be able to watch a symphony concert in your own living room and the sound will compare to that reaching the fifth-row seats of the symphony hall. An entirely new frontier will be opened—a space frontier. You will experience a new "plastic era," that results in an almost complete substitution of synthetic materials for natural material resources. You will see new medicines and health care that add at least 10 years to the average American's life expectancy.

Beyond the technology revolution, what *economic* revolution can be expected? After five to ten years of economic doldrums, an economic growth will begin that will stagger your imagination—and that growth will continue for at least three decades. It will build on an industrial and business surge that results largely from the new technologies already indicated.

What is the *social* revolution? With an industrial surge of almost incredible proportions, the labor classes will share the luxuries previously reserved only for the wealthy. Large numbers of professional women will join men in the workplace. Startling new social programs will be implemented, some of which will benefit a rapidly growing number of elderly people.

Is this the future of tomorrow? No, that future will be even more exciting. This is "the future as it was"—a future projected from the depths of the depression in the 1930s. It was a future based on technologies yet to come, including:

- jet-air travel
- television and hi-fi sound systems
- the Apollo space program
- nylon, polyester, and acrylics
- antibiotics, new vaccines, and advanced clinical testing

Revolutions in technology and their consequences are not new. In fact, an equally dramatic future-as-it-was scenario could have been developed from the perspective of the 1880s. During this period another spectacular surge of major technology innovations occurred, including:

- automobiles
- electrification
- telephones
- photographic films

Those particular innovations of the 1880s (as well as the ones in the 1930s) were so influential in subsequent industrial and business growths that they will be referred to as "macroinnovations." The intent is to draw a clear distinction between them and the more popularly discussed "innovations."

Recollecting the Future is an account of how technologies, businesses, the national economy, and job opportunities grow— and how we can project those growths. It is based on simple principles of growth behaviors. The growths of technologies and the national economy follow a surprisingly consistent pattern of evolution—a pattern of *successive revolutions*.

Recollecting the Future *describes those growth patterns—patterns that can allow you to project future growths.*

Why should you be interested in this exercise in prognostication? Because *Recollecting the Future* can be applied to your own personal and business interests. Purely as a matter of risk aversion, you should be interested in the timing and extent of an unfolding economic growth bust—a growth bust made more omi-

nous by the Crash of 1987. You should be interested in the timing
and extent of a growth boom and concerned about your business
and how it will grow (or decline) in this growth wave, which is
projected to begin in 10 to 15 years. The growth of your own career
prospects—where opportunities will occur and when—should
interest you, and even if you are comfortable with your own career
choice, you may want to know how to guide your children. Clearly,
these concerns involve the future and the aim of *Recollecting the
Future* is to address these and other issues of the future.

The patterns of important growth trends will be described (and
quantified) in the first two parts of this book. Based on a knowledge
of those patterns, the last half of the book will launch excursions
into the future.

A subtle, but important, point should be recognized at the
outset. Most of our business and personal decisions are generally
made as *responses*—responses to events of the times. This book
also proposes approaches that allow decisions to be based on
responses, but in this case responses to recollections of the future.

As a first step toward recollecting patterns of the future, let's
examine the future as it was at two particularly exciting periods—
1900 and 1955.

The Future as Viewed from 1900

Our grandparents saw enormous progress between 1900 and
1930—progress in technology, the economy, and social well-being.
Let's assume your grandfather's birth coincided with the 1880
macroinnovation surge, and he was just entering his independent
working years in 1900 at the age of 20. He and his colleagues would
have shared the following characteristics:

- only 6 percent had completed high school
- less than 2 percent were destined to finish college
- 38 percent would become farmers
- 45 percent would become laborers
- only 17 percent would enter white-collar jobs

The wave of technology macroinnovations had been initiated
around 1880, but in 1900 your grandfather's home was still not
electrified. He probably had no telephone service—only 5 percent

of the homes enjoyed that luxury. Fewer than one in a thousand families owned such a novelty as the automobile, movie theatres were non-existent, and radios were as yet uninvented. The only source of national news was the newspaper or a magazine.

The 30-year growth of new industries between 1900 and 1930 was mindboggling. From the macroinnovations of the 1880s, new industries brought our grandparents homes that were illuminated electrically, local and long-distance telephone service, mass-produced automobiles, movie theatres, rayon fabrics—even aspirin tablets to soothe their headaches.

With that surge of business growth came an unparalleled prosperity that extended well into the 1920s.

What changes in social well-being resulted from the new technologies and industrial growths? Farm workers decreased from about 40 percent of the workforce in 1900 to 20 percent in 1930, resulting in a greater urbanization of U.S. society. The production assembly line was introduced in 1914 and changed the character of labor for, perhaps, 20 percent of the work force. The average U.S. citizen travelled 200 miles per year in 1900 (mostly by railroad). The same citizen traveled 1,000 miles in 1930 (mostly by automobile) as society became more mobile. By the 1920s, motion pictures and the radio were beginning to have important cultural effects on the general public.

As industrial manufacturing grew, the country's energy consumption (especially electricity usage) increased. The electrification of homes, industries, and commercial facilities brought an astounding 30-fold increase in electricity demands between 1900 and 1930. We consumed 20 times more petroleum fuel during that period, due largely to the popularity of automobiles. Clearly, the availability of energy resources was an important factor in economic growth and social well-being.

The growth burst of "high tech" industries in the 1900–1930 period created a demand for more technically trained workers familiar with automotive, electrical, electronic, and chemical technologies. Although 6 percent of teenagers completed high school in 1900, by 1930 that proportion had grown to about 30 percent. In that same period, the percentage of young adults completing college increased from 2 percent to 6 percent. The change in public attitude toward educational needs might have been the most significant social change of the early 1900s.

The Future as Viewed from 1955

Many of us have lived through the 1955–1985 period, but do not fully appreciate the remarkable progress during those years—progress that again included technology, the economy, and our social well-being. Assuming your birth coincided with the center of the 1935 macroinnovation surge, your friends in 1955 shared the following characteristics:

- 60 percent had completed high school
- almost 20 percent would finish college
- 5 percent would become farmers
- 55 percent would become laborers
- 40 percent would accept white-collar jobs

In spite of your general familiarity with them, the impact of the technology macroinnovations of the 1930s on your life was still insignificant in 1955. There were no commercial jet airliners in the United States (although the British had introduced some in 1952), automobiles were only beginning to feature some power-assisted equipment at that time, and superhighways were uncommon.

Stereo phonograph systems were not available in 1955. Black-and-white television sets began to appear in U.S. homes around 1950, and by 1955 50 percent of American homes had a television set. But color TV and the huge TV industry were still several years away. Less than 10 percent of homes had automatic clothes dryers, dishwashers, food disposals, and air-conditioning. Nylon was popular with women in 1955, but polyester fabrics were just being introduced.

The year 1955 marked the beginning of a revolution in industrial and business growths based on macroinnovations that originated in the 1930s.

Air travel, as measured in passenger miles, increased more than 10-fold between 1955 and 1985, and automobile travel tripled. The television industry blossomed into a tremendous money machine, not only through its manufacturing enterprises, but through the entertainment and commercial services that evolved. The manufacturing of new synthetic textiles increased an amazing 30-fold in only 30 years. Plastic materials (such as piping, cabinet veneers, and bottles), detergents, and substitutes for paper also showed enormous growths. Telephone communications quadrupled.

With that surge of business growth, still another boom in economic growth occurred.

The new burst of technology macroinnovations, followed by the surge in business and economic growth, brought about dramatic changes in our *social* well-being—changes we are still assimilating. The growth of automatic home appliances afforded revolutionary career opportunities to women. You might protest that home appliances are not sufficiently high technology to qualify as a macroinnovation, but the business and social consequences were sufficiently influential to so label them.

Superhighways, automobile improvements, and jet aircraft contributed to a more mobile society and to urban sprawl with its share of gridlock and travel frustrations. The pharmaceutical industry introduced wonder drugs that increased life expectancy substantially, putting pressures on our society for the care of the aged. "The Pill" had profound effects on our family planning, life styles and mores—our grandparents might frown on these effects.

The expansion in manufacturing and services brought on by the new industries and businesses resulted in another energy-growth surge. Electricity consumption and petroleum consumption increased. The electronic age demanded even more high-tech knowledge than the electrical age in the 1900–1930 era and our educational system (particularly the colleges and universities) responded to that demand. Our graduate schools became leaders in the world and the U.S. business community received the benefits.

How Progress Flourishes

Although only two periods of growth have been traced in this overview of the future as it was, the rest of this book will pursue a broader assessment of three general principles:

1. Technology, the economy, and social well-being grow in periodic surges.
2. Those growth behaviors can be defined with surprising precision and, therefore, can be put to use in recollecting the future.
3. In the long term, the growth behavior of our society is driven primarily by industrial technology, not government fiscal policies.

Very simply, Principle 1 says that business growth booms and busts have occurred and will continue to occur at regular intervals. Principle 2 claims that both the timing and the magnitude of these booms and busts can be forecast—a bold claim. Principle 3 observes that our current fascination with government tax and money-supply policies as a long-term growth stimulant might be misplaced.

Principle 1, the argument that technology and the economy grow in periodic surges, is not new. The Russian economist, Kondratieff, concluded in the 1920s that the economic growth of capitalistic countries had shown a long business cycle with a periodicity between 45 and 60 years. His conclusions were based on a study of price fluctuation data for commodities between 1780 and 1920. Those conclusions met considerable agnosticism because of the nature of the data and because they covered a period of only 140 years.

A better case for the long cycle was put forward in the 1930s by the Harvard economist, Professor Schumpeter. He authored a scholarly (and complicated) book on business cycles that offered the following explanations for a long business cycle:

- Periodic clusters of important technology innovations create periods of new business growth.
- The periodic surges of new business growths stimulate periods of strong economic growth.
- An ultimate saturation of these new business growths results in severe competition and profit losses that cause a decline in economic growth.

What does all this mean?

In industrialized societies, periods of prosperity result from the growth of economically important technology innovations—the economy flourishes as growth evolves, but erodes after growth saturates.

That sequence of events can hold important lessons for us. We all contribute to and profit from business growth surges—whether we are technologists, entrepreneurs, business managers, engineers, salespeople, or consumers. If we can understand and anticipate new technology, business, and economic growths, we can use this information in our planning and decision-making.

As a first step in recollecting the future, let's look further at Principle 1, the evidence for a long business cycle. Is there evidence that would support the existence of the following?

- periodic technology innovation surges
- periodic business growth surges
- periodic economic growth surges

Parts 1 and 2 of this book will give detailed answers to those questions. Here, we will examine briefly the historical evidence for the three kinds of surges.

The Evidence for Periodic Technology Innovation Surges

There have been four significant periods of macroinnovation surges around 1770, 1825, 1880, and 1935. In the 1770s, innovations in textile machinery paved the way for the Industrial Revolution that began in England. Around 1825, a new wave of macroinnovations included steelmaking processes and the railroad. Let's take a closer look at the 1880 and 1935 surge periods that are more familiar to us.

While some significant technology innovations can be found at almost any time in the late 1800s and early 1900s, the 10- or 20-year period around 1880 was a remarkably prolific one.

Bell's first telephone exchange was installed in Boston in 1877. Edison's Pearl Street electricity station went into operation in

1882, only three years after the demonstration of his incandescent light bulb. Daimler and Benz independently demonstrated automobiles in Germany in 1885. Edison's original phonograph was tested in 1877. Eastman's Kodak camera and roll film can be dated in 1884. Edison's kinetoscope, a motion picture device demonstrated in 1893, took advantage of Eastman's celluloid film. The Germans were introducing synthetic dyes (from their chemical industries) around the 1880s. Even the Remington typewriter was born in this period.

The airplane in 1903, wireless telegraphy in 1895, the electron tube in 1904, and the first radio transmission in 1920 were latecomers to the 1880 innovation wave. Still, the period between 1870 and 1890 was unusually productive.

We tend to identify all of the innovations of this period with famous people. The technology innovations of the 1930s were associated with the institutions or companies that sponsored them. For example, nylon and dacron came from DuPont. Television (in this country) came from RCA, while home appliances came from General Electric and Westinghouse. Jet aircraft, originally developed in Germany and England, were identified with Pratt and Whitney and Boeing in the United States. The electronic digital computer had its origin at the University of Pennsylvania and the Los Alamos National Laboratory; nuclear energy came from Argonne and Hanford. Xerography is usually associated with the Xerox Company. Actually, it was invented by an independent scientist and lawyer, Chester Carlson, and developed by Carlson and others at the Battelle Memorial Institute after 20 large companies rejected the idea as being too harebrained! The innovation was finally sold to Haloid Company, which ultimately became Xerox.

Two important points should be clear:

- *There is strong evidence, even without supporting statistical verifications, that the periods around 1880 and 1935 were marked by surges of technology innovations.*
- *The innovations of the 1880s were largely responsible for new industries, while those of the 1930s were largely responsible for resurgences of existing industries.*

The Evidence for Periodic Business-Growth Surges

The evidence for the existence of periodic business-growth surges is more overwhelming than that for technology-innovation surges. Our grandparents in 1900 were almost completely oblivious to electricity, telephones, radios, and even automobiles—but by 1930 these products were regarded as family necessities.

Giant industries were built in the 1900–1930 era based on macroinnovations involving electricity, telephones, automobiles, movies, and coal-tar chemicals.

Who would have thought in the late 1800s that garments would soon be colored by synthetic dyes coming from coal tar? Or that in 20 to 30 years they would light their homes with electric light bulbs, or telephone family friends a thousand miles away, or drive their children in the family automobile to a theatre to see a movie? The phenomenal growth of these and other new technologies during the 1900–1930 period changed our grandparents' way of life—even changed their careers. What briefly can be said about the rates of business growths in this era?

In 1900, less than 1 percent of our grandparents' friends could boast of electrified homes, gramophones, or family automobiles; and only a little more than 1 percent could claim telephones. None of their friends had seen a movie. Yet by 1910, about 10 percent of urban homes were electrified, and homeowners had telephone service and owned automobiles. Perhaps several folks who had visited the large cities could, almost apologetically, tell of seeing a movie at a nickelodeon—the name given to movie parlors in those days.

Although we read of the "Roaring 20s," business was roaring in the 1910–1920 period but not so feverishly after 1920. Henry Ford introduced and produced 10,000 Model T Fords in 1908. By 1911, production was over 50,000—and in 1915 it reached 500,000! People came to Detroit from all corners of the country to seek employment in the auto industry. When the assembly line was introduced in 1914, production was able to keep up with demand, and by 1920 approximately half the families in the United States owned automobiles. After 1920 the automobile business was primarily catching up with the straggler families and replacing older cars with new models. It is 1910–1920 that must be identified as the most frenzied growth period.

The same can be said about home electrification. The most vigorous growth in home electrification also occurred in the 1910–1920 period, with 50 percent of urban homes electrified by 1920. The peak of telephone growth occurred before 1915, and coal-tar chemicals peaked in the 1910–1920 period.

The movie industry, a novelty in the early 1900s, reached its peak growth in the 1920s. The pioneers of that industry (Zukor, Loew, Goldwyn, and DeMille) were involved as early as 1905 to 1915. Hollywood became the movie capital of the United States between 1911 and 1920. Certainly the period 1915–1925 could be regarded as a brisk period of growth for this economically and socially important macroinnovation.

By 1928, 90 percent of the eligible U.S. families owned automobiles and telephones. Almost 90 percent of urban homes were electrified in the late 1920s; and movies had already seen the largest growth era.

Business growths of the 1880 macroinnovation surge had clearly shown a business surge in the 1900–1930 period—a surge having a peak growth sometime between 1915 and 1925.

Although we are more directly familiar with the 1955–1985 business growth surge, we tend to overlook the signs of growth infancy, growth adolescence (fast growth), and growth maturity for new businesses in our own lifetime. The TV industry was getting underway in 1955 and probably reached its maximum growth from 1965 to 1975. Jet air travel also showed its strongest growth in those years. Synthetic fibers, home appliances, and automobile power equipment all experienced vigorous growths around 1970.

Once again a business growth surge resulted from the innovation surge of the 1930s. It seems probable that most of that growth has now reached a saturation. Most of our homes have automatic kitchen and laundry equipment and new factories for these products are unneeded. New factories for synthetic textiles, TV equipment, and jet airplanes are unneeded.

What does this mean to you? A new surge of macroinnovations is expected in the 1980–2000 period, and new business opportunities will arise in a new business surge beginning only 10

or 20 years from now. We might regard those who capitalized on
the 1900–1930 surge or the 1955–1985 surge as "lucky" or "vision-
ary." After completing this book, though, you should be able to
base your own business planning not on luck or vision, but on
recollecting the future.

The Evidence for Periodic Economic Growth Surges

Of the three questions on innovation, business, and economic
growth cycles, probably the last is the most crucial. To confirm a
long economic cycle, two criteria must be satisfied:

- A valid index of economic prosperity must be defined.
- The index must have a well-documented record extending
  over at least three or four cycles.

The fact that a strong business and economic growth occurred
between 1900 and 1930, and again between 1955 and 1985, is hardly
enough evidence to substantiate the existence of a repetitive
economic wave having a periodicity of some 50 to 60 years.

To test the validity of a long economic wave, we must first
search for a valid indicator. At least four indicators might be
nominated:

- gross national product (GNP)
- gross national energy consumption (GNEC)
- employment statistics
- price indexes of consumer products

The United States has seen two long periods of prosperity
during this century, the 1900–1930 and the 1955–1985 periods. The
country also suffered one extended period of severe depression—
from approximately 1930 to 1940. Those facts are readily confirmed
from GNP, GNEC, and unemployment statistics. It is more
difficult, though, to trace economic trends before 1900.

By looking at the price indexes of various commodities, we
can see that records reach back at least 200 years. These records
were used by Kondratieff to claim the existence of a long economic
wave. But, that evidence has not been universally acclaimed for
several reasons. First, it is not obvious that prices are directly
related to GNP or economic well-being. Second, prices can be

strongly affected by other social disorders such as wars, cartels, boycotts, and pestilence.

How about employment statistics? Isn't the size and intensity of our work force some indication of our economic well-being? Employment levels do not take into consideration the manufacturing contribution of machines. More seriously, employment (or unemployment) statistics are not readily available before about 1900.

That leaves GNP and GNEC. Clearly GNP would provide the most direct measure of our economic prosperity—it is, after all, a measure of all the nation's end products being marketed. Unfortunately, GNP data are based largely on inferences before 1900. Gross national energy consumption is our last possibility.

Business growth in the last 150 to 200 years has, indeed, had a direct and profound effect on one of society's most fundamental resources—the total energy that our nation uses.

When improved housing designs attract new buyers, the home construction business grows and requires increased energy expenditure. When new home appliances attract new consumers, the appliance business grows and requires increased energy for manufacturing (as well as for use of the appliances). The same is true for automobiles, entertainment equipment, clothing, food preparation, and even services.

In most cases, significant technology innovations in consumer products have resulted in new consumer markets. New markets have required new manufacturing operations. And new manufacturing operations have required increased energy expenditure— energy to recover the necessary raw materials, energy to convert those materials into finished products, energy to build the manufacturing facilities and equipment—even energy to support the living requirements of the workers.

Hence, when our product manufacturing and businesses increase abnormally, our national energy consumption will increase abnormally. And, when manufacturing and business activities decrease, our national energy consumption can be expected to decrease. Despite this cause-effect relationship, GNEC has had surprisingly little attention as an economic indicator.

Gross national energy consumption is clearly a basic measure of our "societal industry"—where societal industry is defined in the broadest sense.

Can GNEC tell us about the vitality of our national industry? Is GNEC easily measured? Does GNEC growth show any evidence of boom and bust periods? Most of us are more accustomed to measuring prosperity and well-being by the gross national product. Both gross national energy consumption (GNEC) and gross national product (GNP) have certain weaknesses as absolute indicators of societal well-being—subjects that will be discussed in another chapter. Nevertheless, each of these indicators is useful and a strong correlation between the two exists over successive years—a crucial point.

GNEC can be measured quite easily and accurately by adding the energy-input contributions from all our fuel resources—firewood, coal, oil, natural gas, nuclear fission, hydroelectric, geothermal, and solar energy. Perhaps most significantly, data that date back to 1850 are available on all these fuel uses. Data on coal consumption are available back to 1800. Both the availability and unambiguity of GNEC data make it valuable for examining inferred national well-being over a long period of time—150 years.

Energy consumption data are also useful in tying together technology innovation trends, business growth, economic behavior, and the general welfare of our society. In fact, certain systematics of GNEC growth will provide the very basis for recollecting the future.

The GNEC Long Wave

Does the growth behavior of GNEC show any signs of growth surges? Each individual uses a certain continuing amount of energy simply for subsistence—for food, clothing, and shelter. As our living standards have improved, this *per capita* energy use has gradually increased. Larger houses, electric lighting, more transportation, and better community services all contribute to this increase. Our *overall* national energy consumption, GNEC, has also increased from year to year—partly because of our per capita energy increase—but also because of the large population increase since 1850. Hence, an underlying uniform or steady-state GNEC growth can be easily understood and defined.

Superimposed on this steady long-term GNEC growth is a clear indication of fluctuations or surges, reflecting increased societal industry in certain years or groups of years.

In general, the years that show surges in GNEC also show surges in GNP—they represent years of prosperity.

Month-to-month, or even year-to-year variations in GNEC or GNP can be rather erratic. However, when averaged over five to ten years, the short-term irregularities are minimized and longer-term trends can be recognized.

A remarkable observation comes from an examination of the longer-term GNEC behavior for the period from 1850 to 1985. When the year-to-year data points are compared to the smooth underlying curve approximating the long-range GNEC growth, the data points show periodic variations around the smooth curve. A preview of the wave-like deviations (for both GNEC and electrical energy) is shown in Figure 1–1.

FIGURE 1–1
GNEC and Electric Energy Surges from 1850 to 1985*

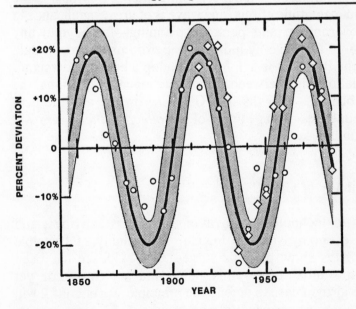

*○Total energy.
◇Electricity energy.

These long energy wave variations show a surprisingly regular periodicity of 50 to 60 years and an amplitude about the median growth curve of 15 to 25 percent. This means that GNEC might be 20 percent higher in a boom year than would normally be expected, but might be 20 percent lower in a bust year some 25 to 30 years later. Coal consumption data dating back to 1800 show the same periodic behavior, which suggests the long energy-consumption wave has a history of at least 185 years in the United States.

The prosperous years of 1900 to 1930 and 1955 to 1985, previously mentioned, both coincide with periods when GNEC was larger than the steady-state growth curve would have implied.

Another remarkable characteristic can be observed: Maximum deviations above the underlying steady growth curve actually occurred in 1915 and 1970. Since the deviation curve showed a turnaround at these years, a 15-year leading indicator signaled that a high-growth period was coming to an end. That leading indicator was also apparent in the earlier energy consumption data (GNEC and coal consumption) for the 19th century.

The GNEC (and coal consumption) data strongly support the existence and timing of a long economic wave. Obviously, the existence and magnitude of this long wave is of great significance to business, government, and personal planning—far beyond any interest simply to the energy industries. Before using growth data to recollect the future, it is helpful to develop a better understanding of the relationships between technology macroinnovations, the subsequent business growths, the GNEC growths, and the economic consequences. Parts 1 and 2 of *Recollecting the Future* will lay that groundwork.

The Projectability of GNEC

The growths of technology innovations, business activities, and our national economy strongly indicate the validity of Principle 1—these growths show periodic surges. Our evidence has been largely circumstantial up to this point and we have not yet developed an airtight case to defend the principle. Parts 1 and 2 will be devoted to a more proper trial of that case.

The systematic regularity of the GNEC growth behavior is, nevertheless, both exciting and suggestive.

The curve showing year-to-year deviations of GNEC from its underlying steady growth trend clearly identifies the existence of a long-wave behavior. Beyond its apparent confirmation of growth surges, the GNEC deviation curve suggests that behavior can be projected to the future. That was Principle 2, and if this conclusion is correct, it can be put to good use in planning our future.

Are we ready to use the simple GNEC growth behavior in our approach to recollecting the future? You might be tempted to compare the 1985–1995 phase of the GNEC deviation curve to that of the 1930–1940 phase, thereby expecting another Great Depression. That inference might be partially true, but there is much more to be learned about growth behaviors, including the relationship of GNEC and GNP, the bands of forecasting uncertainties, and how to interpret the growth behaviors for your personal and business use. Also, growth behaviors of businesses and job opportunities should be of more than casual interest.

Principle 2 has great promise. However, the full potential must wait for other observations on growth behavior.

The Causes of Societal Growth

What can be said about Principle 3? What are the basic causes of progress in our societal growth? A strong clue comes from an examination of societal growth in the highly industrialized countries, including our own.

Basic factors contributing to societal progress include:

- *a strong education system*
- *a competitive free enterprise system*
- *a good climate for R&D*
- *high work productivity*
- *availability of energy resources*
- *a mobility of society*
- *a minimal encumbrance by military requirements*

These factors play an important role in promoting industrial leadership. The United States achieved its position of world leadership between 1880 and 1970. It was not accidental that the U.S. public education system also flourished in the years between 1900 and 1930. Prior to 1900, only elementary school education was compulsory. Most states had also made high school education compulsory by the 1930s. Moreover, most states were developing college and university education systems with good research facilities.

The industrial R&D laboratory had its origin in the German chemical industries as early as the 1870s, and those companies led the chemical industry until 1920. Edison was the pioneer of industrial R&D in this country, founding his first laboratory around 1880. That laboratory was so successful in the 1880s and 1890s that it was imitated by General Electric, Westinghouse, AT&T, and a few other enterprising U.S. companies. Strong R&D has become the basis for hundreds (or thousands) of new businesses created in the United States.

High work productivity made the U.S. auto industry the world leader in 1910–1970. Mass production using standard parts was introduced by the Oldsmobile and Cadillac companies around 1905 and assembly-line operations were adopted by Henry Ford around 1915.

One other factor was of great importance in the U.S. industrial growth of the 1900–1930 period.

While much of Europe was involved in debilitating military confrontations, the United States avoided most of the World War I devastation.

The rise of the U.S. chemical industry owes much of its success to the demise of the German leadership in that industry following World War I. It is ironic that Japan and West Germany— the two most militant countries of World War II—have recently seized much of the industrial leadership. While Russia and the United States have channeled a large portion of their R&D into military research during the 1980s, a very small fraction of Japan's and West Germany's R&D has followed that course. The irony is compounded by Japan's dedication to educational and R&D excellence.

A more basic question at this phase of the long cycle is: What can be done to minimize the adversity of a long-wave economic decline and to assure an early and strong new business growth surge, especially in the face of the 1987 Crash? Two candidates for an economic stimulus are:

1. national fiscal policies and practices
2. national industrial policies and practices

A basic theme for *Recollecting the Future* is that national industrial policies and practices are more important for our *long-term* economic growth. Both government and industry must not lose sight of that long-range objective while responding to short-term fiscal problems. That concern will become more apparent as we learn more about the long economic wave.

Summary

Our history has been marked by periods of extraordinary technology innovations, strong business surges, temporarily prosperous economies, and even significant sociological shocks. Your grandparents born in 1880 saw enormous technology, business, and social changes in the 1900–1930 period—changes that had their genesis in the "high-tech" macroinnovations of the 1880s. Those born in 1935 faced an equally imposing period of change in the 1955–1985 period—changes that came from the wave of macroinnovations of the 1930s. Many of us can relate to this latter period—indeed, we are still learning to cope with cross-country jet lag, smog alerts, televised disasters, husband/wife work careers, space-age education demands, and health problems of an increasingly older population.

Evidence from our GNEC growth behavior and the 1987 stock market crash strongly suggests we are entering the winter of another long economic wave. The Crash of '87 only marks the transition from an economic autumn—where the GNEC deviation curve (in Figure 1–1) was already declining—to an economic winter. The approaching winter should not be interpreted as the result of the crash—the Crash of '87 is simply another sign that the winter is beginning. Throughout this book, the term *after the Crash of '87* emphasizes the dividing point between the economic autumn and the winter of the long GNEC wave. We will be interested not just in the *winter* after the crash, but also the approaching *spring* and *summer*.

Growth patterns of earlier cycles indicate that we can expect another cluster of technology macroinnovations in the 1980–2000 low-growth period to be the forerunner of a new economic expansion—an expansion that should begin in only 10 or 15 years! By understanding what we should expect, we can each profit from the future events. *Recollecting the Future* goes beyond the projection of an economic adversity—the subject of so many doom-and-gloom books and articles. *Recollecting the Future* tells us how to prepare for the much more important new economic boom. When will the boom commence? How will new business opportunities arise? What career opportunities will emerge? Answers will be a primary goal of succeeding chapters, especially those in the last two parts of the book.

As a first step, it is useful to see how things grow—how new businesses grow, how GNEC grows, how GNP grows, and how various social trends grow. The growth behaviors of our economic world are remarkably similar to the weight-growth behavior of our children! Before looking at typical business growths, we will look briefly at human weight growth patterns from birth to maturity. With that background, the growth characteristics of businesses and our economy will not seem so mysterious.

CHAPTER 2

YOUR CHILD'S GROWTH—
ITS IDIOSYNCRASIES
AND UNCERTAINTIES

Can we really recollect the future? Can we recollect the future growth of a new industry? Can we recollect the timing and magnitude of a future bust or boom in our economy? Yes, the key is **growth.**

Wherever growth *is involved, the opportunity exists for recollecting the future—either casually or methodically.*

Most of our recollections are casual or qualitative, but with very little effort they can be methodical and quantitative. Human growth, population growth, business growth, and national economic growth all follow simple growth laws—laws that anyone can learn to use advantageously.

Some parents carefully record the weight and height of their children from year to year. Do they make any special use of those records for health surveillance or diet control? Probably not.

The same is too often true of business growth records. Even when business growth records are kept, they are seldom used to their full benefit. If business volume this year exceeds that of last year, we are pleased—business is growing. If our business volume shows a decrease, we are alerted that something might be wrong. Can't we use growth results for more than just spot checks? The answer is an unqualified yes.

The significance and interpretation of growth behavior can be illustrated first by looking at a child's body-weight growth. The weight increase of a child is slow in the years just after birth, reaching a maximum during adolescent years, and again slowing down at maturity. Your business should show a similar type of growth behavior. Perhaps more importantly, the growths of industry sectors in which your business might participate (air travel, computer equipment, home video equipment, fast-food services) generally show even more distinct growth patterns. You can ask: Is my business involved in an industry that is at the early, intermediate, or final stage of growth? As you can predict how much growth to expect for a child, you can frequently forecast the growth expected for a particular new industrial sector, and therefore, your own business prospects.

Our overall national economic growth shares more similarities with the growth characteristics of a child's weight growth. Our nation's energy consumption (or GNEC) growth began slowly 200 years ago. The year-to-year GNEC growth gradually increased, is now reaching a maximum, and will show a declining growth rate in the next 100 years. But, the national GNEC growth (as well as GNP growth) has another interesting characteristic,—it shows growth booms and busts superimposed on the long-term GNEC (or GNP) growth. Surprisingly enough, the weight growth of a child also shows periods of booms and busts.

The overall growth behavior, the "secular" growth of a child, of your business, or of our national economy, is said to follow an S-growth pattern. Discussions of S-growths have been fashionable topics for authors, lecturers, and even some of our business colleagues. The S-curve is useful as a concept, but would not be particularly helpful for projecting detailed business growths, at least not in that form.

The "growth/ungrowth" curve can be exceedingly useful—with this curve the time for a new product line to reach a 90 percent growth level can frequently be estimated when only 5 percent of the growth has occurred.

The other characteristic growth behavior, the boom-and-bust pattern, is often referred to as the long wave—at least when applied to GNP or GNEC growth fluctuations. Again, the general principle of a superimposed growth fluctuation can be illustrated by the anomalies in a child's weight growth. S-growths and boom-and-bust cycles are not esoteric concepts assigned only to isolated business- or economic-growth characteristics. They are very common characteristics to be found in our everyday life—both at home and in our own business world.

To lay the groundwork for understanding the character of basic S-growth (or secular growth), weight-growth will first be examined in a fictitious world of "Logistica," inhabited by "Logisticans," where growth is not altered by any irregularities. To illustrate the boom-and-bust behavior, weight-growth will subsequently be examined in our earthly world—with all its idiosyncrasies. The Logistican weight-growth characteristics will have special applications in certain business and industrial growths, to be described in Chapter 3. The earthly weight-growth characteristics will have analogies to the GNEC and GNP growths, to be discussed in Chapters 4 and 5. With that distinction, let's look at the Logistican's weight growth behavior.

Growth in the World of Logistica

Logistica is a fictional world where parents are able to forecast with great precision at least one behavior pattern of their children —their growth.

In this simplistic and puristic world of Logistica, growth follows faithfully two very simple rules:

1. Growth behavior is the same for everyone, with full weight at maturity identified as unity.
2. The growth increase in any year is affected by (a) the growth already acquired, and (b) the amount yet to be acquired.

The first rule states that

> The weight of Logisticans (or ETs—extraterrestrials)
> is always measured in fractional units, F

For example, the weight is $F = 0.5$ at 50 percent of the mature or "asymptotic" weight, and $F = 1.0$ at full growth.

The second rule states that

> The *weight increase* in any year
> is proportional to $(F) \times (1 - F)$

More simply stated, the growth rate is proportional to both the fraction *grown* (F), and the fraction *ungrown* (1 − F), in any particular year. In infancy the first term, (F), is approximately zero, and therefore the weight growth per year is small. In adulthood, F is near unity and the second term, (1 − F), is approximately zero, so again the weight growth per year is small. The product of (F) and (1 − F) reaches a maximum when F = 0.5, that is, the weight gain in a year is greatest at the midpoint of growth.

For the mathematically curious reader, related mathematics can be found in Appendix A. For those interested only in business applications of growth, a few figures illustrating typical growth behaviors should be sufficient.

Figure 2–1 illustrates how growth proceeds in Logistica. It is assumed that the ultimate weight of a Logistican adult is 100 pounds, measured on our earthly weight scale, but F = 1 on their scale. It is also assumed that the Logistican birth weight is 5 pounds, F = 0.05, and the almost-mature weight at 20 years is 95 pounds, F = 0.95. At age 10, the weight is 50 pounds, F = 0.5.

FIGURE 2–1
Weight Growth of Individuals on Planet Logistica

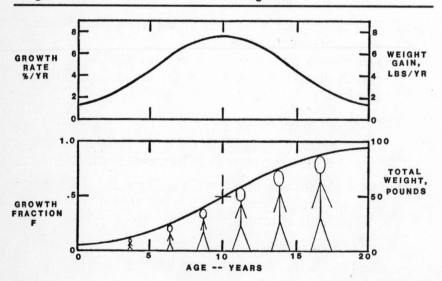

The weight gains in successive years are shown in the top of Figure 2–1. In the first year the Logistican gains only 1.5 pounds, and in the fourth year the weight gain is four pounds (measured on our earthly weight scale). At age 10, the gain is a more impressive 7.5 pounds. Thereafter the gains per year decline, with the gain again 1.5 pounds between 19 and 20.

The overall weight acquired is shown at the bottom of Figure 2–1. At age three, the total accumulated weight of the Logistican is a little over 10 pounds; at age 10 it is 50 pounds; and at age 17 it is almost 90 pounds. Finally, at age 20 it reaches 95 pounds (all measured on our earthly scale of weights). The resulting curve has the shape of an elongated "S" curve.

Mathematicians and futurists occasionally call this S-shaped curve a "logistic" growth curve or a "sigmoid" curve. Most frequently it is simply referred to as the S-curve.

The 23 Pound-Old Logistican

One interesting aspect of the Logisticans' growth is that every individual follows exactly the same growth pattern from year to year. The growth pattern is so common that we can imagine Logisticans identifying their age with their weight. A young Logistican, Alpha Epsilon, might describe himself as 23 pounds old (or 0.23 units old on the Logistican weight scale). An older Logistican, Zeta Omicron, might describe himself as 87 pounds old.

A second interesting aspect of the Logisticans' growth is that their growth/ungrowth (weight-grown/weight-yet-to-grow) ratio has a distinct symmetry to it. As a result, the growth/ungrowth ratio, or $F/(1 - F)$ ratio, leads to a straight line when plotted on a log-linear graph (a scale that increases by multiples of 10 on the vertical axis, and the more familiar linear scale on the horizontal axis). This is illustrated on Figure 2–2, where the Logistican's growth/ungrowth behavior is plotted against his age in years. If the growth follows a *pure* logistic growth, as defined by the mathematician, the plot will yield a perfectly straight line. The mathematical reasons for this are explained in Appendix A, but an understanding of the mathematics is unnecessary for its use.

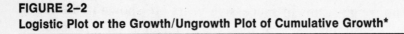

FIGURE 2–2
Logistic Plot or the Growth/Ungrowth Plot of Cumulative Growth*

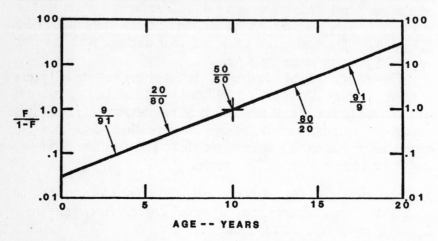

*Numerator shows weight grown; denominator shows weight to be grown. The plot uses a "log-linear" graph scale.

Why is this growth/ungrowth plot of interest? Chapter 3 will illustrate that some very common business growths follow this behavior almost religiously. Therefore, a business planner could have projected in 1905 (when less than 1 percent of households could boast of an automobile) that 50 percent of U.S. families would own autos between 1920 and 1925. The household adoption patterns of refrigerators, TV sets, and microwave ovens could have been anticipated. It can be determined whether the household adoption of a new product is following a pure growth pattern and more importantly, it is easy to project the future adoption pattern from the curve. The approach can also be used to see how rapidly a new technology will replace an old one—word processors versus typewriters, fiber optics versus copper-wire telephone lines, or genetically engineered insulin versus traditional sources. It goes beyond just general trend predictions; it allows specific percentage forecasts of new-product takeovers in future years.

Because of the convenience of the growth/ungrowth projection method, it will be used frequently throughout this book. Moreover, the procedure is being used more and more in business reports and even futurist articles. The important point to remember is:

A straight-line F/(1 − F) plot on a log-linear graph would produce the familiar S-shaped curve for F on a linear-linear graph.

One of the merits of the growth/ungrowth plot is that it can be used by anyone—whether mathematically inclined or not.

Growth in the World of Earth

Space travellers from Logistica visiting our planet Earth would be appalled at our growth idiosyncrasies. In fact, it may be surprising even to earthlings that most of nature's growths (such as the weight, stature, and population of organisms) show more irregularities than industrial growths (discussed in Chapter 3). Chapter 4 will show that one of our most important societal megatrends, gross national energy consumption, shares some of the irregularities of the earthly human weight growth.

The Logistican visitor would immediately note a number of intriguing anomalies in the weight-growth behavior of the earthlings, including:

- a difference between the growths of girls and boys
- a surprising spread of weights from person to person
- a significant deviation of the actual weight growth from that suggested by the pure logistic growth curve

The top curve in Figure 2–3 shows the smoothed logistic plot of the growth/ungrowth for earthly boys. The Logistican would note a particularly significant growth anomaly.

The actual growth/ungrowth points from year to year oscillate about the average underlying logistic growth.

This behavior shows distinct growth booms and busts at different age periods. The percentage deviations of the actual weights, relative to those suggested by the underlying logistic curves, are shown in the bottom of Figure 2–3. What does this mean?

Nature (on Earth) chooses to prescribe an anomalously low weight to earthlings at birth, possibly out of consideration to the

FIGURE 2–3
**A Growth/Ungrowth Logistic Plot for the Weight Growth of Boys and the
Percentage Deviation of the Actual Weights**

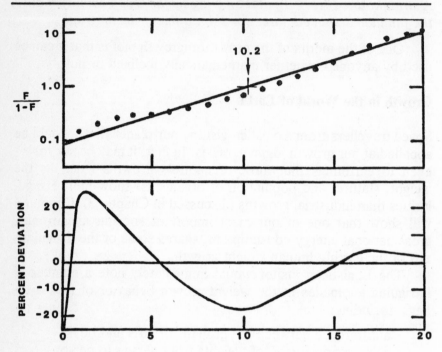

mother. In the first year of the child's growth, the weight level surges from an almost 50 percent deficit (relative to the logistic curve) to a surplus of over 20 percent—a remarkable growth surge. Growth then gradually declines, with the actual growth level crossing the logistic value at an age of about five years. This growth decline will continue for another six years.

The deviation curve shows, next, that a second remarkable growth surge (partly a catch-up surge) begins at the onset of adolescence. If adolescence is defined as the period of this second growth surge, it would appear that adolescence occurs between 11 and 17 years for boys, and about two years earlier for girls. With this surge in growth deviation added to the large growth normally resulting from logistic growth at this time, it is obvious why the blue-jeans industry finds such a lucrative market among teenage clientele. After adolescence, the weight deviation curve again returns to the underlying logistic growth behavior.

The synthesis of the underlying logistic growth curve and the superimposed deviation curve leads to an "oscillation-adjusted-logistic curve." This growth behavior is somewhat analogous to a "cycle-adjusted-logistic curve" that will be found to describe GNEC growth in another chapter.

The "Kitchen Impact" of Weight Growth

Growth requires energy. This principle applies to both biological and industrial growths.

In human weight growth, energy comes from food; in industrial growth, it comes from fuel resources.

Because of this analogy between human and industrial growth, the "kitchen impact" of children's growth deserves some special attention.

The kitchen-impact principle is illustrated in Figure 2–4. Curve A again shows the S-growth, or logistic-growth curve of body weight for an average growing boy. Curve B shows the weight gains per year for the successive years. Both curve A and curve B are shown here in fractional units—similar to the approach used by the Logisticans. Curve B indicates that the weight increase per year reaches a peak at an age of 10 years (as was also the case in Figure 2–1).

It is reasonable to expect larger boys to consume more food than smaller ones, and faster-growing boys to consume more food than slower-growing ones. Therefore,

The food consumption rate is "jointly proportional" to both growth size and growth rate.

Curve C is the product of curves A and B (curve A times curve B), which is a measure of the food-consumption rate for the growing boy. This curve is referred to as the *kitchen-impact* curve associated with growth.

The kitchen-impact curve peaks at about age 14, an age somewhat higher than the growth-rate peak. If the actual growth curve (the oscillation-adjusted-logistic curve) had been used in-

FIGURE 2–4
Illustration of the "Kitchen-Impact" Curve

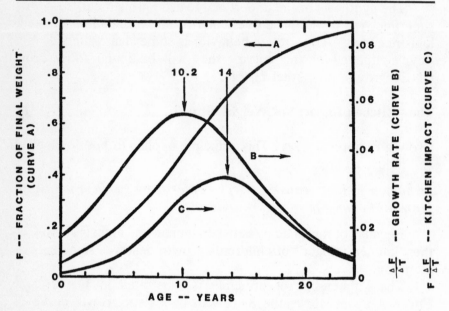

stead of the median logistic growth curve, the kitchen-impact curve probably would have peaked at 15 or 16 years. As any parent of teenagers will know, the kitchen-impact of growth is quite real at around 15.

Although the analysis used here may be somewhat simplistic, the principle is correct, whether applied to our biological or economic behavior. This illustration of the kitchen impact will be recalled later to explain some similar business-related effects.

Forecasts of Population Growth

By now you have learned about the S-growth curve, the growth/ ungrowth logistic curve, various systematic deviations from pure growth, and the kitchen-impact curve. Each of those principles will become more familiar in future chapters as we apply them to business and economic forecasting.

A major attraction of these principles is their usefulness for forecasting various growths related to our business interests—the growths of new technologies, new industries, new careers, GNEC, and GNP.

Growth curves can be useful to us only if they are reliable—or we know just how large an error they might produce. Demographers were among the earliest users of growth methods and their projections of population growth offer us a good opportunity to check the uncertainties of growth forecasting methods. For example, some population forecasts from 1925 allow us to see how large their errors were for projections over periods of 25 and 50 years. The errors associated with population forecasting are especially interesting since a large part of GNEC (and GNP) growth in the United States has come from population growth.

Probably the most important pioneer in the use of logistic-growth forecasts was biologist Raymond Pearl, who was a member of the Johns Hopkins University faculty in the early 1900s. He developed growth methods to describe the weight growth of various organisms, and applied his methods to the study of population growth of fruit flies in closed environments. The work subsequently led Pearl and an associate, Reed, to apply the methods to the projection of population growths of people in the United States and various other nations.

In 1949, the Atomic Energy Commission asked an engineering consultant, Palmer C. Putnam, to study maximum plausible world energy demands for the next 50 to 100 years. In the course of his studies, Putnam reviewed the population projections of Pearl and Reed relative to actual population data some 25 years later, as a test of the logistic forecasting techniques. Data are now available that allow comparisons some 50 years later.

What Errors Should We Expect?

Basically, Putnam concluded that logistic-growth projections were subject to large errors, at least when applied to a few countries, such as Germany and the Philippines. The projections were particularly poor for the less-developed countries. There a population explosion, due partly to increases in life expectancy, created growths far beyond those expected from growth curve extrapolations. Population growths are also significantly affected by wars (as in Germany), by pestilence, by famine and, perhaps, by new social conditions—including better medicine or the use of improved birth control measures.

In spite of these complications, the results of the population projections were reasonably good for industrialized countries—if an uncertainty of 25 percent over a 50-year period is accepted as reasonable. Certainly the application of the S-growth methods offered better results than straight extrapolations or guesses would have yielded. More importantly, Putnam's review—and an update of this review—can allow us to determine typical uncertainties we should expect for similar forecasts over periods of 25 and 50 years.

From Putnam's review, the errors in population projections can be identified for at least seven industrialized regions of the world:

- the United States
- the United Kingdom (including England and Scotland)
- Germany (including East and West Germany)
- France
- Italy
- Scandinavia (including Norway, Sweden, and Denmark)
- Japan

Results of those projections are discussed in greater detail in Appendix B.

Looking at the actual populations 25 and 50 years later (1950 and 1975), the average errors of the 1925 projections can be observed for these typical industrialized countries.

The implied average uncertainties are about 10 to 15 percent for the 25-year projection and 20 to 25 percent for the 50-year projection.

Population projections were much poorer for some of the developing and underdeveloped countries, as already mentioned. In spite of those special problems, one might expect logistic projections of future population growths, at least for industrialized nations, to be somewhat better for several reasons:

- The population levels are drawing closer to ultimate levels for the industrialized countries (i.e., further growths will be smaller).
- The levels of education and industrialization (which tend to stabilize population growth) have increased significantly in the last 50 years.
- The abrupt increases in life expectancy (which have the effect of increasing the number of living people) are now subsiding.

The population of the United States should be predictable for the next few decades within the following uncertainty bands (with a confidence level of at least 50 percent):

15 years	5 percent
25 years	10 percent
35 years	15 percent
45 years	20 percent

The estimated uncertainties for population-growth projections will impose at least one limitation on recollecting the future.

Clearly, the uncertainties of long-range (or secular) growth projections increase significantly with the forecasting time span. For that reason, most of the projections in this book will be limited to 35 years. With that limitation, it will be found that the population-related forecasts (such as GNEC and GNP) to be discussed in Part 3 will not be seriously impaired.

Summary of Growth Principles

Growth is characterized by a growth *rate* that is jointly proportional to a level already grown and the residual level yet to be grown. The growth curve, itself, has an elongated S-shape, beginning at a zero level and approaching some growth limit as an asymptote (i.e., the ultimate growth level). The shape of this logistic growth curve is uniquely defined by a growth rate parameter and the final (asymptotic) growth level. The applications of the growth equation to biological and population growth have a history of over 50 years.

The weight growth of earthly humans shows anomalous deviations from a pure logistic growth curve; but even those deviations yield interesting information about the growth characteristics of children. Since an asymptotic weight level of humans has been defined, within limits, by many generations of evolution, it is relatively easy for us to project the weight of children 5 years, 10 years or 15 years forward.

In contrast, the ultimate growth limit (or asymptotic level) of national populations cannot be defined so precisely and population-growth projections are less precise. However, experience with past population projections, based on logistic-growth methods, allows us to estimate the uncertainties we might expect over 25 and 50 year forecasts. Those uncertainties define a limit on recollecting the future, but projections up to 35 years are *not* seriously impaired.

The growth principles introduced in this chapter will find many interesting and valuable uses in succeeding chapters. As a first example, some relatively simple applications to business competition problems will be illustrated in Chapter 3. Applications to GNEC and GNP growths will be reserved for Chapters 4 and 5.

CHAPTER 3

YOUR BUSINESS GROWTH—
HOW YOU CAN MEASURE IT

Industrial growths can be much more predictable than human weight and population growths. Is that surprising? Perhaps, but industrial growths generally follow remarkably precise patterns.

It is not uncommon for an industrial growth/ungrowth ratio (when properly measured and plotted) to show a straight-line character over an enormous growth range.

What does this mean to you? It suggests you can predict the future growth of a new industry—perhaps an industry affecting your business—after only a few percent of its growth has occurred. It is this special characteristic of growth that is responsible for the distinction between the S-curve as a general principle and the growth/ungrowth curve as a bonafide measurement tool—a tool that can easily be used by any of us.

Two examples will serve to illustrate the extraordinary behavior of industrial growth. One example involves the adoption of automobiles by U.S. families in the first quarter of this century. The other involves the more recent substitution of air travel for railroad travel.

In 1905, only five U.S. families in a thousand (0.5 percent) owned an automobile. Your grandfather might have known two or three families that owned a car. By 1910, only 30 families in 1,000, (3 percent) had become owners. Yet, on the basis of those limited growth statistics, a person familiar with the growth/ungrowth curve could have projected in 1905 that 50 percent of the families in the United States would own automobiles in only 15 to 20 years—a projection both remarkable and accurate. (See Section 2 of Appendix A for additional details.) Embryo automobile manufacturers, potential automobile distributors, car-service venturists, and youngsters with mechanical aptitudes would have relished that information in 1905 to 1910.

The growth of airline traffic relative to rail traffic offers another remarkable example. In 1930, only three out of a thousand passenger miles (0.3 percent) of public travel (air and rail) used airlines. In 1935, it was 17 per 1,000 (1.7 percent), and in 1940 it was about 4 percent. Yet, by 1940 the growth/ungrowth curve would have allowed a person to project that 50 percent of public travel would use airlines before 1960. Remember, jumbo aircraft, jet engines, and radar control were not even on the drawing boards in 1940. This bold projection in 1940 could have forewarned railroads of their impending demise in passenger traffic 20 years before it happened.

What could have been forecast about future career opportunities? In 1920, approximately 30 percent of the workforce was agricultural. Based on workforce statistical data between 1900 and 1920, anyone with a knowledge of growth/ungrowth methods could have determined that agricultural employment would be less than 5 percent before 1970—a 50-year projection!

Growth/ungrowth curves could also have allowed early quantitative projections for the electrification of homes, domestic adoption of telephones, petrochemical competition with coal-tar chemicals, synthetic textiles versus natural textiles, detergents versus soap, radio adoption, TV adoption, home appliance adoptions, the transistor takeover from vacuum tubes, and scores of other growths. Usually, these projections would have been possible when less than 10 percent of the growth had occurred.

Again, it is emphasized that the growth/ungrowth methodology allows explicit *growth projections—not just general trend curves.*

This capability to recollect the future should be of interest to all of us, whether business people, investors, career planners, or potential consumers. Imagine being able to answer the following:

- When will 50 percent of my manufacturing competitors be using robotics for a certain operation?

- When will 50 percent of the real-estate brokers in my city be using computerized searches of listings?
- What fraction of pharmaceuticals will come from genetic engineering in 20 years?
- When will 90 percent of all music recording be on compact discs (instead of LP records)?
- When will 50 percent of new homes be equipped with heat pumps?
- What profession will ensure me the best opportunities in 25 years?

This chapter will outline simple methods for answering questions such as these. Within the last 25 years useful and reliable methods have been developed to project business growths of new technologies. The methods are surprisingly simple, but are unfamiliar to a broad cross section of the business community. They can be valuable to goods- and service-producing companies—particularly those depending on new technologies. Most of this chapter will be devoted to explaining *how* these business-projection methods work.

The business applications to be discussed here are labeled:

- business imitation growths
- product substitution growths
- fractional adoption growths
- successive substitution growths

These four applications are responsive to the following two important questions frequently asked in business analyses:

1. If an aggressive company introduces a new idea, how quickly will other businesses copy the idea?
2. If a new product is introduced in the marketplace, how quickly will it displace the old one?

The first question relates to the "business imitation" application, the second to "product substitution." Each of these growths begins at a zero level and grows to a final fractional level of unity, or 100 percent. Hence, the question of guessing a final growth level, the asymptote, is avoided, which makes the application simple.

Industry Imitation of Innovative Leaders

Industry growth leans heavily on technology innovation.

That theme will be stressed again and again throughout this and subsequent chapters. It is no accident that industry leaders are frequently industry innovators. But industry innovators are usually imitated quickly by competitors. In an influential 1961 article, Edwin Mansfield of Carnegie Tech showed how the logistic growth method could be used to measure the rate of imitation or "catch-up" among businesses within an industry. Why is such a measurement possible?

Imitation growths follow the normal growth rule: The growth rate is affected by both (1) the growth already acquired, and (2) the growth yet to be acquired.

This growth principle (already introduced in the discussion of human growth) is even more rigorously obeyed by business growth. What does the principle mean relative to imitation growth? The larger the number of technology leaders, the more likely it is for other companies to follow the trend. After most of the companies have adopted the new technology, the rate of change will decline because fewer candidates for change are available.

If F is the fraction of companies that has already adopted (or imitated) the new technology, and $(1 - F)$ is the fraction that has not yet adopted it, the principle states that:

$$\frac{\text{The fraction of new adoptions}}{\text{Interval of time}} \text{ is proportional to } F \times (1 - F).$$

Whenever this growth law is obeyed, growth follows the simple S-curve and the growth/ungrowth plot can be applied.

In his study, Mansfield examined how 12 innovations in four different industries were adopted by successive companies. Largely because of the small sample sizes of industries involved (he selected only the major companies), the scatter of points about a logistic growth curve was rather large, but the trends generally followed the normal growth laws.

One of Mansfield's examples was the adoption pattern of by-product coke ovens by 12 competing coke companies.

The by-product coke oven was a technology innovation of special significance.

Why was this technology so important? It had a very direct impact on *two* high-growth industries around 1900 to 1930. Coke was originally made from coal by "boiling" off the various organic and non-organic chemicals. But after 1890, both the residual coke and the by-product distillation chemicals became important in our industrial society. Coke was used as a heat source and a reducing agent to remove the oxygen from iron ore in the iron smelting industry. Benzene became the most important by-product chemical since it was used to produce aniline dyes, pharmaceuticals, perfume, and industrial cleaning agents—all huge growth industries in the 1900–1930 business megatrend.

Prior to 1890, the demand for coke was already large because the iron and steel industry had seen a tremendous growth in the last half of the 19th century. The growth of the chemistry industry was beginning around 1890 (particularly with the growth of the aniline dye industry) and the availability of the base resource, benzene, was to become very important. Although benzene was already being distilled from coal in Europe, the first U.S. industrial distillation plant was built in 1893—a plant designed to produce *both* benzene and coke. The technology was economically attractive to steel companies since the value of the coke by-products was almost as large as that of the coke itself. One large steel company built its own by-product coke oven within eight years of this first plant, and after another three years, two more steel companies had followed. "Imitation growth" was underway.

Imitation growth can be easily illustrated by the adoption pattern of the by-product coke ovens.

The S-curve (or logistic curve) at the top of Figure 3–1 shows the imitation growth for the 12 companies adopting the by-product coke ovens. Shown below the S-curve are numbers indicating the companies that had adopted the new process at specific times, the "growth" numbers, while the numbers above the curve show the companies that had *not* yet adopted the process at those times, the "ungrowth" numbers. The number of adoptions divided by the total number of companies is the imitation fraction, F.

FIGURE 3–1

Imitation Growth in By-Product Coke Ovens Plotted as an S-Curve and a Growth/Ungrowth Curve

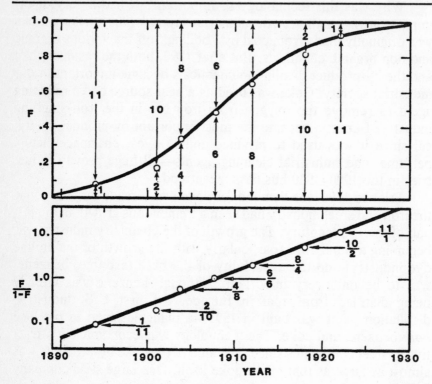

The bottom curve in Figure 3–1 illustrates the growth/ungrowth curve, $F/(1 - F)$ plotted on a log-linear scale. The fraction at each of the points represents the number of adopting companies, F, divided by the number of unadopting industries, $(1 - F)$. In this case, the fraction of adopting companies grew from 10 percent to 90 percent in 25 to 30 years. From his examination of the other business imitation cases, Mansfield found that the characteristic time for growth from 10 percent to 90 percent adoption was in the range of 10 to 30 years.

Mansfield pursued the analysis further. He reasoned that the growth rate of the adoption curve was related to the potential profitability of the process and the financial strengths of the companies. Other possible influences were examined, but were found to be statistically insignificant. It was shown that the imitation rate of companies adopting a leading company's innovation is positively influenced by the expected ROI (return on investment) of the innovation and negatively influenced by the capital expenditures required.

From the imitation logistic, an approach is available for answering the first question—how quickly "catch-up" companies will copy an innovator company.

How can we, as business people, make use of this methodology? Let's assume that we operate a supermarket. In the late 1970s and early 1980s, we might have checked, from year to year, how many supermarkets in our city had adopted the automatic scanning equipment for recording and summing consumer purchases. From a simple growth/ungrowth plot when only 10 percent of competitive stores had adopted this equipment, we could have forecast when 50 percent of our competitors would be using the equipment.

Let's assume we manage a commercial secretarial school. As most knowledgeable secretaries will confirm, this profession has been moving with phenomenal speed into high-technology. But, try to convince an inexperienced young job seeker, or even an experienced secretary who has been away from the profession for 10 years. With only a small effort, school promoters could learn from community businesses what fraction of secretaries in neighboring businesses have been required to use word processors, or any other modern equipment, over the last few years. By plotting the yes/no fraction from year to year, the school could indicate at what year 90 percent of secretaries will be required to imitate those skills.

The growth/ungrowth method can be used for a variety of business imitation studies. The method applies for both goods and services businesses—even for personal-career imitations.

Substitution Growth of Product Innovations

In 1971 Fisher and Pry of the General Electric Company applied the logistic growth approach to the competition between new and old products themselves (instead of the companies involved). Once again, substitution growths follow the normal growth rule:

The growth rate is affected by both (1) the growth already acquired, and (2) the growth yet to be acquired.

In this case, the principle tells us that the larger the number of new products in the total population (new plus old products), the more likely it is that other new products will be chosen over the older ones. But, after most of the population has adopted the new products, the rate of change declines because there is a smaller number of the older products to be replaced. In other words, the rate of substitutions is proportional to both F and (1 − F). That relationship tends to be particularly strong in technology substitutions and as a result, the growth/ungrowth behavior is remarkably regular.

The substitution growth behavior can be illustrated again by the by-product coke oven example. Now we will look at the product growths themselves, instead of the companies using the process. Data from the Encyclopedia Americana indicate that by 1903 some 10 percent of the coke produced in the United States came from by-product coke ovens; by 1917 this had increased to 50 percent; and by 1931 the fraction was 90 percent (using some modest interpolation of their actual data). By converting these data to growth/ungrowth, or F/(1 − F) values, and plotting them with the industry imitation data, as illustrated in Figure 3–2, the two growth curves are similar. However, the product substitution follows the company imitation curve by nine years.

Product substitution lags behind process imitation because of at least two factors:

- The 12 large companies did not immediately convert all their production to the new furnaces.
- Many of the smaller companies may have adopted the new process more slowly.

More importantly the substitution logistic affords another interesting and simple tool for business trend studies. In this role, the substitution logistic can also be an exceedingly useful tool for recollecting the future. The sample sizes in the product-substitution growth curve are usually quite large (sometimes millions of products per year), and this permits better statistical

FIGURE 3–2
Comparison of Substitution and Imitation Logistics for By-Product Coke*

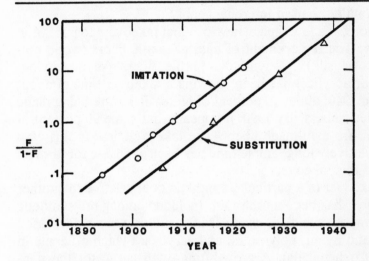

* △ Substitution logistics are measured by tons of output. ○ Imitation logistics are measured by the number of imitating companies.

accuracy than was available from the study of a few competing companies.

Fisher and Pry applied the substitution-growth logistic approach to 17 cases of product takeovers. In subsequent chapters and in Appendix D, the approach is applied to more than 40 new-technology growths. The data are generally observed to fit straight-line growth/ungrowth curves (on log-linear graphs) over some four decades of the $F/(1 - F)$ growths, from about 1 percent to 99 percent takeovers. This means that a production company involved in a new technology venture can forecast, at a very early stage of market penetration, how the introduction of the new technology can be expected to displace its predecessor.

Fisher and Pry have defined "takeover time" as the time for the substitution fraction, F, to grow from F = 10 percent to F = 90 percent, or for $F/(1 - F)$ to grow from 0.111 to 9.0. In the discussions here, a growth-time constant will usually be used, which will be defined as the time for $F/(1 - F)$ to grow from 0.1 to 10.0,—two decades of growth on the $F/(1 - F)$ curve. This growth constant is about 5 percent larger than the takeover time defined by Fisher and Pry. Since the *characteristic growth time* and the *takeover time* (as defined by Fisher and Pry) are so close, the terms will occasionally be used interchangeably.

Let's look at a few typical new-product takeovers to put this in perspective. The replacement of natural textile fibers (wool, cotton, linen, or silk) by synthetic textile fibers (rayon, nylon, polyester, or acrylics) has been showing a takeover time of about 50 years. In 1940, about 10 percent of all textiles were being made from synthetic fibers. By 1990, it appears that some 90 percent of textiles will use man-made fibers. The takeover time in this case has been relatively long; ample time has been available for farmers to adjust to this takeover.

The takeover of a particular synthetic fiber relative to another synthetic fiber has been more rapid. Included among the synthetic fibers are rayon (which is made from cellulosic, or wood-based materials) and nylon, polyesters, and acrylics, (which originate in various petrochemicals). A growth/ungrowth curve for the non-cellulosic versus cellulosic fibers shows a somewhat shorter takeover time—about 30 years. But, the takeover time between different types of petrochemical synthetic fibers has been even shorter. The manufacturers of petrochemical-based synthetic fibers must be very alert to changing technologies.

The takeover times for various electronic technologies are still more rapid. Manufacturers in this technology sector must be prepared for continuous R&D and prompt implementation of the new technologies.

The takeover time can also be a factor in retail stores and even in consumer decisions. The rapid takeover of the compact-disc audio technology can leave some record distributors with obsolete stocks and some audiophiles with obsolete equipment and records. Relative takeover times are important to all of us.

Although the variable, F, is clearly a takeover fraction that varies from zero to unity in all of the growth/ungrowth examples, some caution may still be necessary in defining that fraction. It is frequently found that a new product may not compete for 100 percent of the market held by the original product. For example, detergents will not replace face or bathsoap. These soap applications account for about 15 percent of the total market, so the competition in this case is only for 85 percent of the total market.

Fractional Adoption versus Product Substitution

New technology adoptions *by communities, homes, and systems also follow logistic growth laws.*

New technology is not always a substitution, it can be a new technology *adoption*. Examples include the early electrification of homes, the initial introduction of telephones, or the domestic adoption of radio or television. For these cases, the *fractional adoption* approach to growth measurement can be useful. Here the fractions of communities, households, or even commodities (such as automobiles) adopting a technology innovation can yield important measures of new technology growths. Examples include:

- fraction of urban and/or rural homes with electricity, plumbing, and sewage
- fraction of households with automobiles, radios, television, or selected appliances
- fraction of automobiles with automatic transmission or power brakes

Adoption growth also follows the normal growth rule.

The growth rate is affected by both (1) the growth already acquired, and (2) the growth yet to be acquired.

Here, the principle tells us that the larger the number of the people that have already adopted a new product, the larger the number of their neighbors that will want to "keep up" with them. After most of the families have adopted the new product, the rate of change will decline simply because there will be a fewer number of neighbors. Or, the rate of adoptions is jointly proportional to F and $(1 - F)$. As in the case of substitution growth, adoption growth is remarkably regular.

From the product-substitution and product-adoption laws, an approach is available for answering the second question: how quickly will new products squeeze old ones out of the marketplace?

Much can be learned about business-growth patterns over the last 100 years of business history by using both fractional-adoption and product-substitution data. More importantly, much can be learned about probable business-growth patterns in the future.

Logistic plots of historical data show that reasonable extrapolations for some 90 to 95 percent of substitutions or adoptions can generally be projected for subsequent years when only 5 to 10 percent of the growth has occurred. This characteristic of logistic growth methodology makes it useful for business planning.

Successive Fractional Substitutions

Successive *new technologies frequently replace prior new technologies*.

The previous applications of fractional substitution have involved only two systems: an existing technology and a single newcomer. Marchetti and his co-workers at the International Institute for Applied Systems Analysis (IIASA) in Austria, have extended the "binary" substitution theory to a "multivariate" theory where successive newcomers compete with the prior systems. Here, the growth of a newcomer is interrupted before it reaches maturity, but the growth to the point of interruption (as well as the subsequent decay) follows the usual logistic growth (and attrition) pattern.

Marchetti has described the application of the methodology to the competition of wood fuel versus coal versus oil versus natural gas versus nuclear energy. In this case, it is assumed that as successive new fuel technologies are introduced, each captures a growing fraction of the market previously dominated by former fuels.

Figure 3–3 illustrates an application of the approach to a simplified description of energy-fuel growths and declines in the United States from 1850 to 1980. In 1850, the total energy consumption rate in the United States was only 5 percent of that in 1980, and over 90 percent of the energy production was supplied by wood fuels, as shown in the figure. The use of coal fuel was becoming popular, reflecting the onset of the Industrial Revolution in the United States. As in England, the growth of iron production and the increasing use of steam engines for manufacturing and transportation accounted for much of the coal growth between 1850 and 1900. On the left side of the figure, the scale measures the fraction, F, of a particular fuel used divided by the fraction not including F, $(1 - F)$, or all *other* fuels. The scale on the right side shows the fraction, F, of the fuel used relative to *all* fuel use.

FIGURE 3–3
Fuel Growth Curves Based on the Multivariate Substitution Methodology of Marchetti

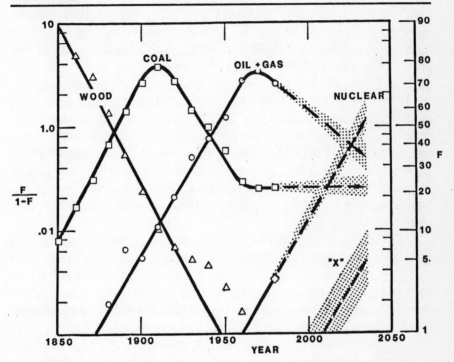

During the 1850–1900 period, national energy derived from coal use increased from less than 10 percent to about 70 percent (as can be seen from the figure), while the fraction of energy from wood fuel decreased from 90 percent to about 20 percent. This fractional growth in coal use faithfully followed a logistic growth behavior in spite of an "energy depression" that occurred between 1875 and 1900.

In the early 1900s, the use of oil and natural gas as energy resources was gaining importance. This was partly due to the convenience of oil products, especially for automobile fuel (gasoline), and partly because of the competitiveness of the fluid fuels with coal fuels for heating uses. The oil and natural-gas fuels have been combined in Figure 3–3 since they tend to be somewhat common in both their uses and their costs (per unit of heat energy).

Marchetti's analysis actually traced the growth of oil and natural gas separately.

As in the coal versus wood competition, the fluid-fuel versus coal competition again followed a typical substitution logistic growth, in spite of an overall energy depression that occurred approximately between 1930 and 1950. As the fractional use of the fluid fuels, oil, and natural gas, increased from about 10 to 70 percent between 1910 and 1960, the fractional use of coal gradually fell from 80 percent in 1910 to 20 percent in 1960. Since some uses of coal (for example those in the electricity-generation and steel-making industries) were not replaceable by the fluid fuels, the fractional use of coal fuel stabilized at about 20 percent in 1970. Beyond 1970, the figure shows a band of uncertainty for the future fractional use of coal. That subject will be revisited in Chapter 11, where the future of energy use and the economy will be recollected.

Returning to Figure 3–3, it can be seen that the growth of nuclear energy between 1960 and 1980 (together with the stabilization of the coal-use decline) has already caused the growth trend for fluid fuels to be reversed from a positive growth to a negative growth (a decay). More will be recollected about the future of solid (coal/nuclear) and fluid (oil/gas) fuel uses in Chapter 11.

Before leaving the subject of the successive growths of fuels, however, some interesting observations can be made about the time scale of fuel substitution growths.

Typically, the time for a new fuel substitution to grow from 1 to 50 percent is about 70 to 90 years. This is significantly longer than the takeover times typical for most other new-technology substitutions (which are 25 to 35 years).

This observation should provide a sobering note to those who suggest that nuclear energy growth should be or could be much faster. The figure also shows the projected growth of an unidentified exotic new energy resource, "X," that might be satellite-solar-energy or fusion-energy technology. Even if such an energy resource could account for 1 percent of our national energy production by 2000, substantial contributions from the new technology could not be expected before about 2070.

What's the Catch?

If there is a "catch," it applies more to organic growths (human weight and populations) than to business growths. Business growths respond almost slavishly to the growth laws of nature. In contrast, eons of evolution have resulted in significant aberrations in our earthly human growth behavior, such as the weight deviations from normal growth at birth and during adolescence that we discussed in the last chapter. Likewise, human ingenuity in agricultural, medical, and regrettably, military technologies have distorted normal population growths. While organic growths can frequently be described by a deviation pattern superimposed on an underlying secular (or logistic) growth, certain kinds of business growths (such as imitation, substitution, and adoption) obey "natural" growth laws directly and rigorously.

In a free competitive society, the rate of growth for a new technology almost always depends only on (1) the growth already acquired, and (2) the growth yet to be acquired.

If these business growth methods are so remarkable, so simple, and so useful, why haven't I heard of them before? The primary answer is that they have been evolving only over the last 20 years or so. Even where they have been identified and used, they have frequently appeared only in technical journals. As the growth/ungrowth principle becomes more generally recognized and understood, its adoption by institutional, business, and personal users might also be expected to follow a growth/ungrowth behavior.

Probably the most extensive use of the methodology has been by Marchetti and his co-workers at the Austrian-based think tank, the International Institute for Applied Systems Analysis (IIASA). Marchetti's earliest work focused on the takeover of various energy technologies in many industrialized countries and the world. In the last 15 years, the IIASA group has applied the methodology to hundreds of growth studies, including:

- the successive growths of alternative energy fuels (as already discussed)
- the growths of transportation technologies (particularly autos and paved highways)

- the growths of military technologies (the replacement of nuclear navy vessels for conventional ones)
- cultural growths (the vocabulary growth of a child, lifetime productivity of artists and scientists, and municipality growths)

It will become apparent throughout this book that the growth/ ungrowth principles can be useful to almost all of us. They can be used in our business planning, our investment planning, our career planning—even our home planning.

Summary of Business Applications

Interest here has focused primarily on how business growth is shaped by technology changes. In particular, we have examined four types of new business growths brought about by technology changes:

- imitation growths (where catch-up companies adopt a new process introduced by an industry leader)
- adoption growths (where a single new technology is adopted in the marketplace)
- substitution or takeover growths (where a second technology displaces an older first one)
- multivariate or successive takeover growths (where a third technology might displace a second one that has already displaced a first one).

In succeeding chapters these business-growth methods will be used over and over, to recollect both the past and the future.

It is important to recognize that these growth methods apply only to innovations that either offer a distinctly novel product where none existed before (such as the telephone, automobile, radio, television) or a significant improvement over prior products (such as polyester textiles, detergents, transistors, or color television). Less spectacular improvements can also be included (such as ballpoint pens, zip fasteners, water-base paints) where the new product might still represent a significant improvement over an existing one.

The methods do not apply to new product brands simply duplicating existing technology without an improvement. They do not apply to product improvements that could be classified as only cosmetic, such as white sidewall tires, gold-plated bath fixtures, or new dress fashions. When properly applied, though, the methods can be truly valuable business and investment planning tools.

It may also be useful at this point to put the product-substitution logistic in perspective relative to various long-term *generic* or *societal* growth patterns. These more general societal growths also show an S-shaped growth behavior, though usually over a much longer period of time. Examples include:

- total passenger-miles of travel
- total event-miles of telecommunications
- gross national energy consumption
- gross national product

These secular growths are difficult to project, partly because the ultimate levels of growth (the growth asymptotes) are difficult to identify and partly because they might have systematic growth anomalies, like human growth. However difficult, some of these growth projections can be so vitally important that a serious attempt to identify patterns of growth can be rewarded. That is particularly true for GNEC and GNP growth behaviors, which will be discussed in the next two chapters.

These overall growth curves generally follow an underlying S-growth behavior, while component contributors to the overall trends typically show growths and declines as they displace, or are displaced by, other technologies.

In energy growth, the growths and declines of wood fuel, coal fuel, and fluid fuels provide such an example. In passenger travel, the successive growths of railroads, autos, and airlines are illustrative. In telecommunications, the telegraph and telephone are good examples. In each of these, the substitution logistic methods can be useful to describe the competitions. The important point is that component technologies can take an increasing share of the market as they displace less efficient technologies, but they can subsequently take a declining share of the market as they are displaced by still more efficient technologies. Hence, these growth curves can rise and fall, instead of following the S-shaped trend. Nevertheless, the growth behaviors will be similar during the growth and declining stages.

Recollecting the Future will make frequent use of *component* growths to understand the rise of new industries. It will also make use of *overall* growths to understand the behavior of our economy. Chapters 4 and 5 will discuss the overall growths of GNEC and GNP. Part 2 (Chapters 6, 7, and 8) will show more clearly how component technology innovations and their resulting businesses grow—as well as the effects of those growths on GNEC and GNP growths. With that background, much can then be recollected about the *future* course of technology, business, and the economy (the subject of Part 3).

CHAPTER 4

NATIONAL ENERGY GROWTH—
ITS BOOMS AND BUSTS

As forecasters, most of us suffer from economic myopia—optimistic in years of prosperity and pessimistic in years of adversity. Even after the market crashes of 1929 and 1987, it was not unusual to find opinions that those setbacks were meaningless in the face of the otherwise sound economy. Are there other economic or businesss signals we might use?

The Commerce Department's quarterly summaries of gross national product (GNP) growths serve as useful indicators of economic behavior for the recent past. And, a variety of economic institutions offer growth projections for the near-term future. But what about the longer range? What GNP growth rate can we expect over the next 10, 20, or 30 years?

The average GNP growth over the last 50 years has been about 3 percent per year.

Economic pundits might tell us an annual GNP growth of 0 to 2 percent would be regarded as an indication of business stagnation—particularly since U.S. population growth is over 1 percent per year. An annual GNP growth between 2 and 4 percent would be considered mediocre; a growth of 4 to 6 percent would be welcomed as a sign of prosperity. These, however, are only general rules. Unusual GNP growths in a single year have been as low as −15 percent (during the Great Depression) and as high as +15 percent during World War II).

GNP is a popular indicator of well-being—we are familiar with its concept and aware of its importance. We are not as familiar with the meaning and significance of the gross national energy consumption (GNEC). This alternative indicator is rarely mentioned in our morning newspapers. We might recognize that a *GNP* growth of 3 percent per year is smaller than the government's target of 4 percent. But, we would be unfamiliar with the significance of a 1, 2, or 3 percent per year *GNEC* growth. Yet, the amount of GNEC growth from year to year is also an important measure of our industrial well-being.

GNEC growth is a key indicator of our national vitality.

What GNEC Growth Can Tell Us

Why should we, as business people, investors, or consumers, be interested in GNEC growth? The answer is quite simple. In years of a relatively large GNEC growth we can expect our factories to be humming, our airlines to be busy, our utilities to be using their full generating capacity—and we will be enjoying the widgets coming from those factories, the cross-country vacations by airline travel, and the full use of our electrical conveniences. However, in years with a weak GNEC growth (or decline), we can expect idle factories, idle airplanes, idle electricity generating equipment, and lower employment.

Historical variations in GNEC can tell us much about national vitality and prosperity in the past.

A reliable projection of GNEC can tell us much about national prosperity in the future.

This is the motivation for understanding energy-growth patterns. This book is not a discourse on energy that debates the merits of natural gas versus oil, or coal versus nuclear, or even solar versus fossil fuels. Energy is important here as a measure of our societal industry.

In the previous chapter, business and industry growth behaviors were discussed. Fundamental growth laws were described that could be used to measure and anticipate our business growths. In this chapter, GNEC growth behaviors will be examined. Again fundamental growth laws will be described—laws to assess and anticipate our overall GNEC (and consequently GNP) growths. These laws cannot tell us *precisely* what GNEC (or GNP) growth to expect in a particular year, but they do tell us what averages to expect over a period of five to ten years. In fact, the results can be surprisingly useful.

The description of business growth involved only one relatively simple growth law—the so-called *logistic* or S-growth law explained in the previous chapter. The description of GNEC (and GNP) growth will involve the combination of two kinds of growth:

1. An underlying, steady S-growth pattern (frequently called the *secular* growth).
2. A superimposed oscillatory or cyclic growth pattern (generally called a *long wave*).

This growth pattern is similar to the weight growth pattern of a child. Assuming such a GNEC growth pattern can be established, three interesting questions can be asked:

- Can we account for the GNEC growth behavior in boom years of the past?
- Can we account for the GNEC growth behavior in bust years of the past?
- Can we project the timing and magnitude of future GNEC booms and busts?

The answer in each case appears to be "yes."

- Yes, we can account for the timing and size of the GNEC booms during the 1900–1929 period and the 1955–1985 period.
- Yes, we can also account for the timing and size of the GNEC bust during the 1930–1940 period—the period of the Great Depression.
- Yes, we can even project the magnitude and duration of the GNEC growth bust following the Crash of '87—and more importantly, the pattern of an ensuing growth boom.

Sound incredible? To lend some credence to these claims, we must examine more carefully the history of GNEC growth. As a first step, let's review how our forefathers used energy.

Society's Food: Our Energy Fuels

We use fuel for heating, transportation, manufacturing, electricity generation, and many other purposes. Each cord of wood, each ton of coal, each barrel of oil contains a definable amount of energy that can be produced by burning.

We can identify our total national energy use by adding the energy contributions from each of the energy fuels we use: wood fuel, coal, oil, natural gas, solar, and nuclear. The U.S. government keeps national records on our year-to-year energy use. The United Nations, the Organization for Economic Cooperation and Development and other world-wide agencies keep international records on energy uses.

Much can be learned about a society by both the quantity and quality of energy it consumes.

Let's look at the average amount of energy a person uses per year from one country to another. Does it differ greatly? Does it suggest anything about the average prosperity of the people?

We might expect that the per-capita GNEC would be somewhat larger in highly industrialized countries when compared to less developed countries. GNEC data for seven of the developing Latin America countries (Brazil, Mexico, Argentina, Columbia, Peru, Venezuela, and Chile) provides a good opportunity for checking this assumption. The average per capita GNEC for these countries is about 15 percent that of the United States. And, what can be said about their relative prosperity? The same seven countries show an average per capita GNP around 20 percent—a percentage ratio very similar to that of the GNECs. Another good check can come from two important countries of Asia: India and China (representing more than one third of the world population). The per capita GNEC for these countries is still smaller, about 4 percent that of the United States—and the average per capita GNP is about 3 percent. In Chapter 1 it was indicated that the prosperity of the United States might be measured from *year to year* by GNEC as well as GNP. The examples here suggest that prosperity from *country to country* might also be revealed by GNEC as well as GNP.

A Historical Profile of Energy Use

The early industrialization patterns of the European and American countries can tell us something about the reasons for energy fuel uses—both the types and the amounts—during the last 150 years.

The earliest reasonably good data for total energy use in the United States indicate a consumption of about 2.3 quads/yr (quadrillion BTUs per year)* in 1850. With a population of 23 million at that time, the per-capita annual energy consumption was around 100 million BTU per person, which will be identified simply as 100 units per person in 1850. That per-capita energy consumption depended largely on the burning of wood, probably for home heating, in the United States, and it remained essentially constant until about 1875.

With the growth of industry—particularly the railroad industry—the U.S. per-capita energy consumption grew a modest 25 percent, to 125 units, by 1900. Then growth became more vigorous, reaching 200 units in 1925, 240 units in 1950, and 340 units in 1975. Today each person uses about 3.5 times as much energy as our forefathers used in 1850. Remember, our grandparents did not own color TV sets, automatic laundry equipment, or air conditioners— and, their grandparents did not have automobiles or electrified homes.

GNEC is the total energy used by all the people in the United States. It combines the per-capita energy use and the total number of people. Since the population increased from about 23 million in 1850 to 216 million in 1975 (about nine times), the total energy consumption increased 30 times between 1850 and 1975—about nine-fold due to population growth and a little more than three-fold due to per-capita energy consumption.

In spite of a dramatic increase in per-capita energy consumption over the period from 1850 to 1975, the larger part of the increase in U.S. GNEC arose because of population growth.

While the United States was primarily a consumer of wood fuel in 1850, the United Kingdom depended predominantly on coal for its energy. Based on fragmentary data for 1850, it appears that the per-capita energy consumption in the United Kingdom had reached about 75 units per person, and doubled, to about 150 units per person, in 1975. During that interval of time, the population

---

*The British Thermal Unit, BTU, is one type of energy unit frequently used. Since we are interested only in relative energy uses—from time to time, or country to country—the absolute magnitude of energy use is not important.

also doubled. Therefore, total energy consumption quadrupled in the United Kingdom—compared to the 30-fold increase in the United States.

Still more can be learned about these societies by examining why and how the GNEC changes occurred.

Around 1850, the population of the United States was shifting to the Midwest. Between 1840 and 1880, the midwestern states grew about five-fold, while growth only doubled in the rest of the country. As the population expanded westward, it was necessary to clear wooded areas for farmland. This abundance of cut wood was a natural resource for fuel, particularly to heat the new farm homes. There is evidence, as shown by the energy scientist Schurr and his coworkers, that this fuel resource was burned very inefficiently in the United States. In contrast, English homes and industry were dependent on coal fuel that was mined and then transported over larger distances for use. Consequently, the English utilized their fuel more efficiently, even in those early years.

A more quantitative analysis of the fuel consumption patterns in the United States and the United Kingdom shows that about 90 percent of the energy consumed in the United States came from wood fuel in 1850, while well over 50 percent of the energy consumed in the United Kingdom came from the superior coal fuel. A major consumer of the coal fuel in England was the rapidly growing industrial sector, since the Industrial Revolution began in the United Kingdom during the 1760—1790 period. In fact, some data from early statistical records of U.K. energy use suggest that *coal* consumption had already increased by 10 times during the 1780—1850 period. The increasing use of the steam engine in British industry was certainly a major factor in the growing use of coal.

From this history of energy use in the two countries, we can draw two important conclusions:

- The English used energy more frugally than the Americans.
- Energy growth in the United Kingdom, both quantity and quality, preceded that in the United States due to earlier industrialization.

Because wood fuel was more available in the United States, per-capita consumption of coal for fuel was only one sixth that in the United Kingdom in 1850, and was about one twentieth in 1800. Even when the Industrial Revolution reached the United States in the 1830–1860 period, wood fuel was still commonly used for steam engines. The use of coal as a primary fuel did not account for 50 percent of U.S. energy use until about 1880. This was surprisingly late, probably because of the abundance and convenience of wood fuel.

The Transportation Revolution

The arrival of the Industrial Revolution in the United States had an important impact on the economy here, but another change was of great significance.

The Transportation Revolution was an especially crucial factor in shaping the United States economy in the 19th century.

Due to the sheer size of the United States (a coast-to-coast width about 10 times that of the United Kingdom) and its rapid expansion westward, the railroad (and to some extent, the steamboat) industry affected energy and economic growth in a profound way. The Transportation Revolution, directly and indirectly, was probably responsible for most of the 25 percent increase in per-capita energy consumption that occurred between 1875 and 1900. It was also a major factor in the transition from a wood-fuel economy in 1850 to a predominantly coal-fuel economy in 1925.

Moreover, the large-scale introduction of automobile travel in the 1900–1925 period extended the Transportation Revolution into the 20th century. Much of the increase in per-capita energy consumption from 125 to 200 units per person between 1900 and 1925 was due to the growth of automobile travel, including its effect on the steel, automobile, and oil industries.

Energy use for transportation continued to grow after 1925. The introduction of heavier, faster cars, the availability of super-highways, and the increasing popularity of air travel were all responsible for part of the per-capita energy growth from 200 to 340 units per person between 1925 and 1975. Electricity generation also started to have a significant impact in that 50-year period.

The purpose of all this background information is to provide you with a vantage point to appreciate how energy consumption has grown—and will continue to grow—from year to year. This chapter hopes to develop enough understanding of GNEC growth to allow a reliable projection of this growth in future years. Based on that ability, we can also hope to forecast GNP as well as GNEC growth.

Let's turn to the subject of describing the growth behavior of both GNEC and electricity energy. First, we'll look at the underlying steady growth of GNEC, and the underlying steady growth of energy used for electricity generation.

The Underlying Steady or Secular Growth of Energy

GNEC in the United States has shown a steady growth from 1850 to 1985, partly due to an increase in per-capita energy use and partly due to a growing population.

The underlying steady growth—the growth curve with irregularities smoothed out—is referred to as the secular growth curve.

GNEC, you'll recall, can be measured by the heat energy from all fuel used in a particular year—the energy from firewood, coal, oil, natural gas, and even nuclear fuels. It is interesting to look at two distinct uses of fuel:

- the use for overall energy consumption (GNEC)
- that part of GNEC used for electricity generation

The latter use is becoming increasingly important as more of our overall energy in industrialized societies is consumed for electricity production.

Figure 4–1 illustrates the growth of total energy consumption, GNEC, from 1860 through 1985, as well as the growth of energy for electricity generation from 1910 through 1985. The scale used for energy consumption tends to obscure the tremendous growth of energy over the period shown. Total energy consumption from 1900 to 1985, for example, grew by almost a factor of 10. During that same 85-year period, the use of energy for electricity grew by an astounding factor of 100. To put this in perspective, your body weight would reach 800 pounds if it grew 100-fold over your lifetime.

The points in the figure show actual values at five-year

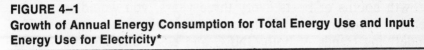

FIGURE 4–1
Growth of Annual Energy Consumption for Total Energy Use and Input Energy Use for Electricity*

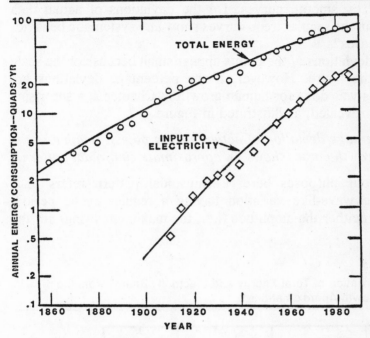

*Data points are shown at five-year intervals.

intervals for GNEC and for energy consumption for electricity generation. The lines represent the smooth underlying curves selected to fit the two growths. (Technical details on the selection of these growth curves can be found in Appendix A.) Basically, this graph shows that the number of points above the curve and below the curve all even out. This means that by looking at the curves, we can get an idea of growth projections and growth variations, such as boom and bust periods. Let's look first, then, for any indication of growth anomalies.

The Energy-Growth Booms and Busts

As a businessperson, you look for overall growth trends in your business and for any deviations from those trends. If you see growth booms or busts every three years, you would search for reasons—either to rectify the erratic behavior or to exploit it. The underlying trends of both GNEC and electricity growths can be described by smooth curves. Do the deviations of actual data points from the secular trend curves show any systematic behavior in these cases?

The deviations of the points appear small because of the scale used in the figure. However, if the percentage deviations are plotted, as was done for human growth in Chapter 2, a surprising pattern is revealed, as illustrated in Figure 4–2.

The percentage deviation of actual energy points, relative to the secular growth curve, shows an approximate sinusoidal pattern.

For our purposes here, a sinusoidal pattern refers to a systematic wave-like variation having a regular cyclic period. Actually, neither the amplitude (i.e., the maximum swing) nor the

FIGURE 4–2
Percent Deviation of Total Energy and Electricity Energy from their Logistic-Growth Approximations*

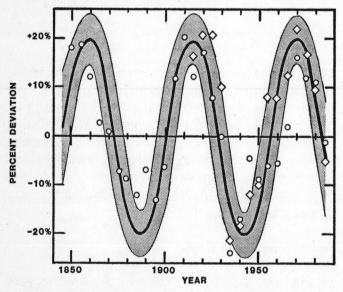

* O Total energy.   ◇ Electricity energy.

time period is perfectly regular in this case. But, over a particular period of 55 years, the deviation generally grows to a maximum of about 20 percent above the underlying curve, then to a minimum of about 20 percent below the smooth curve, and finally returns for another cycle. The shaded area in the figure indicates an uncertainty band from 15 to 25 percent for the amplitude and ±5 years for the timing. Within the uncertainty band of ±5 years indicated, the average period appears to be about 55 years, although in successive cycles the peak-to-peak period can be as little as 45 years and as large as 65 years. To illustrate the variance in amplitude, the peak deviation of actual energy consumption from the secular curve was as small as 15 percent in the years around 1885, yet as large as 25 percent in 1935. Nevertheless, the points fall remarkably well within the shaded area.

There is very strong evidence that both total-energy and electricity-energy consumption grow in surges, having regular cyclic variations about their long-range secular growths.

At this point it's worth reviewing what the long-wave curve in Figure 4–2 has told us and what it means to each of us. In some years energy consumption has been higher than we would have expected—in some years it has been lower. In 1915, and again in 1970, the curve says we used 20 percent more energy than a steady growth curve would have suggested. Stated another way, our industries worked 20 percent harder, our cars traveled 20 percent more, and our homes used 20 percent more energy appliances than we might normally have expected. In 1940, our industries, our automobiles, and our homes used 20 percent less energy than a steady growth would have suggested. In that year, the country was in the depths of the Great Depression.

Can we classify certain periods as energy-growth "boom" years and others as "bust" years? Yes, the energy growth was above normal from 1900 to 1930 and again from 1955 to 1985. Those years are described as boom years. The energy growth was below normal from 1930 to 1955 and those years can be described as bust years (or, more accurately, *energy-growth*-bust years).

Still other messages can come from the long energy wave. Between 1900 and 1915, for example, energy growth was above normal and was growing from year to year. This was the healthiest part of the long wave—the summertime of the energy wave. Had our grandfathers recognized this, they might have consciously oriented their business interests to the new growth businesses of that period—electrification, automobiles, and movies. By 1915, the growth was beginning to decline even though energy use was still above normal. This growth decline was a signal of the end of the energy summer. Had our grandfathers recognized this, they probably would have been cautious about overextending their growth investments, especially in the late 1920s.

Shortly before 1930, energy consumption fell below the level projected by the steady growth curve—the secular curve. Even more ominous was the fact that the deviation curve indicated the decline would continue for another 10 to 15 years. This was the bleakest part of the long wave—it was the winter of the energy wave and it brought with it the Great Depression. Presumably the years from 1985 to 1995 will bring another energy winter. A discussion of how to use this information, will be postponed until the last part of this book.

More on the Booms and Busts

U.S. data on GNEC growth between 1850 and 1985 have allowed us to identify a long GNEC wave including three growth booms and two growth busts. Are there data suggesting still earlier boom or bust periods? Although complete data on GNEC are not available for the years before 1850, data are available on U.S. coal production back to 1800. Again, the growth of coal consumption by itself shows a 50-to-60 year long cycle, even in those earlier years. In fact, the coal wave shows peaks in 1805 and 1855, with a low point in 1825. Energy-related data show the existence of a long energy wave covering 185 years—at least in the United States.

Do energy consumption data for other industrialized countries show the existence of the long energy wave? Yes, the Russian economist, Kondratieff, observed the long wave in coal production (in the English and French economies) dating back to 1830.

Existing data clearly support a long energy wave as an international phenomenon.

Why does a cyclic growth of energy consumption occur in the United States and other industrialized countries? This cyclic growth can be traced to certain business-growth characteristics, thereby lending further support to the validity of the long energy wave.

Recollecting the Future of Energy Growth

Will future GNEC growth depart significantly from its historical pattern? Such a departure would seem highly unlikely. Both the basic secular growth of energy and the boom-and-bust fluctuations superimposed on that growth are too strongly constrained by other causes to expect major disruptions in the near future. This presumption, based on historical fact, underlies the approach to recollecting the energy future.

A "cycle-adjusted-logistic" (CAL) growth can be constructed by superimposing the well-defined sinusoidal deviation curve on the equally well-defined underlying logistic growth curve.

Our first recollection of the future, is illustrated by Figure 4–3, where the boom-and-bust variations have been superimposed on the secular growth curves. The large energy growth from 1955 to 1985 can be clearly seen—although it is equally clear that the boom was coming to a close between 1980 and 1985. GNEC data from 1970 to 1985 are shown on an expanded scale in the inset (with a shaded area to represent a 6 percent uncertainty band). The detailed yearly points show some oscillation within the band, reflecting apparent shorter-term economic cycles that have occurred during the 13-year period. An energy increase during the 1984 economic surge, for example, has only corrected a temporarily large energy decline previously occurring between 1980 and 1983. The more remarkable observation is that the points all fall within the uncertainty band, lending some further credence to the cycle-adjusted-logistic energy growth. In fact, the indicated GNEC curve, and its estimated uncertainty, were originally developed prior to 1980.

The synthesized energy growth curve, shown in Figure 4–3, has an interesting and amusing side story. The curve was described to an audience of policy planners during a lecture in 1979. As can

FIGURE 4–3

Cycle-Adjusted-Logistic (CAL) Growth Curves for Energy Consumption with Extrapolations to 2030*

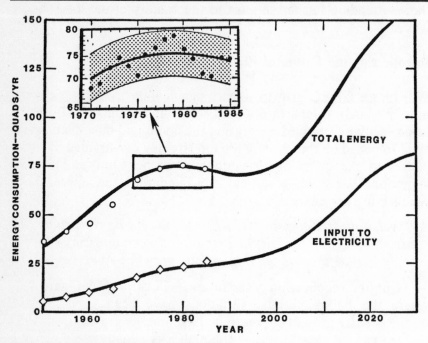

*Inset shows historical data from 1970 to 1985.

be seen from the inset, GNEC was still growing in 1979. Because of the implications of the projections on national energy planning, I was asked to visit Washington to discuss my forecasts and their interpretations. Following the conference, the Department of Energy leaders visited an economics institution to seek an independent view and were persuaded by the economists there that a decline, as projected, would be unlikely. Subsequently, the GNEC has declined by more than 5 percent.

"Very well," you say, "but the comments were on projected energy growths and were directed to an audience of energy-policy planners. What relevance has that to my interests as a business person, an investor, or a consumer?" Again, it is emphasized:

A growing GNEC implies a growing societal industry, a declining GNEC indicates a declining societal industry. A turnover in GNEC growth signals the onset of a decline.

The intent here is not to strike fears of another 1930–1940 depression. That setback was unusually severe and will be discussed in another chapter. It *is* an intent to emphasize that we should not expect a vigorous business growth, such as that between 1950 and 1975, during the 10 years following 1985, especially after the Crash of '87.

Accounting for the Booms and Busts

The questions were already asked:

- Can we account for the size of GNEC growths in boom years of the past?
- Can we account for the size of GNEC growths in bust years of the past?

Quite simply, when the rising phase of the long wave combines with the underlying secular growth, the GNEC growth is amplified. When the declining phase of the long wave combines with the underlying secular growth, the GNEC growth tends to be stagnated. Since half of the long wave is associated with the rising side and half with the declining side, we might expect some 25 to 30 years of abnormal growth and an equivalent subnormal growth. However:

Since the underlying secular growth is an increasing one, the abnormal growths tend to dominate—a happy circumstance for those who welcome a rising GNEC/GNP to ensure good business conditions and job opportunities.

The effects can even be quantified. Let's look at GNEC growth from 1945 to 1970, a period when GNEC deviation was growing from a −20 percent point to a +20 percent rate. The underlying *secular* growth curve would have suggested a GNEC growth of 1.65 times—or about 2 percent per year. But, since the actual GNEC was some 20 percent lower in 1945, and some 20 percent higher in 1970, the real growth was about 2.3 times—or about 3.5 percent per year.

In contrast, the period from about 1915 to 1940 was one where the deviation curve was *falling* from +20 percent to -20 percent. During this period the secular curve alone would have suggested a growth of almost two times, or about 2.5 percent per year. Actually, the growth was around 1.5 times, or about 1.5 percent per year.

Where are we now? The CAL curve in Figure 4–3 suggests there should be no GNEC growth during the 1985–1995 period. The energy-cycle deviation curve (Figure 4–2), indicates we just crossed the zero–deviation line in 1985. An examination of the underlying secular curve would indicate the basic growth between 1985 and 1995 should be about 1.2 times, or a 1.5 percent per year growth. But, since the GNEC deviation curve will fall from the 0 percent level in 1985 to −20 percent in 1995, a 20 percent decline, that decline will just balance the 20 percent rise of the secular growth.

The Approach of the Energy-Growth Winter

These statistics can obscure rather than clarify the picture. Basically, the data indicate that the high-growth period between 1945 and 1970 reflected the combination of a long-term steady growth of GNEC and an upswing of the long wave. The depression period between 1930 and 1940 coincided with the last half of a downswing in the long wave, a downswing that took GNEC growth below that projected by the secular curve. While the GNEC decline beginning between 1915 and 1930 already signaled an economic autumn, the further decline from 1930 to 1940 brought the economic winter—a beginning that included the Crash of '29. The period from 1985 to 1995 again coincides with the last half of a downswing, a sign that another economic winter is beginning—a beginning that included the Crash of '87. The implications of this new winter will be discussed further in the third and fourth parts of this book.

The Reliability of Projections

The GNEC points from year to year bump around the trend line significantly. How reliable will these forecasts be? The whole point of persevering through all these facts, figures, and forecasts is to enable us to use them in our business and personal planning. If the forecasts are incorrect, we can do ourselves a great deal of damage. How much faith can we put in our projections? Let's examine what can cause problems.

Disturbances in energy use due to wars, national strikes, or international embargoes can obviously contribute to *temporary* dislocations in energy growth. Future dislocations that might temporarily occur as a result of major calamities are impossible to quantify and are ignored here.

The more normal uncertainties of GNEC projections can involve both:

- the uncertainty of projecting the continuing secular GNEC growth
- the uncertainty of quantifying the long-wave variations

Each of these uncertainties can be estimated from historical data.

Looking first at the secular growth forecasts, some experience is already available from population projections using logistic growth methods (Chapter 2). From that experience, it appears that:

Uncertainties in forecasts of the GNEC secular growth can be expected to be 5 percent for a 15-year projection and 15 percent for a 35-year projection.

Remember, that the boom-and-bust cyclic swings range from 80 to 120 percent (from 20 percent below to 20 percent above the trendline) of the secular growth—a 40 percent swing. Hence, an uncertainty of 15 percent over a 35-year projection is relatively modest. We must also include the uncertainty arising from the long wave itself—which adds another 6 percent. When the uncertainties of the secular-curve projection and the long-wave projections are combined appropriately (by the square root of the sum of the squares for the two uncertainties):

The overall uncertainty of GNEC forecasts is about 7 percent for a 15-year projection and 16 percent for a 35-year projection.

Using the CAL growth curve (shown in Figure 4–3), a GNEC of 75 ± 5 quads/year is implied for the year 2000 and 137 ± 22 quads/year for 2020. What does this mean? Our societal industry (as measured by GNEC) will grow 1.07 times over the 15-year period between 1985 and 2000—*less than 0.5 percent per year!* Population growth will be more than that. At worst it could fall to 0.93 times the 1985 level—a decline of about 0.5 percent per year. Our business and personal planning should be based on a continuing stagnant GNEC growth and a slow economic growth between 1985 and 1995—in spite of a temporarily strong growth in 1984.

But, between 2000 and 2020, GNEC could grow 1.5 to 2 times, and the growth rate could be between 2.0 and 3.5 percent per year. This is GNEC growth—not GNP growth—the GNP growth will be somewhat larger. This projected GNEC growth implies an impressive new period of prosperity, a boom period, between 2000 and 2020.

A Summary of GNEC and Its Implications

During decades of economic prosperity, GNEC growth has been relatively large in the United States. During decades of economic depressions, GNEC growth has been smaller.

Moreover, from country to country, industrialized nations are characterized by a relatively large per-capita GNEC. Emerging industrialized nations are characterized by a modest per-capita GNEC, and unindustrialized nations are characterized by a relatively small per-capita GNEC.

Author-artist Dr. Seuss once advised aspiring young artists, "Don't start your careers when a Great Depression is also starting." This advice might be paraphrased for aspiring business people, "Don't start your careers when GNEC growth is declining." Or, "Don't be born in countries with a low per-capita GNEC."

As career planners, we don't generally have the luxury of choosing our time or place of birth. But, as entrepreneurs, business leaders, investors, and consumers, we do have some flexibility in choosing appropriate times for important business decisions. Obviously, it can be useful to know the probable course of the economy in the next 5, 10, or 20 years.

There are no forecasting tools that can project with certainty the GNEC or the GNP in any single year, that is, a year precisely three or seven years from now. However, we can project the average GNEC, or GNP, over a five-year span beginning three or seven years from now—not *just* the trend, but the approximate magnitude.

A 130-year history shows that the growth of GNEC in the United States has followed a well-defined, underlying growth pattern with a well-defined, long-cycle variation about the underlying growth. Projections of both the long-term secular growth and the superimposed long wave have some uncertainties, but even these uncertainties can be quantified.

Within a reasonable band of uncertainty, the cycle-adjusted-logistic growth curve can serve as a guide to indicate where the GNEC has been, where it is now, and where it is going.

As will be seen in Chapter 5, the GNEC is strongly correlated with GNP. And Part 2 will confirm the existence of the long economic wave.

CHAPTER 5

ENERGY USE—WHAT IT MEANS TO YOU

You probably never heard of gross national energy consumption (GNEC) before tackling this book. Even now you might regard the year-to-year growth pattern and projectability of GNEC as an esoteric subject, yet:

The course of GNEC growth will have a significant impact on each and every one of us.

The abnormally low GNEC growth occurring now forewarns of slower industry and business growth immediately ahead. The abnormally high GNEC growth projection beginning in the late 1990s suggests thriving businesses and new career opportunities for you and your friends in subsequent years. Two questions might cross your mind:

- Just *why* should GNEC growth be a factor affecting my well-being?
- How much will my *economic* well-being be affected in the approaching years?

The GNEC grew a modest 10 percent from 1970 to 1980, but from 1980 to 1985, it declined almost 3 percent—the first five-year decline since the Great Depression era. What does this decreasing GNEC growth trend imply relative to the economy? Does the Crash of '87 have any special significance in this regard?

Energy pundits have advanced various reasons for the decline of GNEC since 1979. The decline has frequently been attributed to a "successful" national energy conservation effort, partly the result of higher energy prices.

The more likely reason for the recent energy decline, though, is its relationship to the long economic wave.

It is especially important to determine the relationship between GNP and GNEC growths. As an introduction to that subject, a distinction will first be made between two terms, our national *economic prosperity* and our *societal industry*. The ensuing discussion will conclude that:

Just as gross national product (GNP) is an appropriate measure of our economic prosperity, gross national energy consumption (GNEC) is an appropriate measure of our societal industry.

Let's turn to those subjects.

Economic Prosperity

Economic prosperity interests everyone. To the business person, it means good sales volume and good earnings. To the career person, it means job security and growth opportunities. To the consumer, it means sufficient earnings to enjoy a good standard of living.

The degree of economic prosperity can be defined by the total commerce of goods and products within our society.

In our consumption-oriented society, it is customary to equate well-being with national economic wealth, as measured by GNP. The years in which GNP has shown a growth of 4 to 6 percent have been heralded as years of great prosperity.

GNP, measured in inflation-adjusted dollars, will continue to be the traditional index for measuring the dollar value of goods and services produced over successive years. GNP can be measured in either of two ways:

- by the final market value of the output of goods and services in our national economy
- by the total income accruing to business employees, business owners, and government employees.

The two approaches lead to the same value of GNP when properly applied.

Societal Industry

Although not as well recognized as economic prosperity, societal industry should also be of great interest to us. To the business person a strong industry means busy factories and markets. To the career person, it means an abundance of work opportunities. And to the family, it implies domestic services and activities beyond "business" work.

Societal industry will be defined as the total applied industry within our society associated with all *mankind's activities related to goods and services, including those for commerce, government, and the home.*

As our societal industry has moved from the home to industrial and government centers, the term *industry* has become identified with goods-producing, sometimes service-producing, *businesses*. Here the term will be used in the broader context.

Three alternative measures of our broadly defined societal industry might be suggested:

- the monetary value of all goods and services produced, as measured by an index like GNP
- the total employment level in the workforce, as measured by man-hours of work
- the total amount of energy consumed by society to sustain itself

Each of these measures has certain merits and shortcomings.

The monetary value of goods and services may not be an accurate measure of societal industry, since the prices of end products and services, as well as the incomes of individuals, are affected by supply/demand considerations. This can be illustrated by an examination of relative prices during periods of underproduction or overproduction of certain commodities. For example, gasoline prices might fall dramatically during periods of overproduction, yet the fuel effectiveness is unchanged. Also, relative incomes between different professions—medicine, law, engineering, entertainment, education, or manufacturing, (even different individuals within a profession)—might not precisely reflect degrees of contribution to societal industry.

Total man-hours of work contributing to society is probably the least representative of all the potential measures. It ignores the industrial *values* of different work enterprises and overlooks the contribution from capital equipment used for the mechanization of work—machine tools, robotics, and computer technology.

The total energy embodied in our goods and services is the most fundamental measure that can be assigned to our overall societal industry.

Energy analysis and its application to economics has been the subject of considerable work recently. One aspect of that work is the analysis of total energy embodied in the products and services in various sectors of our economy. Energy analysis should not be viewed as a replacement for the more traditional, classical economic analyses. Certainly, kilowatt-hours of energy will never replace dollars on the price stickers of commodities in the marketplace.

The subject of energy analysis is introduced here to emphasize the role of GNEC in our overall societal industry as contrasted to the role of GNP in our overall national economy. To develop that concept, let's examine the basic sources of energy that feed our economy.

Sources of Energy

A society based on organic life would be impossible without some source of energy. Moreover, assuming an equal efficiency of energy use from time to time, the relative level of our societal activities (our societal industry) at any time should be reflected by the amount of energy that society uses.

Our societal energy use includes both the direct *energy expended for our various activities and the* embodied *energy in all the tools devised and used by us as a society.*

Society on planet Earth is sustained by energy resources that can be classified in three categories:

1. Contemporaneous solar-energy resources.
2. Fossil-stored, solar-energy resources.
3. Nuclear-stored, stellar-energy resources.

The contemporaneous solar-energy resources include direct sunlight itself, solar-induced hydropower and windpower, wood fuel (stored over a few years), and various other chemical fuels (usually from organic products). Fossil-stored fuel resources (coal, petroleum and natural gas) have had their origin in organic life that existed many millions of years ago. Nuclear-stored fuel, the fissionable isotope of uranium, had its origin in stellar events that occurred more than 4.5 billion years ago—events that led to our solar system.

Our entire existence and industry depend on the sources of solar and stellar energy.

Dollar expenditures for fuel resources account for less than 10 percent of GNP. In our dollar-conscious society, this can lead to underestimating the full importance of energy. The dollar value associated with energy resources does not even represent an inherent value of energy. The dollar value simply represents the costs of labor, capital equipment, and energy itself to locate, extract, process, and distribute the energy resources to appropriate end points for purchase and use by society.

To appreciate fully the ubiquitous role of energy in our industrial society, let's examine how energy directly and indirectly affects the production of a commodity.

Embodied Energy of Products and Services

Normally, we consider ingredients necessary for the manufacture of a commodity, including:

- raw materials
- capital equipment
- labor
- government services
- direct energy

Assuming that each of these contributions (measured in *dollars* of value) accounts for 20 percent of the product's final value, it might be concluded that energy contributes only one fifth to the "industrial content" of that product. A closer inspection shows that energy is also an essential element in the extraction and processing of the raw-materials component. Energy is also embodied in the capital-equipment component, and even the labor component can be traced to energy required for food, clothing, and shelter. When all factors are considered, the full industrial content of the manufactured product can be traced back to all of its *embodied* energy—the sum of the direct and indirect energy inputs that must ultimately come from the three energy resources of nature already identified. Therefore:

Industry (in the broadest sense) depends on the availability and use of energy. GNEC is the most appropriate measure of our societal industry.

Just as GNP has some problems as a measure of our economic prosperity, GNEC has some problems as a measure of our societal industry. The energy sources from photosynthesis and animal use (such as horses in farming) are difficult to quantify and are usually omitted from energy totals. Also, society has been learning to use energy more effectively from year to year, in two respects:

- through improved thermodynamic efficiencies
- through a broadening application as a replacement for labor

A unit of energy consumption today has a greater industrial value than a unit of consumption 10, 20, or 50 years ago. Despite these apparent shortcomings, GNEC is still the most appropriate measure of industrial activity in our society.

The Relationship of GNP and GNEC

Based on the previous observations, we can conclude:

1. GNP is an appropriate measure of economic prosperity.
2. GNEC is an appropriate measure of societal industry.

Intuitively, we would expect years of high societal industry to coincide with years of strong economic prosperity. In a year when GNEC might be abnormally low (or high), GNP should be low (or high) by a corresponding amount. As an example, in a year when General Motors produces and sells a large number of automobiles, their total energy requirements—both direct and indirect—should be high. The same is true with every other business, including your own.

If a one-to-one relationship exists between societal industry and economic prosperity, the ratio of GNEC/GNP (when GNP is corrected for inflation) should be uniform from year to year.

Although historical data for GNEC and GNP show a strong correlation, the ratio GNEC/GNP has not been constant over extended periods of time, such as decades.

Figure 5–1 illustrates the variation of GNEC/GNP for the U.S. economy during the last 60 years—with some extrapolation to future years. The larger growth rate of GNP relative to GNEC indicates that energy is being used with increasing effectiveness in our economic society.

This means that our steel industries have developed new technologies that use less energy to produce the same amount of steel. Various manufacturing companies have developed new machinery to make automobiles, refrigerators, TV sets—even toilet tissue— with less energy. Electric utility companies have

FIGURE 5–1

Variations of GNEC/GNP and E_{EL}/GNP, 1920–1980, with Extrapolations to 2020

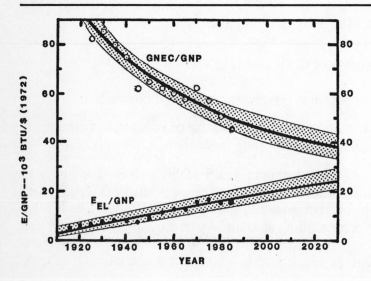

adopted new turbine-generators that generate the same kilowatt hours of electricity with less consumption of coal. We are learning to use our energy more effectively and we are getting an equivalent amount of GNP from an increasingly smaller amount of GNEC.

It has been argued that the fraction of energy used for electricity generation shows a stronger correlation with GNP than does total energy. That ratio, E_{EL}/GNP is also shown in Figure 5–1 (although the E_{EL} used in the figure refers to *input* energy to electricity production). Here, the curve shows a different slope, implying that the electricity energy is growing faster than GNP. This means that a larger fraction of our GNEC is being used each year for electricity generation. Since GNEC/GNP continues to decline, the electricity energy is being used more effectively than the energy previously used for the same purpose.

In summary, it is clear that a strong relationship exists between GNEC and GNP.

Cycle-Adjusted-Logistic Growth of GNP

We will assume that energy usage will continue to improve in effectiveness in the next 35 years and the GNEC/GNP curve will continue its historical trend. We should expect that the GNP growth pattern will follow a cycle-adjusted-logistic behavior very similar to that already projected for GNEC growth—as developed in the previous chapter. Hence, a projected GNP level for future years can be based on the CAL energy growths already discussed.

The projection of the GNEC/GNP curve to the year 2020 was shown in Figure 5–1, with an error band that is estimated at 15 percent. When this error band is combined with the 15 percent uncertainty assigned to the GNEC projection to 2020, a resulting uncertainty of 21 percent is suggested (using the square root of the sum of the squares) for GNP.

The cycle-adjusted-logistic curve for GNP (as well as total energy) from 1960 to 2020 is illustrated in Figure 5–2. We should not be surprised if GNP and energy consumption should show increases or decreases for one, two, or three years that might appear to be inconsistent with the projected long-range trends.

FIGURE 5–2
Projections of GNP and Total Energy Consumption (GNEC) Assuming a Continuing Cycle-Adjusted-Logistic Growth Trend

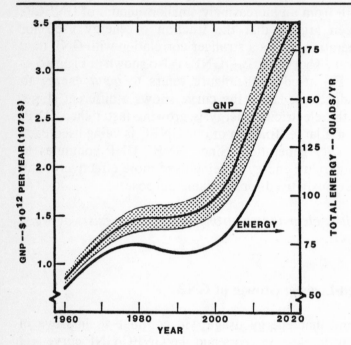

But, over a period of 10 or 15 years, history shows that significant deviations from the CAL curves should not be expected.

This tells us that GNEC will continue to decline over the 1985–1995 period, with the trend turning around in 1995. The average decline will remain within the range of 0 to 1 percent per year, comparable to the 1980–1985 decline. Since GNP is continuing to grow relative to GNEC, the GNP growth should be slightly larger over the same 10-year period—about 1 to 2 percent per year. You might protest that GNP growth was 6 percent in 1984 and 3 percent in 1985, and many economic forecasters projected a 3 to 5 percent per year growth between 1986 and 1990. Don't despair. Those apparent discrepancies will be discussed in Parts 3 and 4. Here, it is suggested that the 1983–1985 growth was the result of a short growth cycle enhanced by the heavy deficit spending of the government. Our own prosperity, if measured by personal spending, would also appear abnormally large if we over-used our credit cards for a year or two.

Does the Crash of '87 have any special significance relative to the approaching economic winter? The percentage decline of the market crash in 1987 was very similar to that in 1929. Moreover, the market behavior in the immediate months after the Crash of '87 closely followed the pattern after the Crash of '29. These similarities emphasize the fact that in each case the crash was another indicator of the transition from the autumn to the winter of the long economic wave. It is unlikely that the winter following the Crash of '87 will bring as much hardship as that following the Crash of '29.

Summary

While gross national product has typically been used as the primary measure of societal well-being, it actually measures only the amount of money traded for goods and services in particular years. GNP is a valid measure of *economic* activity in our society, but can be subject to some distortion arising from factors such as temporarily large deficit spending by the government.

Possibly GNEC provides a more fundamental measure of our basic societal industry. Societal industry, the activity associated with all human endeavors, is closely related to the actual amount of energy consumed by society, both as direct energy and embodied energy in our goods and services. In fact, organic and human life could not exist without some source of energy—solar energy, fossil fuels (such as coal, oil, and natural gas), or nuclear fuel.

Society is learning to use energy more efficiently. There is strong evidence that the energy consumed per unit of societal industry produced is continuing to decrease. This is a gradual improvement, although it is accelerated when energy resource costs increase significantly. In this century particularly, with the large-scale introduction of electricity and more efficient machines, it should not be surprising that we have been learning to produce more GNP with the same GNEC. There is no apparent reason that trend should change.

The superimposition of a long energy wave on the long-term secular growth of energy consumption has been found to describe the growth behavior of U.S. GNEC reasonably for at least the last

130 years. Since the ratio of GNEC per unit of GNP does not seem to be strongly affected by the long wave, one should expect a similar cycle-adjusted-logistic for GNP. This seems to be borne out over the period of history where GNP data are available.

A very important conclusion of this and the previous chapter is that the recollection of historical data describing GNEC and GNP can also provide a useful and interesting basis for recollecting the future growth behavior of our societal industry and economic prosperity.

Some rationale for the cyclic variation of GNEC and GNP is important if we are to accept the use of the cycle-adjusted-logistic curves for forecasting. Reasons for the long wave will be the subject of Chapters 6, 7, and 8 in Part 2 of this book.

PART 2

THE LONG ECONOMIC WAVE AND REASONS FOR IT

CHAPTER 6

TECHNOLOGY MACROINNOVATIONS AS SOURCES OF ECONOMIC BOOMS

The years of the Great Depression, from 1930 to 1940, were bleak for most Americans: unemployment reached as high as 25 percent and most businesses struggled to survive. But, this "winter of despair" was coinciding with a "spring of hope," to borrow from Dickens.

During the 20 years surrounding 1935, the seeds of technology innovation were being sown to create a new surge of economic growth between 1955 and 1985.

Included in the 1935 innovation surge were jet aircraft, television, synthetic textiles, automatic home appliances, and digital computers. From these and other innovations came new industries and business opportunities.

This coincidence of economic adversity and technology rebirth was not unique to the 1935 period. The years around 1875 and 1885 were also marked by a low GNEC and GNP growth. And, it was during the 20-year period surrounding 1880 that an earlier strong surge of major technology innovations occurred. Included in that surge were the automobile, electricity, the telephone, organic chemicals, and snapshot photography.

Was it accidental that the winters of economic despair coincided with the springs of innovation and hope? Were these surges of technology innovations stimulated by entrepreneurs or industries looking for ways out of the economic doldrums? What should we expect as we enter a new economic winter already signaled by the GNEC long wave and the Crash of '87? How can we use these and other signals in a rewarding way?

The primary goal of examining growth patterns of technology innovations, industrial implementations, and GNEC/GNP consequences will be a pragmatic one—to allow us to recollect the future in a personally beneficial way.

In Part 2 of this book, attention will be given to:

- technology-innovation *clustering* (Chapter 6)
- industrial-growth *swarming* (Chapter 7)
- capital-equipment *overexpansion*
- GNEC/GNP growth *busts* and *booms* (Chapter 8)

From this sequence of events, we will be able to appreciate reasons for a long economic wave. We can prepare ourselves to recognize and use the long-wave signals, particularly for the critical years we are now entering.

Why the Long Economic Wave?

Two important explanations have been proposed for a long economic wave, that is, the 55-year cycle of booms and busts:

- the innovation-clustering thesis
- the capital-overexpansion thesis

Briefly, the first thesis proposes that:

Important growth-stimulating technology macroinnovations tend to occur in clusters—generally as the result of a period of business stagnation.

That thesis can be particularly relevant to our business and personal planning in the 1980s and 1990s. The strong business growths arising from the 1935 surge of technology innovations now appear to have run their course. That thesis would suggest that the Crash of '87 was another sign of the economic stagnation that was developing—a stagnation that will bring with it a new surge of important technology innovations creating completely new opportunities for us.

The second thesis proposes that:

Investment in capital equipment tends to overexpand following a peak activity in the overall economy, and some temporary curtailment of construction is necessary until an equilibrium is restored.

Understanding the capital-overexpansion thesis is particularly important for those whose careers are tied to construction or equipment-supply industries. We are at a phase when we should expect capital expansion to be declining.

In this chapter, however, attention will be limited to the timing and character of *technology innovations*. What kinds of innovations should we expect at the forefront of a new GNEC or GNP growth? What kinds should we expect at later times? What signals do these innovations send us about our business, investment, and career planning?

THE CHARACTER OF
TECHNOLOGY INNOVATIONS

The Innovation Hierarchy

An important distinction can and will be made between macroinnovations and incremental innovations, between basic and improvement innovations, between product and process innovations, and even between technology and cosmetic innovations. Both the character and timing of these various kinds of innovations can affect us. Three distinctions are particularly important.

1. Macroinnovations *are innovations leading to entirely new product lines—product lines destined to change the whole course of industry, the economy, and society over a period of decades.*

Your grandparents witnessed the growth of the profoundly important electricity, automobile, chemistry, and motion-picture industries arising from macroinnovations having their births around the 1880s. Your parents saw the growth of jet-air travel, commercial television, synthetic textiles, and digital computers emerging from macroinnovations having their births around the 1930s. Macroinnovations are interesting and significant in our business world because they generally signal *areas* where business growth, and therefore, business opportunities can be anticipated. The beneficiaries are not just the innovating industries, but all the smaller manufacturing, marketing, and service businesses heeding the signals. They involve your neighbors, your friends, and you.

2. Basic innovations *have generally been defined as* individual *technology innovations responsible for major redirections of technology*.

One or several basic innovations frequently contribute to macroinnovations. The steam turbine, the dynamo, the transformer, and the electric light bulb can be regarded as basic innovations contributing incrementally to the electricity macroinnovation. It is not surprising that clusters of basic innovations occur as part of the evolution associated with a macroinnovation.

3. Improvement innovations *are not so radical in terms of industry redirections, yet can be crucially important to competing businesses pursuing a macroinnovation*.

Improvement innovations can vary in degree. The battery ignition system, the spray carburetor, balloon tires, and lacquer paint all contributed—some more importantly—to the evolution of the automobile macroinnovation. Even process innovations, such as parts standardization and assembly lines, can be regarded as significant improvement innovations in the automobile industry.

The Innovation Signals

Why are distinctions in technology innovation important to you as a business person, an investor, or a career planner? They are important because of the signals they send. Macroinnovations, and the basic innovations that contribute to them, are the harbingers of major new business and career opportunities. To the producer, a macroinnovation can allow the introduction of an entirely new product line with no significant competition and, therefore, a better profit possibility. To the merchant, it can allow a larger markup—again with a better profit potential. To the worker, it can demand completely different skills and higher salary or wage opportunities. Macroinnovations (or basic innovations) are more likely to succeed when introduced at a time that industries and the consuming public are looking for bold new directions—when businesses based on older technologies have stagnated.

Improvement innovations occur continuously throughout the industrial evolution of a macroinnovation. They are important because they allow temporary market advantages to the more aggressive competitors. In general, industrial history indicates that even improvement innovations become progressively less significant as the new industry evolves.

It is the improvement innovation that generally gets the most attention in popular literature on technology innovation, but all types of technology innovations have their places and times.

Innovation Clustering

The concept of periodic innovation surges as a cause of the long economic wave is not a new one. In the 1930s, the Harvard economist, Schumpeter, proposed that a few particularly significant innovations (or what we have defined as macroinnovations) have been responsible for the strong economic waves beginning roughly in 1785, 1840, and 1895.

In 1979, some further influential work on innovation clustering appeared in *Stalemate in Technology* authored by Gerhard Mensch. The Mensch team first identified more than 100 basic innovations that made important contributions to our industrial society during the period between 1750 and 1950. The frequency of basic innovations as a function of time was examined to investigate the possibility of innovation clustering.

Figure 6–1 illustrates the frequency distribution of these innovations, based on Mensch's studies. Peaks in the distribution occur at roughly 50- to 60-year intervals. In addition to the clustering effect, the data indicate a larger number of innovations in the 1880 and 1935 surges—an effect probably due to the larger number of technologists and the greater organization of research work during these periods. In contrast to the clustered distribution of basic innovations, the Mensch team found that the distribution of fundamental scientific discoveries or inventions was more random. These conclusions deserve special emphasis.

FIGURE 6–1
Innovations per 10-Year Interval Based on Mensch's Data

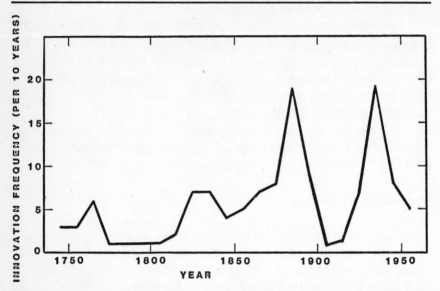

Although fundamental discoveries and inventions tend to occur somewhat randomly, basic innovations occur in clusters at regular intervals.

As discussed in Appendix C, the Dutch economist, Van Duijn, selected basic innovations and their dates which led to a distribution that was not as sharply peaked as Mensch's distribution curve. His results led him to a somewhat different interpretation of the role of technology innovations in the long economic wave. However, the basic importance of innovation surges, as a factor in the long wave, is not altered.

Mensch's work on innovation clustering focused on basic innovations—not particularly on the macroinnovations to which they contributed. Schumpeter's attention was aimed more toward a few macroinnovations and the economic effects that resulted. Since many macroinnovations have been the source of profoundly important industries, let's examine just how various basic and improvement innovations contributed to a few of the most significant macroinnovations. To do this, we can look at macroinnovations assigned to the four important innovation periods—1770, 1825, 1880, and 1935.

THE 1770 MACROINNOVATION PERIOD

Figure 6–1 suggests a first historically significant innovation cluster occurred around 1770.

Perhaps history's most significant megatrend was the Industrial Revolution—which was initiated primarily by the textile macroinnovation.

The textile macroinnovation had its birth in England, at about the time of the American Revolutionary War. It evolved from a number of basic innovations between 1765 and 1790 related to:

- the mechanized spinning of cotton or wool fibers into threads
- the weaving of the threads with weaving looms
- the application of power equipment (mostly water power at that time

The new textile technologies offered enormous improvements in production efficiency and quality over textiles being produced with home equipment—but the new equipment was generally too expensive and too large for domestic application. Many of the traditional domestic activities moved out of the homes to more capital-intensive work centers. Other industries also responded to the industrialization signal coming from the textile macroinnovation.

While history has justifiably accorded great importance to the sociological changes brought about by the Industrial Revolution, it was basically the new textile technology *that led to the restructured industrial society.*

Largely as a result of the textile industry, England became a leader in the important Industrial Revolution, beginning in the late 1700s. Although an embryo textile industry had appeared in the United States as early as the 1790s, a significant growth did not occur there until around 1820 or 1830.

THE 1825 MACROINNOVATION PERIOD

The steel, steam-engine, and railroad macroinnovations were crucial to a second long economic wave that began in the 1840s.

Steam-engine technology had been evolving before 1790 and was being pioneered for some applications, such as operating water pumps, driving factory equipment, and propelling ships. One example was Fulton's steamboat in 1809. However, even the commercial use of steamboat transportation did not become important until around 1830 or 1840, when railroad transportation was also becoming significant.

One of the earliest demonstrations of a railway steam carriage occurred in England around 1804. However, it took 20 years (until 1825) to identify the beginning of the railroad macroinnovation. At that time, the first practical experiments were conducted on a "train,"—a locomotive with attached cars. Five years later, train service was introduced in the United Kingdom, using a relatively modern, high-speed train that could travel an astounding 40 miles per hour! The first train service also appeared in the United States around 1830.

The railroad industry—like the textile industry in the previous wave—depended on a number of basic innovations. Three basic technology innovations included the steam locomotive, the coupled train, and the iron-rail technologies, all in the early 1800s. These basic innovations, and many subsequent improvement innovations in several countries, contributed to the rapid business growth of the industry between the 1840s and the 1870s.

THE 1880 MACROINNOVATION PERIOD

The surge of macroinnovations centered around 1880 was very influential on industrial, economic, and sociological growth. Beyond the notable technology macroinnovations of this period, an eventful institutional innovation—the industrial research laboratory—appeared. That innovation, more than any other, changed the future course of industrial technology in the free-enterprise world. What was the origin of this industrial innovation? What was its impact?

The Industrial Research Laboratory

With the possible exception of Edison's early laboratory, industrial research laboratories had not yet been adopted in the United States prior to the 1880s. Technology innovations before 1900 came largely from individuals, not laboratories. Edison, Bell, and Eastman were representative of American innovators responsible for electricity, telephone, and photography macroinnovations in the 1880 innovation surge. These macroinnovations had strong U.S. roots, but the automobile and chemistry macroinnovations had their roots primarily in Germany. Otto, Daimler, and Benz were three important German innovators contributing to the automobile macroinnovation.

Edison's laboratory contributed to at least four technology macroinnovations: electricity, telephones, phonographs, and kinetoscopes (motion-picture equipment).

In spite of those monumental technology contributions, Edison's most profound innovation may have been the concept of the industrial research laboratory.

The Edison laboratory, established in 1876 at Menlo Park, New Jersey, demonstrated that technology innovation could be an important business. Out of that laboratory came 2,000 patents, many of which led to commercial products having a substantial impact on Edison's own business interests as well as national and international economic growth between 1895 and 1925. This institutional innovation appeared in the German chemical industries at about the same time, and was soon copied by other large companies in the United States and Europe.

The chemical industry research laboratory had its origin in Germany as early as the 1880s.

When coal tar, the by-product of coke production, was still regarded primarily as a nuisance, the Germans were already isolating valuable organic compounds from these tars for use in the chemical dye, synthetic perfume, and pharmaceutical industries. As business prospered, they plowed more of their profits into scientific research, which effectively gave them a world-wide monopoly in the chemical industry. This was probably the earliest example of industrial research laboratories being used by aggressive businesses to establish and maintain strong competitive positions.

The German monopoly of the chemical industry was finally broken by government seizures and subsequent leases of German patents to U.S. companies during and following World War I. The Du Pont Company, in particular, acquired a large number of important patents which enabled them to expand their interests, in the 1920s, far beyond their prior interest in explosives.

In 1900, General Electric became the first large U.S. company to organize a structured industrial research laboratory. The benefits to GE were slow in appearing, but after 10 years the venture became very rewarding. Due to some brilliant research on tungsten metallurgy and on electron emission from hot filaments in inert gases through the 1905 to 1915 period, the GE Research Laboratory developed patent positions that assured them a virtual monopoly in the profitable lamp business. They maintained this position for over 50 years. In addition, research work allowed GE to diversify into other businesses, such as medical products (through the x-ray tube), thermionic tubes, the radio, chemical products, and high-strength materials. The early adoption of a strong research laboratory, and the effective use of its resources led to GE's supremacy over electric-equipment competitors both in the United States and Europe.

In 1907, Bell Telephone was also beginning to recognize the importance of research. They established their research laboratory in 1911, a laboratory destined to become one of the foremost industrial research organizations in the world. Early developments from the Bell Laboratory included the perfection of the "triode" vacuum tube. This allowed the amplification of telephone and radio signals, which enabled coast-to-coast telephone communications to be introduced commercially in 1915. As with GE's domination of the lamp business, AT&T dominated the telephone industry largely through patent positions coming from their research activities.

In the chemical, electrical, and electronic industries, these and other research laboratories became important contributors to the success of large companies.

By 1915, the number of industrial research laboratories in the United States exceeded 50, and by 1930 the number had grown to more than 1,000. This growth ushered in a new and important mechanism for accelerating technology innovation—a step destined to stimulate more new business growth and its economic consequences.

Let's look at some of the 1880 technology macroinnovations themselves.

The Diversity of Macroinnovations

Macroinnovations are significant not only because they represent new *technology* systems, but more importantly, because they are the sources of new economic megatrends. From our perspective today, at least 10 prominent macroinnovations can be identified with the 1880 surge:

1. Electricity.
2. Automobiles.
3. Telephone.
4. Chemicals (including pharmaceuticals).
5. Photography (including movies).
6. Phonographs and records.
7. Typing and typesetting.
8. Food canning.
9. Aluminum.
10. Reinforced concrete.

Each of those macroinnovations offered industrial opportunities to hundreds of enterprising manufacturers. More significantly, they signaled thousands of opportunities for related sales and service industries.

What can we learn about the pattern of inventions, basic innovations, and subsequent improvement innovations in the evolution of the various macroinnovations? A more detailed look at two of the most important macroinnovations of that period—electricity and the automobile—will provide some insight.

The Electricity Macroinnovation as an Example

By the year 1800, the Industrial Revolution was well underway in England. A new era of technology was emerging in factories and mills—even in transportation. England led this technological revolution, but by 1800 it had spread to the European continent and the United States. In spite of this surge in technological progress, almost nothing was known about electricity. Electric-generating equipment did not exist, electric motors were completely unknown, and electric lights were not even an idea.

In 1800, an Italian scientist, Alessandro Volta, invented the electric battery, which paved the way for studying electrical behavior resulting from electric currents. By using batteries as a source of electrical currents, the English scientist Humphery Davy was able to demonstrate the potential of a novel electric arc lamp in 1810, as well as an even more novel hot-wire "incandescent" lamp that burned dimly for a few minutes.

Perhaps the first major scientific step toward electricity generation and its use, was the work by the English scientist, Michael Faraday, between 1820 and 1830. His experiments showed that electric currents could be generated by moving a coil of wire through a magnetic field and that these currents could be used to drive a simple electric motor.

From these very primitive experiments, it became apparent that electricity generation, electric lighting, and electric motors were all practical possibilities. Innovative minds soon turned their attention to applications of these principles.

A burst of electrical and electromechanical innovations occurred both in Europe and the United States, especially between 1860 and 1890, laying the groundwork for electrical industries.

The gestation time from the discovery of fundamental electricity and electromechanical principles to the burst of basic innovations was 50 to 75 years. By 1870, the industrial climate was right for these first seeds of technology innovations to initiate the electricity macroinnovation.

A typical pattern of basic and improvement innovations contributing to a macroinnovation, in this case the electricity macroinnovation, is illustrated by Figure 6–2. The degree of radicalness is indicated at successive times for a few of the electricity innovations. In particular, the figure traces the innovation evolution for two electricity industries—those involving electricity generating systems—Curve A, and those associated with incandescent lamps—Curve B. Other lines of development could

FIGURE 6–2
Evolution of the Electricity Macroinnovation with Trendlines for Incremental Innovations

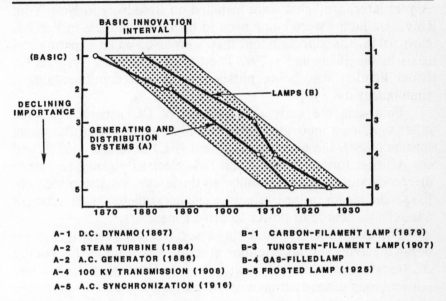

A-1	D.C. DYNAMO (1867)	B-1	CARBON-FILAMENT LAMP (1879)
A-2	STEAM TURBINE (1884)	B-3	TUNGSTEN-FILAMENT LAMP (1907)
A-2	A.C. GENERATOR (1886)	B-4	GAS-FILLED LAMP
A-4	100 KV TRANSMISSION (1908)	B-5	FROSTED LAMP (1925)
A-5	A.C. SYNCHRONIZATION (1916)		

have been included, such as arc lamps, electric motor applications, and electrolysis.

The first direct current (DC generator, by the German inventor Werner Siemens in 1867, is identified as a basic innovation beginning Line A in Figure 6–2. This invention was more than just a laboratory experiment. Siemens was interested in applying electricity to his mining industry. In fact, an early electric locomotive for use in his mines was demonstrated in 1879. But many other industrial inventors were working on still other applications of electrical systems in the 1870s—both in Europe and the United States.

Most of the development work on electricity generating equipment, in the 1865–1885 period was motivated by interests in electric lighting.

The American inventor, Charles Brush, developed a commercial dynamo in 1876 that was used as a source of electricity for his arc lamps. In 1879, the Brush Electric Light and Power Company was the first public company in the United States to generate and sell electricity for lighting streets in San Francisco and Cleveland. A year later, arc lights were installed on Broadway in New York City. Arc lamps were being used to light a few streets in Paris as early as 1878, and in London, they were used on an experimental basis in the 1878s and 1879s. The use of generating systems for street lighting was being pursued in several countries almost simultaneously.

Following the early development of DC generators, three other significant innovations appeared in the mid-1880s: the steam turbine (1884), the alternating-current (AC) generator (1886), and the AC transformer (1887). Until 1884 electricity generators were driven by steam engines, similar to those used on steam locomotives. The steam turbine offered a smaller, quieter, more efficient and reliable source of power to drive generators.

The AC generator and the associated AC electric system began receiving serious attention around 1886. With the help of the AC transformer, electricity voltages could be stepped up to allow efficient long-distance transmission and, subsequently, reduced to a more convenient level at locations where it was to be used. The battle between proponents of DC and AC systems was particularly bitter in the late 1880s, with the merits of the AC system winning universal recognition around 1890.

Further improvements, shown in the figure, were the adoption of higher transmission voltages and the synchronization of the alternating currents at separate generating sources. These developments were important, but not as basic as some of the earlier developments.

The evolution of the incandescent light bulb, shown by Line B in Figure 6–2, is also illustrative. In the late 1870s, Edison had correctly observed that arc lamps were not really ideal candidates for domestic lighting because of their unpleasant glare and their complexity. In 1877, Edison turned almost the complete attention of his Menlo Park laboratory toward the development of an incandescent lamp system—in spite of the success he was realizing from another of his innovations, the gramophone (1876).

Even before this time, the English inventor, Joseph Swan, was experimenting with filament lamps. In fact, Swan successfully demonstrated a carbon filament lamp before Edison (both in 1879). However, Edison's more grandiose goal was to develop an entire commercial system for electric lighting—including generation equipment, distribution lines, lamps, sockets, switches, even electric meters. Edison began generating electricity at his Pearl Street station in New York in 1882, serving 70 customers and 400 light bulbs. Within a few months, the number of lamps being supplied had increased 10-fold.

The early incandescent lamps used carbon filaments—Swan's used carbonized cotton thread and Edison's used carbonized paper (but carbonized bamboo fibers soon thereafter). Lamps with carbon filaments predominated until 1907 when metallurgists learned to make tungsten filaments using a powder metallurgy technique. The more sophisticated ductile-wire tungsten filament, developed by GE in 1911, was the result of some truly ingenious metallurgical research.

In 1912, it was found that the lamp efficiency and lifetime could be improved still more by using inert gases (nitrogen and argon) instead of a vacuum inside the bulb. The frosted lamp introduced in 1925 is indicated in Figure 6–2 only as a relatively simple improvement, although an extremely important one commercially.

By the 1890s, other important applications of electricity were being introduced, particularly for manufacturing and transportation. The electric trolley car appeared in Cleveland and Kansas City by 1884, and by 1890, most of the large cities in the United States had similar systems.

Even at the most remote levels of the innovation hierarchy— equipment supply, home installations, factory applications, and service enterprises—business opportunities were offered by the electricity macroinnovation.

This observation seems obvious in retrospect. Yet, business pioneers in electrical-equipment manufacturing and servicing were probably regarded as venturesome or foolhardy by many people around the turn of the century. New business and career opportunities can occur from macroinnovations for those who are alert, enterprising, and willing to learn new technologies.

The Automobile Macroinnovation as an Example

A burst of automobile engine and motor-car basic *innovations occurred between 1870 and 1890, which initiated an automobile industry—primarily in Europe—around 1895.*

An innovation pattern, similar to that indicated for the electricity macroinnovation, is illustrated in Figure 6–3. Again, a much larger number of technology innovations contributed to the automobile evolution, but the examples have been chosen only to illustrate the general progression from basic innovations to the less radical improvement innovations. The two lines of evolution, in this case, are Line A for technology innovations, and Line B for process innovations.

  Beginning with the technology innovations, the development of the four-stroke (intake, compression, explosion, exhaust) inter-

FIGURE 6–3
Evolution of the Automobile Macroinnovation with Trendlines for Incremental Innovations

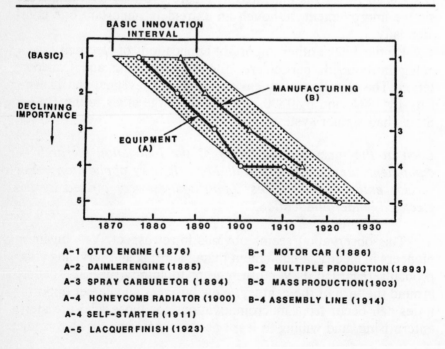

A-1 OTTO ENGINE (1876)	B-1 MOTOR CAR (1886)
A-2 DAIMLER ENGINE (1885)	B-2 MULTIPLE PRODUCTION (1893)
A-3 SPRAY CARBURETOR (1894)	B-3 MASS PRODUCTION (1903)
A-4 HONEYCOMB RADIATOR (1900)	B-4 ASSEMBLY LINE (1914)
A-4 SELF-STARTER (1911)	
A-5 LACQUER FINISH (1923)	

nal combustion engine was a key basic innovation, in 1876, by the German inventor, Nikolaus Otto. Otto's engine used coal-derived gas as a fuel and was intended primarily for stationary applications. Gottlieb Daimler and Karl Benz independently developed a smaller four-stroke engine that used petroleum-based fuel in 1885, that was the forerunner of the modern automobile engine. Both of these Germans used their engines in motorized carriages around 1886—with some contention about who was actually first.

Although the birthplace of the automobile was Germany, credit for the first significant production of automobiles belongs to the French.

Both Benz and Daimler sold patent rights to French companies for the production and sale of their automobiles. The Panhard and Levassor Company acquired rights for the Daimler automobile in 1891, and it was this company that generally designed the automobile layout as we know it today. The engine was moved from under the seat to a hooded location in the front, using a drive shaft, a clutch, and a sliding gearshift mechanism. In 1893, this same company introduced the spray carburetor and in 1895 adopted an in-line two-cylinder engine. In 1899, the more efficient honeycomb radiator was developed allowing the Mercedes of 1900 to achieve a speed of 35 miles per hour.

Figure 6–3 shows the self-starter, introduced in 1911, as an improvement innovation. Obviously, this innovation was a very important one for the man in the pinstriped suit and the lady in the silk dress. Many other improvement innovations between 1900 and 1925 were also notable. How often would we drive 30 miles to a play or a concert, if we had only a 1915 vintage car?

The evolution of automobile technology was surprisingly slow in England and the United States. The delay in England was created by the "Red Flag Act" that required a person carrying a red flag to precede any motor vehicle on British roads. This Act, promoted by the railway industry to protect itself, remained in effect until 1896. Automobile progress in the United States was probably delayed by the more inherent problem of unsatisfactory roads.

The second line in Figure 6–3, Line B, illustrates the progress of manufacturing technology from year to year. It has been argued by some that the assembly-line techniques introduced by Henry Ford in 1914 should be ranked on a level with some of the most important basic technology innovations. A good case can be made for that argument on the grounds of its economic impact. However, the introduction of interchangeable (standard) parts by Cadillac and mass production techniques by Olds in the 1901–1903 period were necessary forerunners of the assembly line. The important point is that manufacturing process development can be just as important as equipment technology development, especially in high-volume businesses.

Other Examples

The electricity and automobile macroinnovation have been selected as two important examples of macroinnovations, although the telephone and chemistry macroinnovations could also have been selected. In terms of economic and social impact, the phonograph and photography macroinnovations might be regarded as less significant. However, if the associated entertainment industries are included, the economic consequences of these industries cannot be lightly dismissed. Let's look at some of the implications of the photography macroinnovation.

The photography macroinnovation was initiated by Eastman's box camera and roll film, but was extended by Edison's kinetoscope and the subsequent emergence of a large and profitable motion picture industry.

In 1884, Eastman developed a paper with a photosensitive emulsion that could be rolled onto a spool. By 1885, his company was selling the paper negatives, and by 1888 had developed a simple box camera that could be mass produced. In 1889, Eastman's paper negative was replaced by a transparent nitrocellulose film that was the forerunner of negative black-and-white film used today. This was the beginning of the Kodak Company organized by Eastman.

Having heard of Eastman's success with photographic film, Edison acquired a strip some 50 feet long which he tested in 1888 as a possible film for use in his motion picture machine, the kinetoscope. The success of this venture led Edison to establish the first motion picture studio. A variety of motion pictures were produced in the studio, featuring famous personalities of the time such as Annie Oakley, Buffalo Bill and Gentleman Jim Corbett. The first "peep show," using these films, was opened in 1894 on Broadway, New York City.

Within another year others had contributed to the development of a "vitascope" projection machine—a machine that was subsequently manufactured and sold by the Edison company. In 1896, a vitascope movie was shown in a New York music hall and was an instant hit. Improvement innovations involving the movie art form were also important. "The Great Train Robbery" is generally regarded as the first movie telling a story—a movie that was produced in the Edison studios in 1903. Shortly thereafter, some of the earliest motion picture studios and movie theatres were springing up.

From these motion-picture technology innovations came opportunities for people in all phases of this new business— equipment technicians, producers, artists, theatre operators and, possibly, even popcorn vendors. Once again, the alert and aggressive people of that era were able to carve out a variety of interesting and profitable careers.

THE 1935 MACROINNOVATION PERIOD

Although our greater familiarity might breed some contempt of our more recent history, the 20 years surrounding 1935 can be credited with as many macroinnovations as already indicated for the 20 years surrounding 1880. Let's remember that macroinnovations (by their definition) must be selected on the basis of their economic and social consequences, as well as their technological originality. For example, the discovery and civilian application of nuclear energy might be judged by some as the most scientifically advanced breakthrough of the 1930–1980 period, yet its contribution to economic growth during those years cannot compare to the economic impact of television, jet-air travel, or polymer chemistry (synthetic textiles and plastics).

Although there could be some debate on a selection of the most significant macroinnovations of the 1935 wave, the following list of 10 can certainly be identified as important ones:

1. Polymer chemistry.
2. Television.
3. Jet-air travel.
4. Office equipment (including computers).
5. Automatic home appliances.
6. Automatic automobile equipment.
7. Superhighways.
8. Antibiotics.
9. Space systems.
10. Nuclear energy.

A strong case could also be made for including frozen-foods, supermarkets, and the mass production of homes.

Possibly some of the most significant, yet least appreciated, new technologies of this century have been those resulting from the chemistry industry. As an illustration of an important 1935 macro-innovation, let's examine the evolution of the polymer-chemistry macroinnovation.

The 1935 Macroinnovations—Polymer Chemicals

What are polymers and why are they so important to us? Polymers are extremely long, chain-like molecules, or macromolecules. Natural polymers include proteins, cellulose (wood), rubber, amber, and even DNA. Man-made polymers include nylon, polyester, synthetic rubber, acrylic floor tiles, and some detergents. One of the marvels of our age is that scientists have been able to duplicate some of the chemistry processes in nature and even improve on nature with many of our synthetic products.

Most of the chemicals we are familiar with, like water, salt, sand, glass, and most gemstones, are made up of molecules having combinations of only two, three or, perhaps, ten atoms as building blocks.

In contrast, polymers might have thousands or millions of atoms combined in a single molecule.

But even in these seemingly complex molecules, there is usually a simplicity of structure. For example, polyethylene is made by joining together, or "polymerizing," thousands of ethylene molecules—molecules having a basic constitution of only six atoms. When long chains of these macromolecules are produced, they have a tenacious character we identify as "plastic."

The *use* of polymers, even the chemical reconstitution of polymers, is not particularly new. The rayon and celluloid technology innovations date back to the 1880 innovation wave. At that time it was found that cotton linters or wood pulp could be dissolved in a solvent and subsequently forced through tiny holes (or spinerets), with the emerging threadlike material solidified to create rayon. A similar process could be used to make sheets of celluloid. The products, in these cases, were simply reconstituted polymers, not synthesized polymers. Nevertheless, even this relatively primitive chemical process led to the very important rayon industry in the early 1900s.

In the 1920s, the Du Pont Company recognized that a synthetic textile industry could be an even more profitable venture than their explosives industry. They created a team of organic chemists in their research laboratory to search for new and better polymer products. In 1928, Du Pont recruited the brilliant organic chemist, Wallace Carothers, from Harvard University to help in the pursuit of their work.

In 1935, Carothers developed a process for polymerizing two relatively simple carbon compounds into a long-chain molecule—a substance we now recognize as nylon.

By squirting his polymer through very fine apertures, he was able to produce a threadlike material that could be stretched and braided into a nylon thread. Unlike rayon, nylon was found to have properties actually better than silk and consequently gained almost immediate popularity—though not without the help of some clever promotional effort by Du Pont.

Like the previous schematic figures for electricity and the automobile, Figure 6-4 illustrates the evolution of synthesized polymer (or plastic) materials. Two traces are shown, one for synthetic fibers and one for other plastics. The development of nylon qualifies as a basic innovation initiating the synthetic textile evolution and contributing to the polymer-chemistry macroinnovation. The British chemist, J. R. Whinfield, was subsequently responsible for the development of another important synthetic

FIGURE 6–4
Evolution of Plastics and Synthetic Textile Macroinnovations with Trendlines for Incremental Innovations

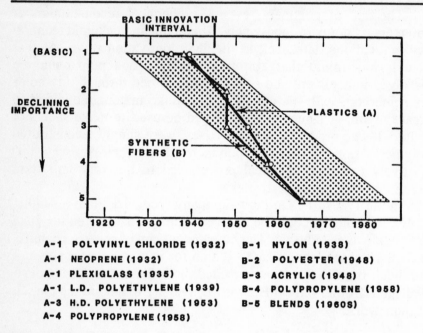

A-1 POLYVINYL CHLORIDE (1932)	B-1 NYLON (1938)
A-1 NEOPRENE (1932)	B-2 POLYESTER (1948)
A-1 PLEXIGLASS (1935)	B-3 ACRYLIC (1948)
A-1 L.D. POLYETHYLENE (1939)	B-4 POLYPROPYLENE (1958)
A-3 H.D. POLYETHYLENE (1953)	B-5 BLENDS (1960S)
A-4 POLYPROPYLENE (1958)	

fiber, polyester (known as Terylene in England, and Dacron as a Du Pont product). Both because of the complex technology involved and its economic importance, this synthetic fiber must also be regarded as a basic or near-basic innovation.

Many other synthetic fibers have evolved, each having different characteristics and different applications. Your sweater probably contains an acrylic, a textile that approximates natural wool. The carpeting in your home may use a polypropylene. Spandex, the elastic textile, may hold important parts of your anatomy in place! Perhaps the lowest in the hierarchy of innovations would be various blends such as polyester and cotton or polyester and wool.

In the late 1920s, chemists in some of the German industries were also showing success in the polymerization of plastic materials. One of the earliest of these plastics was polyvinyl chloride, which finds uses in home plumbing, garden hoses, and phonograph records. Another especially prominent plastic is polyethylene. A low-density polyethylene, developed first by the British chemical industry in 1934 finds applications in plastic bags (to replace paper), protective films in building construction, and in piping. In the early 1950s, German chemists developed still another process for producing a high-density polyethylene, which had a higher tensile strength and higher melting point than the low-density variety. This material has been used for making bottles and pipes where more strength is necessary.

Other important plastic materials were developed in the 1930s and 1940s. Acrylic resins, commercially known as lucite and plexiglass, have become popular for uses in lenses, windows, kitchenware, and even furniture. Teflon was discovered at Du Pont in 1938 and was brought into commercial production in 1948. Amino plastics (such as formica) are found on your kitchen counter tops and as furniture veneers.

Both the plastics and synthetic textile industries showed tremendous commercial growth between 1950 and 1980 with at least a dozen chemical companies in the United States profiting from the development and production of these materials.

Although the biggest uses for polymer-chemistry products have been in the plastic and textile industries, other applications have been found for these remarkable materials. Synthetic polymers are now used extensively in paints, dyes, synthetic rubber, synthetic leather, detergents, and even pharmaceuticals. It has been said that if all the synthetic polymer materials in our household were suddenly converted back to their raw material sources, most of our furniture fabrics, floor coverings, counter tops, kitchenware, bathroom amenities, TV cabinets, wire insulation, and hundreds of other objects would end up as a pool of oil on our floors. Even more embarrassing, most of us would be left practically naked, only covered by layers of glistening oil.

Other Examples

Although the polymer-chemistry macroinnovation was one of the most important arising from the 1935 wave, several others also had tremendous impacts on the economy of the 1950 to 1980 period.

The television macroinnovation, beginning in the late 1930s, has obviously had a profound effect on our national economy and our lifestyles.

The television macroinnovation actually started in England before it was significant in the United States. The British Broadcasting Company was already televising programs in 1936, and by 1938 the country boasted over 3,000 home television receivers in the area around London. At that time, the United States had fewer than 100 sets and broadcasting was essentially on an experimental basis. Following World War II, television saw a surge of growth in both the United States and Europe.

The evolution of television was also stimulated by incremental innovations. Perhaps one of the most important was the introduction of color television in 1953. Magnetic tape, that is video tape, was being used by 1956, and satellite broadcasting was underway in 1969. In addition to these technological innovations, television—like motion pictures before it—saw many innovations in the production and artistic processes associated with this important macroinnovation.

The federal government, and even our military organizations, have been sources of basic innovations—especially in the air-travel industry.

The jet aircraft engine is one of the technologies that arose from military development.

Both the British and Germans were working feverishly on the development of jet aircraft engines and airplanes during World War II. Although the Germans apparently demonstrated a working airplane using this technology around 1941, the British actually developed and put their jet aircraft into production somewhat ahead of the Germans. As with other macroinnovations, jet air travel was characterized by a number of incremental innovations, both in the type of engines used, the airplane designs, and related air travel technology. For example, the development of radar by the British not only was important in its military applications, but has become an essential factor in the control of civilian air travel.

The introduction of automated home appliances probably cannot be ranked technologically with other basic innovations, but this macroinnovation again had profound effects on the economy and our pattern of living.

Electrified home appliances such as refrigerators, washing machines, irons, and vacuum sweepers were already in use before the 1935 innovation wave. The important distinction was that the new wave not only offered greater conveniences to the housewife, but freed her from a full-time housekeeping responsibility. Women were able to enter the workforce in large numbers. The economic consequences were felt not only by the appliance manufacturers and electricity supply companies but also by society itself through the enlarged base of workers and family incomes.

Automatic equipment for automobiles can also be regarded as a significant macroinnovation, in spite of its rather modest technological advance. The introduction of power steering, power brakes, and automatic transmissions in the 1930s made automobile travel simpler and more convenient.

However, the little-recognized impact of superhighways may have had an even more important impact on automobile transportation than did automobile equipment itself in the post-war period.

In 1937, the State Legislature of Pennsylvania purchased an uncompleted railroad bed between Pittsburgh and Harrisburg owned by the Pennsylvania Railroad Company. A Turnpike Commission was authorized to construct and operate a toll road on this route, with some support from federal funding. The Pennsylvania Turnpike was such a success that other states moved forward with plans for superhighways shortly after the end of World War II. The superhighway macroinnovation has had an enormous impact not only on automobile travel but also the trucking industry. It has made our travel more convenient, opened new areas for housing development, made fresh farm products more accessible, and created dozens of new job opportunities.

Still other macroinnovations resulting from the 1935 surge should be acknowledged. Automated office equipment macroinnovations—including digital computers, Xerox machines and, subsequently, word processors—have been crucially important to harried secretaries and demanding bosses alike. Obviously, the introduction of antibiotics, space systems, and nuclear energy have also had important impacts on our economy and living standards.

As a postscript, it is significant to note that all macroinnovations need not come from industries. Federal and state governments can also be sources, as in the case of nuclear energy, jet air travel, and superhighways.

The Exceptions

As a final observation on innovation clustering, it must be recognized that all macroinnovations—and the basic innovations providing the leading edge—do not fall within the innovation surge period. For example, the airplane macroinnovation was an important one that had its birth around 1910, some 30 years after the 1880 peak and 25 years before the 1935 peak. The radio macroinnovation had its birth around 1920, 15 years before the 1935 peak. More significantly, the commercial growth of radio—both in terms of equipment consumption and the broadcasting industry—was quite substantial between 1920 and 1930, which marked the end of the business growth wave associated with the 1880 macroinnovation.

Still, the important conclusion is that a remarkable number of macroinnovations did have their births in the 1870 to 1890 surge and again in the 1925 to 1945 surge.

Summary

Technology innovation has become critically important in industrial societies—both to each of us individually and to the economy at large. While specific innovations cannot, in general, be anticipated with any certainty, history shows that the directions of macroinnovations can be identified early in their evolution. Like giant currents in a river, these macroinnovations can alter the entire course of society over a period of a half century, and there is strong evidence that several of these currents can begin at roughly the same time.

What is the implication of these new directions on you as an individual? Most importantly, an early identification of these macroinnovations can alert you to new career opportunities, to better business opportunities, and to interesting investment possibilities. It is easy to look with awe at the few successful companies, or individuals within companies, who might have pioneered such a macroinnovation. But, it is more important to examine the many opportunities a macroinnovation can present to each of us—in new engineering, production, marketing and service activities. Particularly during the threshold of a new innovation surge, as we might expect between 1985 to 2005, the emergence of macroinnovations can tell us much about new business opportunities and the need for career training or retraining.

Are we making use of the opportunities offered? Can we get a headstart on the next surge of macroinnovations? That is one of the goals of *Recollecting the Future*.

As a cautionary note, innovations should be compared to life itself. An innovation, and particularly a basic innovation, represents only the birth of a new technology. What about the subsequent growth of products belonging to a macroinnovation? For the answer, we must turn to an examination of business growths and their consequences.

CHAPTER 7

THE SPAWNING OF BUSINESS MEGATRENDS

Why has special emphasis been given to the subject of technology macroinnovations? Because those macroinnovations are the seeds of industrial and societal growths—growths that affect each of us.

From technology macroinnovations come new industries, new business opportunities, new surges of economic growth, and even new sociological directions.

Macroinnovations are *only* the seeds. Those seeds are essential, but it is the subsequent industrial and business growths that create prosperity, career opportunities, and sociological progress. What time interval should we expect between the germination of macroinnovations and a surge in business growth? What can we learn from the industrial growth surges of 1900–1930 and 1955–1985? In particular, how can growth curves be used to describe the business growths resulting from the economically important macroinnovations identified in the previous chapter?

Using Growth Curves

As a first step, an S-growth curve can be useful as a simple means for indicating the "growing-pain" years, the "growth-boom" years and the "over-the-hill" years in our business planning. But, we can extract much more information from our business growth data by making use of the more definitive "growth/ungrowth" relationship, the $F/(1 - F)$ data explained in Chapters 2 and 3. By using this more explicit approach, we can actually lay the groundwork for recollecting the future.

We can use growth/ungrowth curves to describe—and frequently project—the growth of major industry *sectors* having their origins in macroinnovations.A knowledge of these overall industry growths can guide our business planning into promising growth channels. It can tell us how fast new industries will grow and how fast older ones will decline. Such information is invaluable to you when deciding on career readjustments, business redirections, and long-term investment planning.

As a second application, we can examine the substitution growth of new products or services resulting from improvement innovations within an industry sector such as the takeover growths of LP records, transistorized electronics, and polyester textiles. These kinds of growths can often tell us something about our own competitive position. Are we ahead of the pack, or behind?

As a third especially interesting application, we can examine how the "swarming" of new industry growths has contributed in the past—and might be expected to contribute in the future—to the overall national economy. In this case, the growths of several large new industries might happen to coincide, so that their combined impacts could have a profoundly important effect on long-term economic growth.

Although a clustering of basic innovations and macroinnovation births can plant the seeds for a surge of business growths, it is the resultant swarming of industrial growths that actually produces economic-growth surges.

Proper industrial-growth projections lie at the very heart of recollecting the future—the future of growth booms and growth busts. The three growth surges that built on innovation surges centered around 1825, 1880, and 1935 will be examined here.

The Railroad Growth Surge—1840 to 1870

The railroad industry affords a good first example of industrial growth building on a number of basic innovations. Prior to 1830, long-distance travel across land was limited to carriages, wagons, horseback, or foot. Between 1800 and 1830, practically all large cities in the eastern United States were connected by stagecoach lines. These coaches typically traveled at speeds of 5 to 10 miles per hour—about the speed of a jogger—and usually over rough roads. Even as late as 1850, much of the transportation in the United States was by stagecoach.

The railroad macroinnovation was destined to change that. By 1840, railway systems were beginning to grow in several countries, but particularly in the United Kingdom with 1,300 miles of railroads in service, and the United States with 2,800 miles in service. By 1860, the mileage of track in the United Kingdom was 10,000 miles and the United States, 30,000 miles—a 10-fold increase in only 20 years! Another three-fold growth occurred between 1860 and 1880.

What was the business significance of that huge expansion? In this context, we usually think of the famous business tycoons and Wall Street financiers who profited handsomely from the railroad enterprise. But those profits, lofty though they were, represented only the tip of the iceberg. Thousands of people in the railroad industry and many more in related equipment supply industries—including the steel and coal industries—benefited from the railroad growth. More importantly, opportunities were opened for freight transportation in much larger volume and over much longer distances than ever imagined.

The railroads had a historically profound effect on the economies of frontier regions of the United States. Between 1850 and 1860, a major part of United States railroad growth was in the midwestern states of Ohio, Indiana, and Illinois. The railroad was responsible for a population surge as well as an economic surge in those states. That was only the beginning of the railroad expansion and the "Transportation Revolution" in the United States.

Before the Civil War, some consolidation of railway systems was already occurring, with the formation of the New York Central, Pennsylvania, and Illinois Central systems. In those early years of strong growth, serious competition between the giants was not an important factor.

Another surge of growth (and consolidation) in the United States occurred again after the Civil War, including the formation of the Union Pacific, the Northern Pacific, and the Santa Fe systems in the western United States. With the initial surge of railway growth now beginning to saturate, and even overlap, competition became more vigorous in the 1870s. Disastrous price wars developed in the 1870s and 1880s, and profitability was seriously damaged. In fact, the railroad industry was almost devastated in the subsequent panic of 1893.

Even though a further growth of railroad passenger and freight usage was to occur in the next industrial growth era, the first large expansion of railroad mileage was already showing a slowdown by the 1880s—some 50 years after the railroad innovation.

Other Industrial Growth Surges—1840 to 1870

The railroad industry was not the only one based on a macroinnovation originating around 1825. The blast furnace opened a new era for steel production. Steam-engine applications to riverboats led to the growth of inland water travel at about the same time as the railroad growth. The invention of the reaper was an important factor in agricultural growth, and the invention of the telegraph was responsible for a completely new communications industry in the 1800s.

Many of these industries continued to show a significant growth (or regrowth) after the 1880 stagnation period. But generally, the first large surges of growth for these industries occurred in the 1840 to 1870 period. Those business growth surges were impressive, but the 1895 to 1925 business growth surges—that followed the 1880 innovations were even more impressive.

THE 1895 TO 1925 PERIOD: INDUSTRIAL GROWTHS

A Diversity of Business Growths

As already emphasized, the 1870 to 1890 period was remarkable for technology innovations. Five especially significant macroinnovations—electricity, automobiles, photography, the telephone, and organic chemicals—created entirely new businesses.

The growths of these five industries began slowly after the 1880 innovation surge, reached a peak growth some 30 to 40 years later, then showed a growth saturation about 50 years after the innovation surge.

In general, the five industries showed significant growths in the 1895 to 1930 period, though the individual growth peaks varied by about ±5 years from a median curve. The individual growth curves are more remarkable for their similarities than for their differences. The overall behavior is frequently described as a swarming of industrial growths.

Perhaps even more interesting, the growth behavior for as much as 90 percent of the individual growths could have been forecast by the time some 10 percent of the growth had occurred. The automobile industry growth provides a particularly fascinating illustration of this remarkable growth behavior.

The Prophetic Growth Surge of Automobiles—
1900 to 1930

The automobile growth/ungrowth curves were almost miraculously uniform over a hugh span of growth. In Figure 7–1 the S-growth curves for (A) the fractional substitution of automobiles for horse-drawn carriages, and (B) the fractional adoption of automobiles by United States families are shown at the top of the figure. The bottom shows the growth/ungrowth ratio (on a "log-linear" scale) for the same two examples. Curve C (the dotted bar) indicates an approximate average of Curves A and B—an average that is used in Figure 7–3. Note that the points fit a straight line over a remarkable range of almost 0.001 to 10! The upper curves are not particularly revealing, but the bottom curves certainly are.

The growth/ungrowth line indicating the substitution of automobiles for carriages shows that the growth data follow almost perfectly the "logistic-growth" behavior from less than 1 percent to at least 90 percent of the total substitution. A similarly good behavior appears for the automobile adoption curve (here it is found that about 15 percent of the families were not destined to be candidates for car ownership in the 1920s).

The remarkable behavior of the substitution growth indicates that by 1905, when only 3 percent of all vehicle sales (autos and carriages) were automobiles, it could have been forecast that autos would account for 90 percent of sales by 1920. (See Section 2 of Appendix A for more details.)

FIGURE 7–1
Growth Behaviors for Automobiles

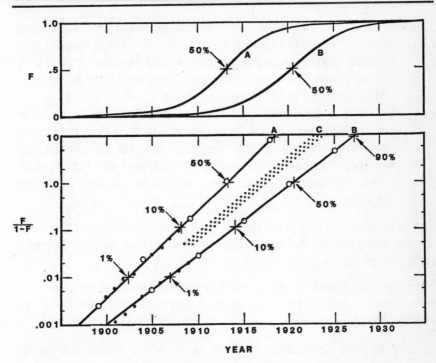

Why is this growth curve so remarkable? What is so unusual about a straight-line relationship?

This straight-line curve was foretelling history 10 to 20 years before it happened, indeed, the growth/ungrowth curve appears to have almost a mystical quality. In 1905—when only one family in 200 would own an automobile, when paved roads outside urban areas did not exist, when the automobile was only an expensive toy for affluent sportsmen—the growth/ungrowth curve was suggesting a mechanical, industrial, and sociological revolution in the next 20 years. For example:

- By 1905 (before the Model T Ford, before electric starters, and before acceptable roads), it was already ordained that automobile sales would make the horse-drawn carriage business practically obsolete by 1920 (with carriage sales at less than 10 percent)!

- When only 20,000 cars were being produced (in 1904), it would be apparent that the production rate could be over a million in 1920!
- By 1905, when a horse-drawn carriage cost $50 to $100, (less than one tenth the cost of an automobile at that time) it was implied that automobile prices would decline and family wages would increase sufficiently to allow some 80 percent of the families to afford automobiles 25 years later!
- By 1905, when only a handful of people were working in automobile businesses, it could be inferred that enormous opportunities would be opening for automobile-factory workers, sales distributors, mechanical-service technicians, filling-station operators, and even road-construction workers!

These projections could be made by you or me—without the help of the complex digital-computer programs that would become available 50 years later.

Without exaggeration, the growth/ungrowth method must be acknowledged as a simple, but enormously powerful tool for forecasting business futures.

As already emphasized, there were some staggering problems—technical, manufacturing, financing, and even social—that required resolutions in the 1905 to 1920 period in order for the growth/ungrowth forecasts to be realized. Let's look at the history of the automobile to see how those resolutions evolved.

The Automobile Growth History—1895 to 1925

Peak Growth Year: 1917   Takeover Time: 12 years

In spite of Germany's leadership in automobile technology during the 1880s, it was France that became the leader in automobile production during the 1890s. In 1896, some 300 cars were produced in France—more than in the United Kingdom and United States combined. By 1900, world automobile production had reached almost 10,000 per year, with the United States, France, and Germany as the leaders. Admittedly, the automobiles at that time were little more than motorized carriages.

Automobile production became significant in the United States in the first decade of the new century.

Although an embryo automobile industry began in the United States during the late 1890s, it was really the little one-cylinder "curved-dash" Oldsmobile that launched this country into something resembling mass production.

In fact, a strange accident introduced the mass-production concept in those early years. In 1901, after their factory was destroyed by a disastrous fire, it was necessary for Oldsmobile to purchase automobile parts from a variety of suppliers. The specification of components led to a need for parts standardization, which turned out to be the key to mass production. With this approach, some 1,000 cars were produced in 1901 and production doubled in 1902. By 1905, the company was producing more than 5,000 cars per year.

Henry Ford truly revolutionized the automobile industry and, in many respects, American industry.

Some historians have suggested that Ford's industrial management policies of the 1910 to 1920 period may have had a greater impact on the labor class of the world than Lenin's Bolshevik policies. Although Ford had entered the automobile business as early as 1895, his real fame dates from 1907.

In the early 1900s, automobiles were either too primitive (little more than "horseless carriages"), too expensive, or both. Ford decided to solve this problem by producing a stripped-down automobile, but with a 4-cylinder engine and a practical body design that would be appealing and affordable to a larger cross section of the public. The resulting Model T Ford was purchased by some 10,000 people in 1908. By 1911, Model T sales had reached 70,000, in 1912 over 150,000, and in 1914 some 250,000.

But the Ford revolution went far beyond manufacturing and sales. Between 1908 and 1912, the company was able to decrease the price by almost a factor of two. In 1914, Ford shocked the industrial world by announcing that his company would establish a $5 per day minimum wage at a time when the average was less than half that level. His argument was that a move toward higher labor wages would ultimately benefit industry as well as the working public. In a sense, the Ford policies constituted a social as well as a production revolution at that time.

Let's refer once again to Figure 7–1. The seven years between 1907 and 1914 might logically be called the "growing-pain" years. During those years, the auto registrations per household (the adoption curve) increased from 1 percent to 10 percent, Or, in effect, the manufacturing equipment and labor force had to accommodate a 10-fold increase in production. Again it was largely Ford who found the answers to this challenge presented by the logistic growth prescription. Mass production techniques were continually improved between 1911 and 1915, and Ford introduced the famous assembly line in 1914. Although the assembly line has been popularly believed to be one of Ford's most significant innovations, there is ample evidence that this particular technique was borrowed (though embellished) from other successful industries such as the firearms, the clock-making, and even the meat-packing industry (where Ford, it is said, got the idea). Nevertheless, the careful optimization of the assembly-line technique by the Ford industrial engineers was a very important contribution to the manufacturing industry at that time.

Ford maintained his leadership in the automobile industry into the 1920s. However, the company adhered to its Model T concept too long. As other companies, particularly General Motors, introduced the concept of annual model changes, Ford finally lost its preeminent position. Ford belatedly introduced some radical changes in the late 1920s and 1930s, but by then the primary market position was lost.

What can we conclude about the overall character of automobile growth? First, the substitution growth curve in Figure 7–1 shows that in 1914 the number of automobiles produced was equal to the number of carriages. And second, by 1921 half of the candidate families in the United States owned automobiles. Growth had peaked, between 1914 and 1921. Perhaps more importantly, some 90 percent of the growth had occurred by 1928. This is not to suggest that automobile sales were coming to an end. It only means that the annual *growth* of this important industry was ending. Hence, auto sales, auto service work, and related job opportunities were finally reaching a plateau.

Although automobile sales remained brisk between 1921 and 1928, the industry was no longer a growth industry in the late 1920s.

The Electricity Growth Surge—1900 to 1930

Peak Growth Year: 1915   Takeover Time: 30 years

We frequently forget the conveniences provided by electricity. As some perspective, the typical home in 1880 was illuminated with candles, lanterns, or gas burners, and heated with wood- or coal-burning pot-belly stoves. Meals were prepared on wood-burning kitchen stoves, clothes were washed in tubs, and bathing was made more comfortable with the help of a tea kettle of hot water.

In contrast, today we light our homes with the flip of a switch. We control room temperatures by a thermostat that activates a furnace or an air conditioner. Food is removed from the electric refrigerator, prepared by an electric processor, and cooked on an electric range. Even the disposal of garbage is handled by electric equipment. Clothes are washed in automatic washers and dried in automatic dryers. We turn on a faucet for hot water. All of these amenities, and many more, have appeared in less than 100 years—in the Electricity Age.

New businesses, and even new lifestyles, evolved from the electricity and electromechanical innovations occurring around 1880.

How did new electricity businesses grow? Some very early electricity generating systems, primarily for street lighting, were appearing in the United States and Europe around 1879. However, practical electricity began in 1882 with the Edison Illuminating Company that installed systems for home and commercial lighting, both in London and New York. The Pearl Street Station in New York initially supplied electricity for about 60 customers within a one-mile radius of the station.

By 1886, only four years later, some 500 generating stations had been built, most of them to supply electric lighting for factories and textile mills. Even then, the number of buildings illuminated by electric lights was minuscule compared to those using gas lamps.

While the growth rate of electricity was spectacular in those early years, the total impact was destined to be small for several years.

Electricity growth in the 1882 to 1900 period was following the very slow growth associated with the early part of a typical S-growth curve.

A serious problem with Edison's DC supply systems was that direct current could not be transmitted efficiently for distances exceeding about a mile, therefore requiring a large number of relatively small generating stations. That problem was resolved around 1886 when commercial generating systems began using alternating current, with transformers to step the voltage up for longer-distance transmission. The AC innovation allowed generating stations to use much larger generators with significant improvements in the economy of electrical supply.

Another important innovation was the steam turbine, which began replacing the reciprocating steam engines in the late 1890s. The turbines were simpler in design, more reliable, and less expensive.

The growth/ungrowth curves in Figure 7–2 tell us something about both the overall electrification megatrend and some of the technology substitutions that occurred. Curve A shows the growth/ungrowth relationship for household adoption of electricity, in urban areas, between 1900 and 1935. Again, a straight line can be superimposed over growth points. Though not shown in the figure, only 1 percent of the growth had occurred by 1892. By 1906, only 14 years later, 10 percent of the urban homes were electrified and by 1920, 50 percent electrification had occurred.

Actually, other electrical industry growth curves would have shown somewhat faster takeover times. For example, the adoption of electric lighting by factories and stores would have shown a 50 percent adoption before 1920. The adoption of electric trolleys by large cities, as shown by curve B, was unusually early and fast. The overall growth of trolleys, as measured by track mileage, showed a 50 percent growth by 1905. An estimated overall growth of domestic and commercial electrification, then, is shown by the dotted curve D.

FIGURE 7–2
Electrification Growth and Technology Substitutions

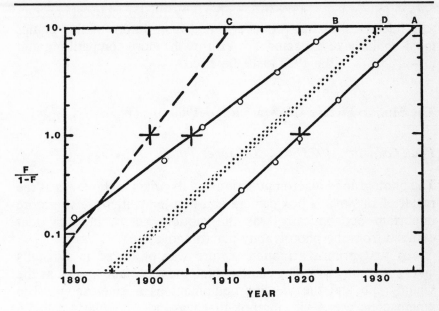

The dashed curve, C, illustrates the takeover of AC versus DC electricity generation and steam turbines versus steam engines. These redirections occurred rather early in the history of the electricity industry and the takeover times were, apparently, 20 years or less. Even faster takeovers probably occurred for tungsten versus carbon filaments and gas-filled versus evacuated electric light bulbs.

What would all these statistics have told us in the early 1900s? By 1906, it could have been seen that 90 percent of the home electrification business would still be available to people choosing to enter the electrical wiring profession—the "high-tech" industry of the early 1900s. Utility companies could have planned their urban expansion activities with considerable confidence. And, electrical fixture manufacturers, distributors, and store outlets could have foreseen a growing business opportunity.

From the same growth curves, it could also have been seen that 50 percent of the initial home electrification growth would be completed (at least in the urban areas) by 1920. Electrical contractors, electrical-fixture producers, and distributors of this equipment could have expected slower growth, more competition, and lower profits in the 1920 to 1930 period.

The Motion Picture Growth Surge—1900 to 1930

Peak Growth· 1923   Takeover Time: 34 years

The photography macroinnovation had its origin in the 1880s as the result of Eastman's box camera and film innovations. Even more important economically was the motion picture industry that evolved from the photography macroinnovation.

A first primitive motion picture was produced in Edison's laboratories in 1889. The camera equipment became known as the kinetograph and the viewing equipment as a kinetoscope. The kinetoscope was a viewing box that was more popularly called a "peep show." The films for these peep shows were about one minute long, and did not involve any ribald subject matter. Two New York speculators, seeing the potential of the peep-show devices, bought a number of them and opened a few kinetoscope parlors in penny arcades on lower Broadway in 1894. The peep-show kinetoscope was an immediate commercial success, which led Edison to produce a number of short movies in a studio he created in his laboratories.

Other entrepreneurs, seeing the potential of picture-projection equipment that would allow a larger audience, urged Edison to develop such a projection machine. While Edison showed no immediate enthusiasm for such a development, experimenters in France, England, and the United States pursued the idea quite vigorously. After some success in 1896, a relatively obscure American developer, Thomas Armat, persuaded Edison to manufacture his projector or "vitascope" as it was called. Now convinced that the idea had a commerical potential, Edison undertook the enterprise with renewed enthusiasm.

The first motion-picture theatre using the vitascope opened in Los Angeles in 1902. (Movies were already being shown in France, by the Lumière brothers, even before 1900.) Not surprisingly, the success of the projection movie exceeded that of the peep show. "Nickelodeons"—theatres that charged a nickel admission fee— began to spring up throughout the country. By 1910 the number of theatres had grown to some 10,000, with locations in practically all the large cities of the United States. Already by 1904, the Edison studio was busy producing large numbers of films, featuring running times of up to 15 minutes.

Soon, a number of other film-production studios began to appear, largely in the Los Angeles area. Many of the improvement innovations that followed were based on improvements in art form, in contrast to the technology innovations of earlier years. Though less technical in character, these improvement innovations were, nevertheless, crucially important in the vigorous competition between the various studios.

The growth of the motion-picture industry, which depended largely on the film-making studios after 1910, made a strong contribution to the U.S. economy in the 1910 to 1930 period.

Can reasonable growth data be developed for this important industry? Two approaches are possible. Census data for movie attendance are available covering the period from 1922 to the present. To examine growth in the earlier years, data on the number of projectionists are available back to 1910. The records show that attendance reached a maximum level around 1930 and remained relatively stable until 1950. Using the peak number of projectionists, which also occurred around 1930, fractional growth data for earlier years can be developed. The fractional growth data, developed in this way, show that the growth from 10 to 90 percent occurred in 34 years, with the peak year around 1923.

Following 1923, the actual growth of the motion-picture industry was beginning to decline.

As with the automobile industry, the growth saturation beginning in the late 1920s did not mean an end to the motion-picture business. It simply was ceasing to be a growth industry.

The Telephone Growth Surge—1895 to 1925

Peak Growth Year: 1910   Takeover Time: 30 years

In 1875, telegraph communications by Morse code were possible to almost any place in the U.S. and even to Europe. However, there was no way in which a person could communicate by speech with a friend, relative, or business associate only a mile away—at least without a rather arduous and time-consuming buggy ride.

Alexander Graham Bell applied for the first telephone patent in 1876, and in the same year demonstrated his device to an awestruck audience at the Philadelphia Centennial Exposition. Only one year later, a private telephone line was built in Boston to augment a burglar alarm system. In the next year, 1878, the first commercial telephone exchange was built to serve about 20 telephones in New Haven, Connecticut. Several other exchanges rapidly appeared in the ensuing years. By 1884, a two-wire telephone line had been built between New York and Boston, and by 1885 a multiple-wire line was completed between New York and Philadelphia. By 1892, telephone communication between New York and Chicago also became possible.

The enormous capital investments for telephone lines and equipment quickly made it impossible for Bell and his original investors to finance the industry growth. Through a succession of organizational changes, the corporate structure of the company evolved into the AT&T parent company in 1900, with control over a number of regional companies to handle local services.

The adoption of telephones in homes began earlier than automobile adoption, and extended over a longer period of time. Although the growth/ungrowth curve for telephone adoption was not quite as uniform as the curve for the automobile and home electrification adoptions, it still showed a significant uniformity between 1890 and 1930. The data for this first-generation growth of telephone adoption suggested that about 50 percent of the U.S. homes were candidates for telephone service (because of location or economics). The takeover time from 10 to 90 percent adoption among these candidates was about 30 years, and the growth peak occurred around 1910.

The Chemical Industry Growth Surge–1900 to 1930

Peak Growth Year: 1912   Takeover Time: 28 years

A huge growth in organic chemicals occurred following the 1880 innovation period. From this industry came synthetic dyes, perfumes, dry-cleaning fluids, explosives, and pharmaceuticals. Reconstituted cellulose fibers (such as rayon) and films (such as celluloid) also came from the same period.

In spite of the German monopoly of the organic chemistry industry in the 1880 to 1915 period, a significant growth was also beginning in the United States during the early 1900s.

One of the best measures of growth in the organic chemical industry might be the annual production of organic chemicals separated from coal tars. Several chemical and steel industries discovered, shortly after 1900, that the coal-tar by-products of coke manufacturing could show as much profit to coke producers as coke production itself. Two good measures of the growth of organic chemicals are the imitation and substitution growths of by-product coke furnaces, relative to the simpler coke ovens that did not recover coal tars.

The peak year for the imitation growth was 1908 and that for substitution growth was 1917. The takeover time in each case was 28 years.

By the 1920s, the growth of the by-product coke industry was beginning to saturate.

If data from the German industry had been included, the saturation time for the production of coal-tar products would probably have been earlier. Once again, the important observation is that the strongest growth was occurring sometime between 1900 and 1920, with growth declining thereafter.

Industrial Growth Swarming—1895 to 1930

Automobiles, electricity, motion pictures, telephones, and organic chemicals are five dominant industries that had their origin in the

1880 innovation surge. Not only did those industries contribute importantly to the national economy, they were also responsible for significant sociological changes. In each case, the growths were distinguished by a notable characteristic.

Prior to 1880 these five industries did not exist, yet in the 1900 to 1930 period their contribution grew from insignificance to a substantial fraction of the overall national economy.

Figure 7–3 illustrates the typical growth/ungrowth curves for the indicated five growth industries. If we had plotted the fractional growth, F, on an ordinary graph (instead of the growth/ungrowth curve), the five industries would each have shown the familiar S-growth behavior. The contribution in most of the cases would have been less than 10 percent in 1900, yet by 1920 most would have reached or passed their peak growth period. Shortly after 1920 the growth would have been declining in all cases. The shaded area, from 1925 to 1935, represents a time when most of the growth had been completed and growth stagnation had occurred.

Apparently a swarming of the new industry growths occurred as the result of the technology innovation cluster around 1880. Or, it might be argued that an especially favorable business climate in the 1895 to 1925 period encouraged new industry growths based on the prior innovations.

Still other industries based on the 1880 macroinnovations could also be shown to have similar growth patterns in the 1895 to 1925 period. The phonograph industry was beginning to show a substantial growth around 1900. The commercial food-canning industry had already started growing before 1900. Technology innovations in newspaper printing created a new growth surge for that industry around the turn of the century. The reinforced concrete innovation led to a surge of construction in large industrial buildings at about the same time. Although the peak growth year is not always easily identifiable for these industries, all of them certainly contributed strongly to the 1895–1925 business growth surge. Moreover, practically all of them were beginning to show a growth saturation in the 1920s. Even the radio industry, a late starter, showed a household adoption (among electrified

FIGURE 7-3
**Typical Growth/Ungrowth Behaviors for five important industries of the
1895-1925 Growth Wave**

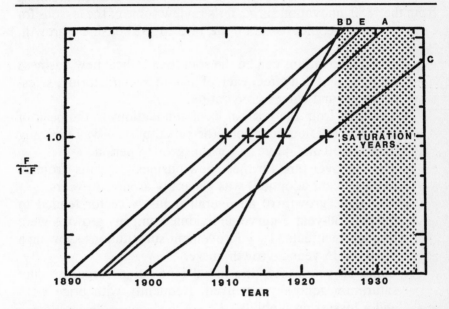

A—Electricity adoption.
B—Automobile adoption.
C—Movie growth.
D—Telephone adoption.
E—Coal-tar recovery for organic chemicals.

homes) with a peak growth around 1925. It should not be surprising that 1930 would mark the beginning of an economic slowdown.

Are these growth curves accurate representations of growth resulting from the macroinnovations? The growth curves are, indeed, accurate for the cases chosen. But a comprehensive growth of the electricity industry should include more than just electrification of homes and street cars. Growth was also occurring in commercial lighting, factory power equipment, early appliances, and dozens of other related businesses. The average electrification growth curve chosen was only representative (though reasonably representative) of the overall electricity industry growth. Similarly, the growth curves for the other cases are only representative.

Before leaving the subject of the industry growth resulting from the 1880 innovation surge, let's review some of the lessons for us as business people, based on the 1895 to 1925 business growth.

- Basic innovations can be the source of radical new business growths that can affect each of us—in manufacturing, sales, services, and career preparation.
- The time from the peak of basic innovations to the peak of macroinnovation adoptions (or substitutions) was typically between 30 and 40 years for this growth period.
- The takeover time for these new business growths (from 10 to 90 percent adoption) was generally around 30 years.
- While the growth of an overall industry sector tended to follow a 30-year S-curve, individual company growths were frequently affected by improvement substitutions showing a 5, 10, or 15-year S-growth curve.
- Some 50 years after the initial innovation surge, product saturation generally occurred, frequently with price wars and a loss of profitability.

Let's turn our attention now to some of the business growths between 1950 and 1980, resulting from the innovation surge of the 1935 period.

THE 1950–1980 PERIOD: INDUSTRIAL GROWTHS

A Diversity of Business Growths

Economic growth between 1895 and 1925 may seem like ancient history to many of us. However, many of us have lived through the business growth surge between 1950 and 1980. This last surge was largely initiated by basic innovations having their origin in the 1925 to 1945 period. The business growths in the 1950 to 1980 period can be illustrated by reference to five of the significant macroinnovations indicated in Chapter 6: polymer chemistry, television, jet air travel, automated home appliances, and automated automobile equipment.

Before examining the effects of these macroinnovations, some further observations can be made about a rejuvenation or extension of growths associated with the previous wave. Although home electrification growth was already saturating in the 1920s, all uses of electricity were not saturated. In the 1930s new ways were being found to apply electricity, for work conveniences rather than illumination. Likewise, the number of automobiles per family began to grow beyond a single unit after the 1930s, partly because of a more affluent society after 1950, but partly also because of automated and power-assisted equipment that made the automobile more appealing to other members of the family. Telephone usage saw another growth surge after the 1930s, as did organic chemicals, radio equipment, and photography. Most of these growth rejuvenations depended on basic or near-basic innovations in existing technologies, such as improved auto equipment, hi-fi sound, and color photography. However, other new industry growths were based almost completely on new technologies.

You can probably remember several of the 1950–1980 business growth surges that had significant effects on our economy. One of the most important of these new businesses was the polymer-chemistry revolution.

The Polymer-Chemistry Growth Surge—1950 to 1980

Peak Growth Year: 1964   Takeover Time: 29 years

Much of the organic-chemical-industry growth between 1895 and 1925 was based on the availability of coal tar as a by-product of the coking industry. A particularly important chemical coming from the coal tar was benzene—and its various derivatives. In the 1930s, the organic chemists turned to petroleum products as a larger and richer source of these important chemicals.

Even though the petrochemical industry accounted for less than 10 percent of the total petroleum refinery products—a small amount relative to fuel products—the chemicals from this by-product created a huge new feedstock industry.

By 1950, some 10 percent of the benzene feeding the organic chemical industry was now coming from petroleum instead of coal—and by 1957 it was 50 percent. Once again, a growth/ ungrowth curve shows a remarkably precise logistic growth behavior, beginning in the 1940s. The takeover time (10 to 90 percent takeover) was a relatively short 15 years and the peak growth occurred some 22 years after the 1935 innovation surge. This was only a small part of the organic-chemicals revolution that was to become enormously important in the 1950 to 1980 business growth surge.

Organic chemicals had already found some applications in the textile and plastics industries in the 1895 to 1925 business growth surge. However, the extraordinary discovery that long-chain carbon compounds—the polymer chemicals—could be synthesized, opened a whole new industry that has had profound effects on textile, plastic, detergent, and pharmaceutical technologies in the 1950 to 1980 growth surge.

The growth of the synthetic fiber industry is an excellent example of the remarkable consequences of the polymer-chemistry revolution.

Following the synthesis of nylon in the Du Pont laboratories, nylon hosiery was already being introduced in the marketplace before World War II. Nylon was an immediate success because, for the first time, a synthetic fiber was actually as good as, or better than, the silk fiber previously used for our most luxurious garments. The nylon industry was completely diverted to military products, such as parachutes, during the war, but afterward showed another huge growth in civilian applications.

Polyester fiber had also been developed in the United Kingdom before World War II, but was delayed by the war. Du Pont was able to introduce its own polyester fiber called Dacron in 1953 as well as an acrylic fiber, Orlon, in the 1950s. The growths of these synthetic fibers have surpassed the sensational growth of nylon. Polyester fibers have almost completely taken over the garment industry previously dominated by cotton, while polyester and acrylic textiles have largely replaced wool textiles.

The remarkable growth of these non-cellulosic fibers can be illustrated by the substitution growth of these fibers relative to the cellulosic fibers, for example, rayon. The peak growth year for this substitution was 1964 and by the 1970s growth saturation was beginning to occur. The takeover time, from 10 to 90 percent substitution, was 29 years. The time interval from the peak of the innovation surge (1935) to the peak substitution (1964) was also 29 years.

The Television Growth Surge—1950 to 1980

Overall Peak Growth Year: 1965 Overall Takeover Time: 30 years

Some primitive television broadcasts were already occurring before World War II, especially in England. Following the war, some 10 percent of homes in the United States had acquired black-and-white television sets by 1949.

In only eight years, the household adoption of television increased from 10 percent to 90 percent—the peak growth year occurring in 1953.

Still another strong surge in television sales took place in the 1960s, when color sets came on the market. While not quite as fast as the original adoption of television sets, the substitution of color for black and white was still surprisingly fast. In 1966, 10 percent of the black-and-white television sets had been replaced by color, with 90 percent replaced only 12 years later. These technology takeover times were surprisingly short—an apparent characteristic of technology growths in the electronics industries.

The *overall* television industry growth is somewhat harder to quantify, but can be approximated by the number of industry employees and revenues. From these very rough numbers, the overall takeover growth began at about the time of 10 percent adoptions for black-and-white sets and reached 90 percent at about the time a 90 percent takeover had occurred for the color versus black-and-white TV substitution.

As with the movie industry, the TV production industry probably has had more impact on our economy than the TV manufacturing industry itself. Job opportunities were created for those people who were sufficiently alert and aggressive to seize the opportunities. However, the television industry apparently reached its peak growth in the mid-1960s and can no longer be identified as a growth industry, though still an important one.

The Air Travel Growth Surge—1945 to 1975

Peak Growth Year: 1958   Takeover Growth: 26 years

The air travel macroinnovation was already acknowledged as one that had its origin midway between two innovation surge periods. But, the large growth of air travel had to await the 1950 to 1980 business growth wave. Like the automobile around 1905, the air travel technology in the 1930s required significant technology improvements, especially in airplanes and air-traffic guidance, before substantial growth could be ensured. The jet aircraft engine and radar flight-control technologies paved the way for this large growth.

Again, like the automobile/carriage substitution, the air-travel/rail-travel takeover could have been forecast at least 15 years before long-distance rail travel was destined for obsolescence in the 1960s. The air-travel/rail-travel takeover faithfully followed a growth/ungrowth linear curve with a peak growth year some 25 years after the peak of the 1935 innovation surge. But, by the 1960s the air-travel industry growth was also beginning to saturate. Price wars and carrier consolidations have resulted from the fierce competition that has developed in the industry.

The Home Appliance Growth Surge—1950 to 1980

Peak Growth Year: 1967   Takeover Time: 26 years

The primary motivation for home electrification in the 1895 to 1925 growth period was an immediate interest in electric illumination. Nevertheless, some home appliances were also becoming popular, including electric refrigerators, washing machines, vacuum sweepers, and irons. However, the home appliances of the 1950 to 1980 growth period were distinctly different in objective.

Home appliances in the 1950 to 1980 period were aimed at woman emancipation from full-time household commitments.

That goal was largely motivated by women's interest in the simplification of food storage, food preparation, kitchen maintenance, laundry activities, and other household chores so they could pursue industrial work opportunities on a more even basis with men. As a consequence, home appliances have had a profound effect on the economy, not only through the appliance manufacturing and electricity consumption effects, but through the effects of a broader workforce base and greater take-home pay. Perhaps more than any of the other macroinnovations of this period, the automatic home appliances have been responsible for a major sociological revolution—a revolution that will probably continue until all vestiges of sexual discrimination have been eliminated.

Once again, the household adoption of home appliances can be traced by growth/ungrowth curves. In most cases, the logistic-growth fits of adoption data suggest that between 50 and 75 percent of all homes will *ultimately* be equipped with automatic dishwashers, disposals, laundries, automatic dryers, and air conditioning. Although there is some dispersion in the growth curves for different appliances, typically the peak growth year appears to be around 1967. The average takeover time for these adoptions has been 26 years and the time from the peak of the innovation surge to the peak of the adoption growth has been a little more than 30 years. Once again, the growth of an important new industry has begun to show a saturation.

The Automobile Travel Resurgence—1945 to 1975

Peak Growth Year: 1962   Takeover Time: 28 years

By 1930, 80 percent of the families in the United States owned automobiles—a truly astounding growth achievement. However, the Great Depression of the 1930–1940 period magnified the woes of an automobile industry that had already ceased to be a growth industry. In the years following World War II, a new growth surge occurred in automobile ownership, as well as automobile use. The growth in ownership resulted partly from important basic technology innovations, such as automatic transmission, power steering, and power brakes that increased the appeal of automobiles still more.

Growth in automobile use also resulted from another kind of innovation, the superhighway. Growth data for the superhighway growth are not readily available, but the Pennsylvania Turnpike was constructed just before World War II, and a vigorous highway growth in other states occurred shortly after the war. Superhighway growth probably reached a maximum in the 1960s.

The adoption growth of power equipment in automobiles can be identified rather precisely from Department of Commerce data. As might be expected, this adoption rate has also followed very closely a typical growth/ungrowth straight-line curve. Taking the average of the adoption data for all automatic equipment, the peak growth year appears to be 1962.

Industrial Growth Swarming—1950 to 1980

Polymer chemicals, television, air travel, and automatic home appliances are four dominant industries that grew largely from basic innovations having their origins around the 1935 era. If automobile power equipment and superhighways are included, then the resurgence of auto travel can also be traced to this innovation surge. By comparing the growth characteristics of these industries to those of the prior growth surge, a common thread is apparent.

Prior to 1935 these industries either did not exist at all, or they had only the potential for a substantial new growth surge based on significant technology innovations—but grow they did.

Many other industries based on the 1935 macroinnovations contributed importantly to the 1950 to 1980 business growth surge. Included were digital computers (including microelectronics and microchips), nuclear energy, space travel, hi-fi audio equipment, frozen foods, and mass-construction of homes among others. Growths of these other industries could also have been indicated here—but in practically every case they would have shown characteristics similar to the five cases already selected and discussed.

Figure 7–4 illustrates the typical growth/ungrowth curves for the five cases. In general, the takeover time was around 30 years and the peak growth time occurred about 30 years after 1935 (the

FIGURE 7–4

Typical Growth/Ungrowth Behaviors for the Five Important Industries, 1950–1980

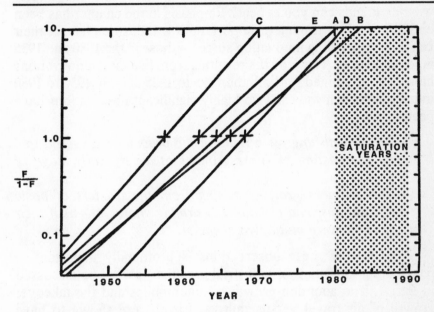

A—Non-cellulosic versus cellulosic synthetic textiles.
B—Television adoption.
C—Air versus rail travel.
D—Home-appliance adoption.
E—Auto-equipment adoption.

peak of the innovation surge). Again, a shaded area from 1980 to 1990 indicates a period of growth saturation for these five growths. With the growth stagnation has come a decline in the GNEC growth and, more recently, the Crash of '87. More on the significance of the industrial growth stagnation will be reserved for discussion in Chapter 8 and Part 3.

A swarming of new industry growths was stimulated either by a surge of basic innovations or a more favorable business climate in the 1950 to 1980 period. The role of basic technology innovations and macroinnovations in our business and personal lives should be apparent.

Summary

Now that you have invested your time and energy into this chapter what dividends can you expect? Emphasis in the chapter has been on the growth swarming of important new industries having their genesis in preceding innovation surges—those in the 1880 and 1935 innovation eras. The growths resulting from five macroinnovations have been examined for both the 1895 to 1925 and the 1950 to 1980 industrial growth waves. Two highly significant observations have been made:

- *The growth/ungrowth relationship provides a powerful tool for forecasting business growths at a very early stage of growth.*
- *The business growths arising from the clusters of basic innovations tend to have a swarming character—as if their growths were mutually beneficial.*

The first of these observations is profoundly important in recollecting the future of industrial growths—as will be discussed in Part 3. The adoption growth of automobiles and the takeover growth of air travel versus railroad travel were shown to have almost mystical qualities. These growth behaviors are typical for many other types of industrial growths. But, it is the growth/ungrowth curve, the $F/(1 - F)$ curve, that really makes growth forecasting a definitive and usable procedure.

The second observation, on business-growth swarming, is also important relative to understanding at least one mechanism contributing to the long economic wave. The behavior of industrial growths in the last two growth waves, strongly suggests that the swarming of business growths might be even more dominating than the clustering of innovations. For example, the basic innovation for the radio occurred between the 1880 and 1935 surges, but the industrial growth followed closely that of other industries in the early 1900s. In contrast, the basic innovation for the airplane also occurred between the latter two innovation surges, yet its large industrial growth waited for the next growth wave between 1950 and 1980. The microchip appeared well after the 1935 innovation surge, but still rode on the final part of the last industrial growth wave.

Some of the coincidences of business growths arise simply from the favorable economic conditions already resulting from a few strong business growths. Nevertheless, the relationship between technology innovation surges and industrial growths cannot be overlooked. It will be useful, then, to look more carefully at the various factors that apparently contribute to the long economic wave.

CHAPTER 8

THE LONG WAVE CONNECTION

Two severe stock-market crashes have occurred in this century—in 1929 and in 1987. Each crash happened at the same phase of the long GNEC wave. In this same period, two remarkable industrial growth booms have occurred—one during the 1900–1930 period, and one during the 1955–1985 period. Each boom also occurred during the same phase of the long GNEC wave.

Over the last 150 years, the timing of technology-macroinnovation clustering, industrial-growth swarming, and business-growth economic stagnations has shown a consistent pattern relative to the long GNEC/GNP wave.

Can we identify the link between the industrial growth surge and the GNEC growth cycle? Are there still other business or societal behaviors related to the long economic wave? How can we as business and career planners use that information in recollecting the future?

At least one aspect of the long economic wave is apparent. Whether a cause or effect, there is little doubt that a clustering of economically important macroinnovations can have a significant impact on subsequent business growth—and ultimately on the economy at large. Important though macroinnovations are, very few of us will be fortunate enough to be "insiders," i.e., involved in them *at their inception*. Still, just the knowledge that macroinnovation clustering predominates during a particular period of the GNEC/GNP wave is a useful piece of information. The 1980s and 1990s should mark one of those periods.

The real value of macroinnovations to most of us is that they are signals.

By recognizing macroinnovations sufficiently early, we have an opportunity to adjust our businesses and careers to benefit from the radically new industrial directions they signal. It is the consequent industrial growths that bring dollars to our business coffers, our national economy, and our family purse. We should be prepared to recognize the signals and act accordingly.

Let's carefully examine the relative timing and growth behaviors associated with technology macroinnovation clustering, industrial growth swarming, and GNEC/GNP surges. Let's also examine other features of the economy such as industrial equipment requirements, work productivity, and psychological factors that can play a role in the long energy or economic wave.

The Innovation-Growth/Industry-Growth/ Energy-Growth Relationship

In earlier chapters, we learned that:

- Basic technology innovations showed surges around 1880 and 1935.
- New industries showed strong growth surges during the periods 1895–1925 and 1950–1980.
- GNEC/GNP growth has shown a long wave with two of the peaks occurring in 1915 and 1970.

Can we establish a more precise relationship between these growths?

Figure 8–1 shows all three of those growth characteristics superimposed on a common time scale. The bottom of the figure shows the technology innovation and business implementation *rates* of growth as two bell-shaped curves. The innovation-rate curve shows a peak rate at about 1935, consistent with the Mensch data discussed in Chapter 6. The delay time between the innovation midpoint and the composite business-growth midpoint is about 30 years, consistent with observations in Chapter 7. A shift of that curve by two or three years in either direction would not change the conclusions significantly.

The impact of business growth on societal energy needs (GNEC) is affected by both the growth rate and the growth size of the industrial market demanding energy. The resulting energy

FIGURE 8–1

Timing of the Technology-Innovation, Business-Implementation, and Weighted-Implementation Growth Curves Relative to the Long Energy Wave

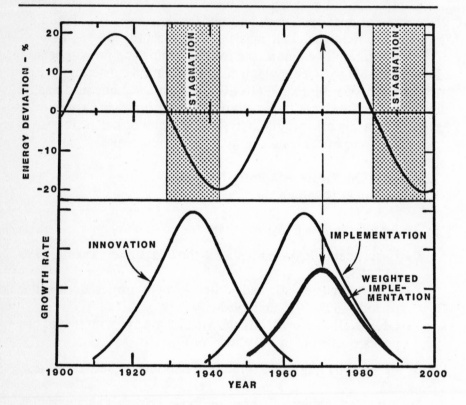

demand is very similar to the food demand, based on the growth rate and growth size of the teenage boy, discussed in Chapter 2. Hence, the heavy curve (labeled "weighted implementation") is simply the "kitchen impact" of business growth on its resources—including its energy resources.

The striking conclusion is that the size-weighted, growth-rate curve (the kitchen impact) peaked at about 1970—precisely the year the long energy (and economic) wave peaked.

That correlation confirms that gross national energy consumption is intimately related with the growth of new industries, just as food consumption is related to the growth of children. It can also be seen that the 1935 innovation surge peaked at about the middle of the 1930–1940 stagnation period—the period between the time the energy-deviation curve crossed the zero-axis and the time it reached a minimum. The market crashes of 1929 and 1987 coincided approximately with points where the declining GNEC moved from above to below the underlying logistic growth curve. Probably more significantly, it marked points where the growths of new industries (from earlier macroinnovations) were reaching growth stagnation. The figure appears to be a dramatic illustration of how all the pieces fit together.

Having inferred this correlation of growths, how can we use the information in our own business planning?

Using the Long Wave in Business Planning

Technology innovations are clearly the seeds for new business and industry growth. But to most of us, the business growths themselves are the basis for our monetary rewards. Still, attention to basic technology innovations and macroinnovations is or should be an important part of business planning for the industrial giants— companies like Du Pont, GE, IBM, AT&T, Exxon, and Boeing. Among these giants, it is crucially important that research laboratories give attention to the possible big leap forward, as well as to the more modest improvements in existing technologies. A recognition of the success probabilities of various kinds of technology innovations at different phases of the long economic wave can be particularly useful for research planning in those companies.

Realistically, most of us have little hope of being sources of macroinnovations. Nevertheless, it is just as important for us to recognize the signals of business redirections.

Two signals for redirection are (1) the long-wave timing, and (2) early growths that can be extrapolated by the growth/ungrowth principle.

Around 1880, for example, industry leaders familiar with the characteristic of the long wave could have expected big changes in industry directions. By the year 1900 or 1910, they could have deduced, from growth/ungrowth projections, the likely growths of electricity, automobiles, and movies. Likewise, in 1930 or 1940 industry leaders could have again expected significant redirections from the historical behavior of the long wave. In 1950 or shortly thereafter, growths could have been projected for a number of large industries such as synthetic fibers, plastics, TV, and air travel. Even the growth adoption of home appliances could have been forecast and the sociological implications might have been anticipated. Perhaps equally as important, the declines of several older industries such as railroads, rayon textiles, coal-tar products, and even coal itself could have been anticipated—and their rate of decline in the following years could have been projected quite accurately.

The period from 1987 to early in the new century will offer extraordinary opportunities for recollecting the future—a future with dramatic changes from the prior decades. At this time the industrial giants should be reassessing their future. Some will find new business opportunities, some business obsolescence. It probably will be 1990, perhaps even 2000, before reliable growth/ ungrowths can be projected. Nevertheless, even now a few can be forecast—a subject to be discussed in Part 3.

These recognitions are equally important to wholesale distributors, retailers, service technicians, and perhaps most importantly, educators. Only a few companies are involved in a new product at an early date. These new business opportunities gradually diffuse not only to other companies, but to specialty stores, service organizations, and training schools. Traditionally, it has been the people with pioneering spirit that have profited most by early initiatives.

The Capital-Overexpansion Thesis

As previously discussed, a compelling case can be made for innovation clustering as a source of the GNEC and GNP long wave. Can other possible sources of the long wave be indicated?

A strong case can also be made for capital overexpansion as a source of the long economic wave.

The capital-overexpansion thesis, as a fundamental cause of the long wave, has been suggested by a number of economists, but special attention here will be focused on the work of Forrester and his colleagues at the MIT Sloan School of Management. Even accepting the capital overexpansion thesis, innovation clustering can still be regarded as a strong catalyst or at least a corollary to the long wave. Or, accepting the innovation-clustering thesis, capital overexpansion might still be regarded as a catalyst or a corollary.

Looking again at industry growths associated with various macroinnovations, many of them were strongly dependent on the support of capital equipment—particularly electricity, telecommunications, air travel, superhighways, and the chemical industries.

If there is any nonuniformity of capital equipment growth for capital-intensive industries, we can expect nonuniformities in the associated equipment-supply businesses and their employment levels.

What has been the history of capital expansion associated with industries arising from a few of the macroinnovations? Three examples can be used for illustration—the textile industry in the Industrial Revolution, the railroad industry in the Transportation Revolution, and the electricity-generating industry in the Electricity Revolution.

One of the significant features of the Industrial Revolution, beginning in the United Kingdom around 1760, was the transfer of textile activities from homes to more centralized work locations. That transition occurred because the efficiency of mechanized textile equipment exceeded that of simple manual labor; yet the cost of the necessary capital equipment was far beyond the means of individual households. A potential problem of these new "capital-intensive" industries, as history has subsequently borne out, has been the necessity for a careful balancing of market demand with capital-equipment acquisition to fulfill that demand.

As industrial equipment became more complex, particularly with the evolution of power-driven equipment, the careful planning of equipment expansion became increasingly important to avoid overexpansion.

A good illustration of the perils of capital overexpansion is the early growth of the railroad industry. In the years between 1880 and 1883—when growth saturation was already beginning—about

10,000 miles of railroad tracks were being added each year, a growth rate of about 10 percent per year. The expense of this expansion, together with the fierce competition that was already developing, was a major factor in a financial panic that occurred in 1884. Expansion was sharply curtailed for a few years, but another substantial overexpansion occurred shortly thereafter that contributed to the almost-disastrous panic of 1893.

The early history of the railroad industries offers a graphic example of the tendency toward capital overexpansion at the end of a strong growth period.

An even more quantifiable example of periodic capital overexpansion can be found from the records of electricity growth in the United States during the last 80 years. Since good data are available for both consumption and capital-equipment growths in this case, it deserves special attention.

The Electricity Industry Long Wave As a Case Study

The electricity industry is a very large contributor to the gross national product and is characterized by the huge capital equipment investments it must make. For example, about 50 percent of the cost of generating electricity is associated with the cost of the generating equipment itself. When distribution equipment (electricity lines and transformers) are included, the financial commitments for equipment are even larger.

What does this mean to us as electricity customers? More than half the dollars the consumer pays for electricity are generally used to finance the equipment. This investment money must come from banks, financial investors, and stockholders. In contrast, only about one fourth of the consumer's money is used for labor and less than one fourth for fuel (mostly coal and uranium). If all electricity customers reduced their consumption by 50 percent, the electricity companies could not afford to reduce their bills by 50 percent—they would have to continue payments on financing costs. As a consequence, a reduction in electricity consumption by all customers would require an *increase* in the electricity rate (the cents per kilowatt-hour) that you would pay.

It is crucially important for capital-intensive industries to plan their equipment expansion carefully.

Unfortunately, it usually requires five to ten years to plan and construct large generating plants (as well as plants in other capital-intensive industries). Hence, if the growth of consumption decreases after new plant constructions begin, a company can find itself with excess generating capacity. Under those circumstances, the company profitability will generally be impaired and the electricity bills to customers might be higher than necessary. However, if an overly conservative approach is taken by utilities, the effect might be insufficient generating capacity, local blackouts, and unhappy customers. Obviously, long-range construction planning receives careful attention in all capital-intensive industries.

Capacity Growth versus Consumption Growth

With this background, let's look at the record of electricity generating-capacity growth relative to electricity consumption growth. The historical growth of U.S. electricity energy consumption can be described by an underlying secular growth curve with a long-wave variation superimposed. The amplitude of the electricity-consumption long wave has been about 20 percent and the average period about 55 years, which is consistent with the GNEC growth behavior.

What about the growth of the generating capacity? This growth also shows the 55-year long wave. Perhaps surprisingly, the amplitude is 30 percent instead of 20 percent—50 percent larger. Moreover, the historical data show the peaks of the generating-capacity wave extend about five to ten years beyond the peaks of the electricity-consumption wave.

Figure 8–2 indicates the pattern of the generating-capacity long wave (the dashed curve) superimposed on the electricity-energy wave. The technology innovation and business implementation surges are again shown at the bottom of the figure (as in Figure 8–1). The labels A, B, C, and D show successive phases of the electricity-consumption (and GNEC) long wave.

FIGURE 8–2

Relationship of Innovations, Implementations, and Weighted Implementations to the Long Electricity-Consumption and Generation-Capacity Waves

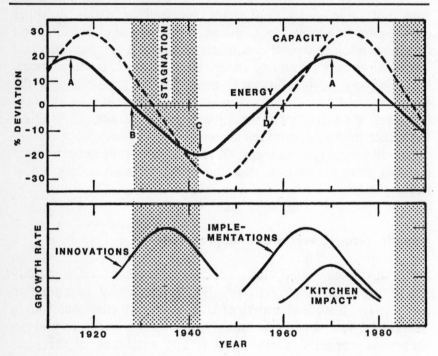

It is occasionally argued that the timing of capital-growth is a more important trigger event—both for economy declines and rejuvenations—than the apparent technology-innovation and business-implementation growths. Again using the electricity industry as an example, it does appear that the peak turn-around for the capital growth curve is closer to the beginning of the stagnation period. Likewise, the trough turn-around for capital growth does come just before 1950, the beginning of the 1950–1980 business growth surge.

For more on the importance of the capital growth relative to the long economic wave, let's look at some interesting computer-modeling work that has been reported by MIT.

The MIT System Dynamics National Model

For at least 10 years, the System Dynamics Group at the MIT Sloan School of Management has been developing and using a computer model that simulates the socioeconomic behavior of our society.

The MIT System Dynamics Model simulates social and psychological factors as well as economic factors involved in decision-making within the various sectors of society.

An important feature that distinguishes the System Dynamics Model from the more common econometric models is that decision-making in the various sectors is modeled to reflect observed business, government, and individual practices—in contrast to the optimal economic practices generally followed by econometric models. In other words, the MIT model recognizes what people *actually* do—not just what people *should* do.

Because of the complexity of the MIT model, it is not an approach that could easily be adopted by any business or institution as a working tool. However, the completenesss and versatility of the model make it a useful national resource for studying probable socioeconomic trends under real societal conditions. An especially attractive feature of the model is its ability to study the possible consequences of alternative national policy directions. Clearly, that is an inherent limitation of simpler trend analysis approaches.

Results of studies with the MIT System Dynamics Model have been widely reported in technical, economic, and financial journals. A significant observation of the studies is that the three following distinct economic cycles appear in their results:

- a short cycle of 3 to 7 years
- an intermediate cycle of 15 to 25 years
- a long cycle of 45 to 60 years

The long cycle has been described as a particularly dominant one in the model studies.

The MIT studies indicate that the long wave is generated by interactions of the capital-goods-producing and the consumer-goods-producing sectors of the economy.

Basically, the oscillation reflects a sequence of events that includes:

- a small demand for capital expansion during an economic depression
- a deterioration of the existing capital stock during this low-growth period
- a subsequent need for equipment replacement
- an accelerating need for new equipment during a new growth period (stimulated not only by capital needs in the consumer-goods-producing sector, but also by its own capital needs in the capital-goods-producing sector)
- a buildup of a capital-equipment order backlog
- an overexpansion in capital goods

Also involved in this chain of events are the labor shifts between sectors. This proposed mechanism for the long wave is important, not only because of its implications on business growth, but also because the studies imply an explanation for the long wave even without a requirement for innovation surges.

The Role of Innovation in the Capital Overexpansion Model

In the systems studies using the MIT National Model, innovation was not introduced explicitly. The long economic wave was observed simply as the consequence of a strong buildup of capital equipment, the ultimate overexpansion of that buildup, and the subsequent curtailment of capital growth, thereby leading to surplus labor and unemployment. The results of the model studies also imply that the cessation of the capital-equipment growth tends to persist for a period of some 20 years. During this period existing structures and equipment deteriorate, creating a need for replacement. When this replacement commences, the beginning of a new growth surge is signaled.

Although the introduction of new technology growths is not necessary to account for the long cycle in this model, it has been pointed out by some of the MIT workers that innovation can be an important complementary factor. Graham and Senge of MIT, for example, have observed that industrial investments in new technology directions are strongly discouraged after a growth cycle is underway. To put this in perspective, ask yourself: Would you invest your company's money predominantly in research or in manufacturing equipment when sales are outstripping production capabilities?

During a strong business growth, the most cost-effective way to use financial resources would appear to be further investments in the production enterprises already showing a handsome return.

In contrast, the climate for innovation is most conducive after growth has been exhausted and industry finds itself in the economic doldrums with its traditional product lines. Both the Mensch and the Forrester schools seem to agree that innovation is strongly stimulated at that time. Moreover, it would appear that the magnitude of the capital-growth requirements to establish new lines of industries might actually be greater than that simply to renovate existing industries.

The spate of new capital-goods requirements following the 1935 innovation wave offers a good example of the emphasis on new types of capital growth. A need for aluminum-production equipment for the aircraft industry created a need for capital expansion in that industry. The renewed growth of the auto industry after the depression created a critical need for highway construction and new oil refineries. The TV industry created new requirements for capital investments in manufacturing and broadcasting facilities. The same was true for the petrochemical industry, the synthetic textile industry, and the air-travel industry.

Both schools of thought note apparent trends toward mini-innovations or pseudo-innovations at the end of a long economic cycle. Certainly a stalemate in technology innovation could be an important factor in diminishing the need for new capital formation. However, it has been argued by some that the precise timing of the innovation wave does not clearly establish innovation clustering as the primary driving force for a new economic cycle. In this particular argument, more attention would be focused on capital investment cycles. Although the overall effect is not greatly changed, it's rather interesting and informative to examine some of the controversies.

Long-Wave Issues

There is general agreement among the long-wave proponents that technology innovation is a relevant factor. There are, however, disagreements on its degree of impact, its timing, and its role in the cycle (is it a cause or effect?) Some critics of the innovation-clustering thesis have argued that the innovation wave is more diffuse than indicated by the Mensch data, though this criticism is largely a matter of degree.

The distinction between the arguments of the two long-wave schools of thought tends to be rather subtle.

One school would argue that the "clustering" of innovations is a trigger mechanism for initiating a "swarming" of commercialization; critics would argue that basic innovations are only inhibited during prosperous times.

Some of the critics also argue that commercialization swarming is much stronger than innovation clustering. They would conclude that capital-equipment trends might be more significant in triggering economic growths or declines, largely because the economy is more sensitive to capital expenditures. An example would be the current slowdown in utility orders for new generating equipment, thereby causing a decline in equipment supply and plant construction businesses. That position leans more toward the Forrester thesis.

Critics of the innovation theory as a long-wave source have another objection. They point out that some of the very important innovations, such as railroads, automobiles, airplanes, and electrification, have had equal or greater impacts on national economies in cycles following the innovation than during the cycles in which they were introduced. An example is the enormous growth of the air-travel industry in the 1945 to 1975 period. In contrast, capital overexpansions have always occurred at the end of strong growth cycles.

Clearly some of the macroinnovations have extended over more than one long wave. However, much of the second-cycle growth might be attributable to subsequent innovations—such as automatic automobile equipment and superhighways that stimulated a new automobile growth, or jet engines and radar air-control which improved the efficiency of air travel, or even innovations in electricity usage (such as home appliances) which gave new impetus to electricity growth. In support of the innovation-clustering thesis, it does appear that many of the large business growths in the commercial swarming are strongly coupled to technology innovations preceding them—as was discussed in Chapter 7.

Other factors can be important in the long wave. The British long-wave economists, Freeman, Clark, and Soete, have noted that heavy demands on the labor resources during a period of prosperity lead to higher labor costs, lower productivity, and profit erosions. This can lay the groundwork for economic difficulties toward the end of a commercialization growth cycle. Most of us in business can relate to these arguments also.

Controversies on causal mechanisms can easily obscure the more important conclusions regarding the long wave.

Whether the various factors are causes or effects might be quite important to economic theorists trying to understand the most probable triggering mechanisms for the long wave. A better understanding might also help future policy planners to minimize effects of the long wave. For using the long-wave behavior in our business planning, all of the contributing factors must be regarded as significant. Remember, our interest as business people is recollecting the future—using the results for our own business and investment guidance.

Putting the Pieces Together

The contributing factors to the long wave can be summarized as follows (referring again to Figure 8–2):

- The level of GNEC, GNP, and electricity consumption begins to decrease at point A, but the installed capacity of generating equipment (and factories) continues to grow beyond immediate needs.

- Technology innovations during this period probably are directed largely toward improvements (or pseudo-improvements) of existing consumer products.
- At point B, economic stagnation has become obvious and plans for future capital expansion are severely curtailed.
- Around point B, technology innovation efforts are beginning to focus on more radical technological changes in consumer products. This does not necessarily imply any increase in R&D, but rather a reorientation.
- The appearance of a few dramatic technology innovations between points B and C might result in some further innovations in other sectors of the economy.
- At point C, new products are beginning to be implemented, though the kitchen impact is very small at this stage,
- The capital construction suspension draws to an end around, or shortly after, point C—both because the surfeit of equipment has now been attenuated and the growths of new products, resulting from radical innovations, demand new investments.
- The recovery gains momentum between C and D, fueled both by new products and facility equipment expansions.
- Improvement innovations probably begin to dominate R&D around point D—particularly process and manufacturing innovations.
- As the GNEC/GNP curve passes through point D, commercial implementations become important, and the kitchen-impact curve begins to be significant.
- At this stage, an increasing demand for labor resources, both in the product and capital-equipment markets, leads to higher labor costs and lower productivity, thus beginning to squeeze industry profits.
- Finally, as the kitchen-impact curve reaches its maximum, energy consumption reaches a new peak at point A and the cycle begins anew.

Again it is emphasized that no attempt has been made here to establish whether technology innovations or capital-equipment growth behavior triggers particular energy-consumption transitions.

Many factors can and do contribute to the long wave—from our point of view, the relative importance of triggering events need not be a topic of controversy.

To use the long-wave theory, it is more important to know where we are in the wave, what we should expect at this time, and how we should plan our business activities to exploit our knowledge. The factor that is the predominant "triggering" mechanism can be left to the theorists.

Other Factors in the Long Wave

Technology-innovation surges and capital overexpansion are both important factors in the long economic cycle. It can be argued that still other factors are contributors. For example, the average working career of an individual spans 40 to 50 years. People in the workforce at the end of a particular economic cycle have no direct memory of the problems that occurred at the end of the last cycle. Can you remember what business conditions prevailed in the 1920s? Even the similarity of the stock market behaviors following the 1929 and 1987 crashes has been a surprise to many of us.

Moreover, the prosperous years of high growth prior to the peak of a cycle undoubtedly have an adverse conditioning effect on management, labor, and government, resulting in some deterioration of productivity at the end of a cycle. All of these problems can propagate the long business cycle in spite of the increased knowledge and capability of human enterprise. Moreover, each of the possible causes for the long wave appears to have a periodic character of some 40, 50, or perhaps 60 years, making the identification of a primary source even more difficult.

The factors involved in the long wave make it apparent that the long-range national economy is primarily a product of industry practices—not the converse.

Government economic policies are generally reactive to, not independent of, industrial and economic trends. True, government policies can undoubtedly be important in the shorter range. It is an interesting observation, though, that monetary, taxation, and government-spending policies seem to have more unpredictable longer-range effects during a growth stagnation period. Again, it implies the *industrial* policies tend to be more dominating in the long range.

In that respect, it seems that government policies directed toward revitalizing technology innovations and capital re-investment in industry could be exceedingly important during the time of the long-wave *transition*. Those policies might involve education, training, cooperative R&D, technology transfer, and federal and state projects aimed at *new* technologies, and perhaps, appropriate tax initiatives encouraging high technology growth— both innovation and prompt implementation. Those points will get further attention in Part 4.

Summary

Two major factors have been identified as contributors to the long energy/economic wave:

1. Innovation clustering with a resulting new-industry swarming.
2. Capital overexpansions.

Still other factors, such as the average worker's lifetime and work productivity, can contribute.

As business people, investors, and career seekers, it is important to know both where we are in the long cycle and how to respond. These responses might involve R&D, engineering, manufacturing, equipment investments, marketing, personal investments, and/or career planning. The purpose of this chapter has been to show how all the pieces fit together in the long-wave connection.

With the background from the three chapters in Part 2, we are now ready to apply our knowledge to recollecting the future. Part 3 will take us on that excursion.

PART 3

THE FUTURE ACCORDING TO RECALL

CHAPTER 9

TESTING THE CREDIBILITY OF RECALL—ENERGY AND THE ECONOMY

The Crash of '29 marked a significant transition point in the long economic wave. At that approximate time, the GNEC growth crossed the "equinox" between an economic "autumn" and a "winter."* The average annual GNEC growth subsequently fell to below-average growth rates, that is, the growth of energy use by industries, transportation, commerce and households had sunk to a lower-than-normal level. Moreover, the economic prosperity of the country (and the world) was destined to reflect that lower level of overall societal industry.

Before the Crash of '29, little thought was given to the possibility of an approaching economic adversity. Even after the crash, at least for several months, the likelihood of a prolonged recession or depression was generally dismissed by political, financial, business, and economic leaders.

Would the economic outlooks at that time have been different if there had been a recognition and appreciation of the GNEC (and GNP) long wave? Even before the Crash of '29 is it conceivable that an exceptionally knowledgeable long-wave analyst could have projected the general economic trend of the 1930s? Could the average GNEC (or GNP) *growth rate* have been estimated for the

---

*In this respect a difference exists between our calendar seasons and the economic seasons defined here. In our calendar seasons, the autumnal equinox marks the transition from summer to autumn (around September 22). In the economic seasons, the autumnal equinox has been chosen arbitrarily to mark the transition from autumn to winter.

next 10–15 years—or the following 30 years? Actually, a forecast of only the *general* economic trend should not be regarded as incredible.

As early as 1926, the Russian economist, Kondratieff, was forecasting an economic slowdown in the 1930s based on his analysis of long-term fluctuations in the prices and production levels of various commodities.

However, the possibility of forecasting *quantitative* GNEC (and GNP) average growth rates at that time for the approaching bust and boom periods would almost certainly be regarded as beyond the pale. But growth forecasts, within reasonable limits, could have been credible if we allow two important presumptions:

- The forecaster was familiar with logistic growth laws and possible regular deviations from logistic growth.
- The forecaster was aware of the close relationship between GNEC and GNP growths.

To suggest that any forecaster or forecasting enterprise might have such prescience in the 1920s or 1930s could, admittedly, stretch our imaginations inordinately. However, since we are interested only in the credibility of *applying* the growth principles, we will assign that exceptional wisdom to a mythical growth analysis company, RECALL (Recollection Enterprises using Cycle-Adjusted Logistics and Logistics), Inc. It will be assumed that RECALL was unusually steeped in the knowledge of growth methodology as early as the 1920s.

The credibility of RECALL will be tested (in this chapter) by examining how successful the company might have been in forecasting energy and economic trends for a subsequent 25 to 50 years, based on its knowledge in the 1920s and later. In Chapter 10, the credibility test will be extended to the projectability of technology and business growths in various manufacturing and service industries. If the company passes these credibility tests, we might more willingly endorse its forecasts of economic and industrial growths for the 1985–2020 period. Let's start, then, with an examination of RECALL's projection capabilities in the 1920s.

Before the Crash of '29—The Confusing Signals

The economic signals prior to 1929 were generally encouraging. GNP grew about 15 percent from 1923 to 1928, an average growth rate of about 3 percent per year. During this same five-year period, the market index for industrial stocks increased an astounding 150 percent or 2.5 times—an average annual increase of 20 percent per year. Unemployment was around 4 percent in 1928. And, the federal government revenues exceeded expenditures by more than 20 percent. As President Hoover was to say, even following the 1929 Crash, "The fundamental business of the country . . . is on a sound and prosperous basis."

Could a more detailed analysis of the GNP fluctuations during the 1920s have told a different story? Probably not, at least on the basis of the year-to-year changes over a short period of time.

Year-to-year changes in GNP can be quite misleading, even during times of normal growth, since these changes can vary from less than zero to as much as 10 percent within an interval of only a few years.

The GNP annual growths during the 1920s did not deviate from this general rule of perversity. As an example, the GNP growth during 1925 was about 8 percent when corrected for inflation; yet in 1927 it showed a zero growth. On the average, the economy of the 1920s would generally have been regarded as healthy, when measured by inflation-corrected GNP.

As is legend now, the stock-market behavior during the 1920s (prior to the Crash of '29) was painfully misleading—especially to the many speculators seeking rewards for their Wall Street labors. Stock speculation had reached epidemic proportions fueled by the over-confidence of investors, a broad participation of financiers (including various financial institutions), the evolution of holding companies (allowing the pyramiding of investments), and the availability of low margin requirements for stock purchases. The speculative fever invited disaster—and disaster befell. But, the October crash was only a beginning. From its peak value in 1929 to its low in 1932, the average value of stocks decreased almost eight-fold. In fact, the market decline due to the Crash of

'29 was relatively modest—much less than two-fold. The largest decline began in the spring of 1930, when the Great Depression commenced.

The depth of the depression in the 1930s was of devastating proportions relative to any prior depressions in U.S. history. As a measure of the severity, the GNP fell by 10 percent in 1930, another 8 percent in 1931 and about 15 percent in 1932, for a compounded decrease of about 30 percent over the three-year period. Undoubtedly, the many bankruptcies of financial institutions, companies, and individuals, as well as the absence of any safety nets such as bank insurance, unemployment compensation, or social security contributed substantially to the severity of the Great Depression.

With that backdrop, let's look at the probable forecasts (or recollections) of the fictional company, RECALL. As a first step, we'll see whether the year-to-year variations of GNEC were any more revealing than those of GNP. In two of the years—1921 and 1923—the GNEC variations were even more dramatic than those of GNP. However, as a general rule, the GNEC tended to rise and fall quite consistently with GNP.

The GNEC trends can be more informative when looking at growth rates averaged over 10-year intervals. For example, between 1900 and 1910, the average GNEC growth rate was 5.6 percent per year. Between 1905 and 1915 it declined to 3.0 percent per year. The decline continued in subsequent 10-year intervals, reaching 1 to 2 percent per year for the 10-year intervals ending in 1926, 1927, 1928, or 1929. But, remember, the GNEC long wave was not known at that time.

RECALL's Approach to GNEC-Growth Projections— Before the Crash of '29

Could the longer-range growth behavior of GNEC have been recognized before the Crash of '29? Could it have furnished some forewarning of the 1930s adversity?

Assuming RECALL had been familiar in 1925 with the GNEC long wave, the onset of an energy-use decline could, at least, have been anticipated.

The basic question is whether RECALL could have observed the long GNEC wave by the mid-1920s, and whether it could have developed a reasonable description of the wave pattern from historical data. Although those data on GNEC growth were not nearly so well documented as they are today, it is conceivable that some astute RECALL analysts could have observed an indication of a cycle-adjusted-logistic (CAL) growth pattern for GNEC, based only on data available from 1850 to 1925. Admittedly, barely one and a half cycles would have been discernible as a wave-like perturbation on the underlying GNEC secular growth. However, data showing a long cycle in coal consumption between 1800 and 1925 could have added another 50 years of evidence. The projection of a CAL growth pattern for GNEC would undoubtedly have evoked considerable agnosticism among energy analysts and economists, and probably justifiably so at that time in history. Quite remarkably though, the amplitude, period, and timing of the cycle for GNEC could have already been approximated quite well by 1925.

Figure 9–1 shows the growth of GNEC from 1850 to 1925 based on the historical GNEC data. Even with the simplest kind of curve-fitting, a straight line on the log-linear plot, it would have become apparent from a deviation plot of actual data points that the year-to-year GNEC points were oscillating about the base curve (or, really, the base straight-line). With that simple observation, a cycle amplitude of about 15 percent (instead of 20 percent) and a period of some 50 to 60 years would have been identified.

The straight-line fit would have implied a continuing steady (exponential) growth of GNEC, a continuing constant percentage increase each year in the basic growth. The energy analysts in RECALL would have known that the concept of a continuing constant growth rate would violate nature's laws and, therefore, would have sought a logistic fit instead of an exponential one. Just how they would have proceeded, or what they would have concluded can only be the subject of conjecture. However, their final conclusions on the probable course of the economy after 1925 would have been remarkably good, almost independent of the uncertainties in the precise choice of the underlying secular growth curves (or straight line).

FIGURE 9–1
**Growth Data on GNEC to 1925 with Exponential Extrapolation (solid line)
and Logistic Extrapolation (dashed line)**

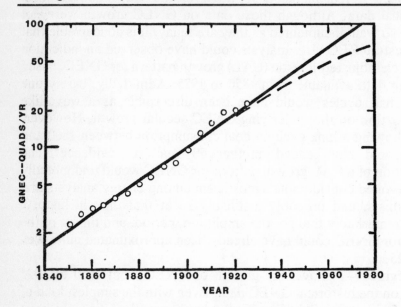

There is some hazard in trying to predict what energy (or economic) forecasters might have projected, since a viewer from the 1980s might assign his own knowledge of historical events to the forecaster of 1925. Nevertheless, an attempt will be made here to recreate a credible 1925 forecast by RECALL—based only on the premise that the RECALL analysts would have been familiar with logistic growth principles and would have had at least a suspicion of the long energy wave.

RECALL's GNEC Growth Projections—Before the Crash of '29

As a first attempt at re-creating some conceivable RECALL energy-growth projections in 1925, let's seek only average GNEC growths over two future periods: a 15-year period from 1925 to 1940, and a subsequent 30-year period from 1940 to 1970. To gain some perspective on average GNEC growth rates, let's look at the history of GNEC growth.

*Maximum GNEC growth rates (associated with prosperous years)
have typically been in the range of 4 percent per year when
averaged over 15 years. Minimum GNEC growth rates (associated
with economic adversities) have typically been in the range of 1
percent per year, again when averaged over 15 years.*

Could RECALL have related GNP growths to GNEC
growths? That relationship might have been particularly difficult to
establish in the 1920s. From our perspective in the 1980s, it appears
that our GNP growth rate has been exceeding GNEC growth rate
by about 0.5 to 1.0 percent per year, on the average. It is possible
that RECALL could have estimated (and rationalized) a similar
relationship in the 1920s, but probably with a larger uncertainty
band. Because of the difficulty of establishing such a relationship in
the 1920s, our attention here will be limited primarily to the GNEC
growth rates.

Remember, a realistic forecast of GNEC growth must take
into account both the underlying secular growth and the superimposed growth oscillation. The RECALL analysts would already
have observed the amplitude and timing of the growth oscillation,
though they would have assigned an amplitude around 15 percent
instead of 20 percent to the cyclic swing. The projection of the
underlying secular growth would have been more difficult. Somewhat surprisingly, the uncertainty in secular growth would not
have seriously affected the general conclusions of the RECALL
analysts. The simplest (and most optimistic) projection would have
assumed a continuing growth of 3.3 percent per year, as shown in
Figure 9–1.

How badly would RECALL have erred with that *upper-limit*
secular growth assumption? The projection of 3.3 percent per year
would have led to a forecast some 15 percent high for the 15-year
projection beyond 1925 (i.e., to 1940) and more than 50 percent
high for a 45-year projection (i.e., to 1970)—based on historical
information as we know it today. A 50 percent error may seem very
large—even for this relatively long time span—but that error
would be equivalent to a prorated error of only 1 percent per year.

RECALL might also have assumed a *lower-limit* secular
growth rate of 1.7 percent per year—one half the previously
assumed rate. Such a projection would have led to a forecast that

FIGURE 9–2

GNEC Average Growth Rates, 1925–1940 and 1940–1970 as Estimated by RECALL in 1925*

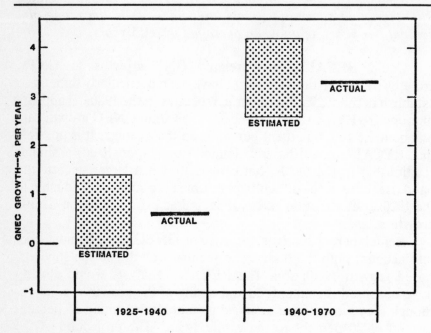

*Solid lines to the right indicate actual growths.

was 5 percent low for the 15-year projection beyond 1925 and 20 percent low for the 45-year projection. It is possible that more careful reasoning could have improved on the uncertainties, but probably no better than on the population uncertainties discussed in Chapter 2.

The above projections were only for the underlying secular growth curve. On these various secular growth possibilities, RE-CALL would then superimpose the cyclic variation based on an assumed amplitude of 15 percent. The projected RECALL average growths for the 1925–1940 and 1940–1970 periods are shown in Figure 9–2. The projected ranges of growths are shown by the shaded area, with subsequent historical growths shown by the solid lines to the right.

In summary, RECALL would have projected:

- A GNEC growth between 0 and 1.5 percent per year for the 1925–1940 period—compared to the actual average growth rate of 0.6 percent per year.
- A growth between 2.6 and 4.2 percent per year for the 1940–1970 period—with the actual growth at 3.3 percent per year.

These are the GNEC projections—the average GNP growth rates might have been projected to be slightly higher, possibly around 1 percent higher. Not only could RECALL have foreseen an abnormally low growth between 1925 and 1940, it could have actually projected the *size* of the GNEC growth rate within reasonable limits. Moreover, RECALL could have projected both the timing and the approximate magnitude of the more remote growth boom.

Admittedly, these are *average* growth rates over fairly large time spans. Still, the conclusions are striking. Perhaps most striking is the observation that:

Seemingly large uncertainties in the secular growth are not particularly significant in the overall conclusions.

It is once again emphasized that these projections would have been made in 1925, well ahead of the stockmarket crash in 1929. Such projections, even with the apparent uncertainty bands, could have been of inestimable value to business clients of RECALL.

RECALL's GNEC Growth Projections—After the Crash of '29

We are generally optimistic in times of prosperity and pessimistic in times of adversity. For this reason, RECALL can be particularly useful during transition periods, especially during the autumn and winter phases of the long wave.

Even during the first few months after the Crash of '29 there was general optimism that the succeeding years would be generous ones. As late as the early 1930s it was widely believed that the market crash was only a localized phenomenon affecting a small percentage of people across the United States. As the Great

Depression descended on the country, this feeling of optimism was gradually replaced by a feeling of despair.

Few people in the mid-1930s would have accepted the premise that a new business boom of remarkable proportions would begin in only another 10 years.

Not only can RECALL be useful in the deceptive times immediately preceding an economic winter, it can be at least as useful during the winter of despair. By the mid-1930s, more GNEC data points were available, albeit abnormally low points even relative to the cycle-adjusted-logistic curve for GNEC growth. RECALL could have alerted industries and society that a new surge of GNEC growth would begin around 1945.

As already seen from the vantage point of the pre-crash 1920s, average GNEC growth would increase from around 1 percent per year in the 1930s to some 3 percent per year in the 1950s and 1960s. Factories would again be humming, travel would be booming, jobs would be plentiful—all of us would be enjoying a new wave of prosperity. Moreover, with additional GNEC growth data available in the 1930s, RECALL could have improved on its forecasts of the 1920s. True, even the RECALL forecasts might have been slightly pessimistic in the 1930s because of the abnormally large GNEC decline during the Great Depression. Yet the RECALL forecasts would have been much better than the forecasts of others, projected from the depths of the depression.

Some important conclusions can come from the RECALL experiences of the 1920s and 1930s. First, it should not be expected that RECALL could foresee *short-term* economic trends that occur from year to year. Secondly, although a 15-year forward forecast from 1925 could have suggested an economic adversity, there is nothing to indicate that the RECALL projections could have foretold a stock market crash to occur specifically in the year 1929. Finally, the full magnitude of the 1930s depression could not have been predicted. The Great Depression was abnormally severe, relative even to a RECALL-type forecast. In fact, the exact timing and depth of the depression were probably affected by a number of factors, such as the degree of financial speculation, and various industrial and government policies. Nevertheless, RE-

CALL's forecast of a GNEC (and GNP) decline would have been generally correct.

Reading History from the GNEC and GNP Curves

Let's look more closely at the actual year-by-year GNEC and GNP historical data points relative to the cycle-adjusted-logistic (CAL) growth curves. A fascinating conclusion of this examination is that much can be seen about the history of the United States by studying the variations of these GNEC and GNP points from the smooth curves. Figure 9–3 illustrates these variations from 1915 to

FIGURE 9–3

Cycle-Adjusted-Logistic Curves for GNEC and GNP Growths with Uncertainty Band*

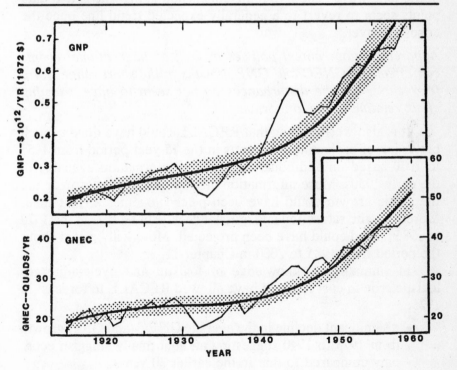

*Fine line shows year-to-year values.

1960. The solid CAL curves and the shaded uncertainty bands, shown in the figure, are based on 1980 knowledge.

It can be seen that total energy consumption, GNEC, increased during 1927 to 1929, at a rate slightly faster than the CAL curve would have predicted—consistent with the GNP growth spurt just prior to the 1929 crash. It is very apparent that the plunge in the curve from 1929 to 1932 was particularly severe, relative to the CAL curve, with a GNEC between 1931 and 1935 considerably below the uncertainty band—*attesting to the extreme severity of the Great Depression*. Finally, the abnormally high points from 1942 to 1945 reflect the heavy government spending and the dedication of the national effort during the World War II years. The short-term irregularities generally reflect short-term business cycles, government economic policies (or failure of policies), and international events. Those events, as previously implied, could be expected to alter, to some extent, the precise timing and magnitude of the long wave. The intriguing conclusion is that the actual data points seem to revert to a generally expected trend line once the crises are over.

Apparently, government policies as well as international events can affect the GNEC and GNP growths in the short range (for a few years), but the disturbances do not seem to have a lasting effect relative to the long wave.

It is also worth noting that RECALL could have done a much better job of projecting the trends in the 15-year period from 1955 to 1970 based on additional background information available in the early 1950s. More information on both the secular growth and the cyclic growth could have been pieced together at that time. Moreover, the saturation and gradual decline of GNEC in the 1970 to 1985 period could have been projected. More will be said about the period from 1985 to 2000 in Chapter 11.

In summary, a knowledge of logistic and cycle-adjusted-logistic growth curves could have allowed RECALL to forecast in 1925:

- a significant decline in the average GNEC (and GNP) growth from 1925 to 1940 suggesting an abnormally sluggish economy compared to that in the earlier 30 years.
- a robust recovery in the average growth from 1940 to 1970.

Although some paucity of historical GNEC and GNP data from 1850 to 1925 might have limited the accuracy of the actual projections in 1925 for the period 1925 to 1970, the general trends in the economy already could have been anticipated. Based on the updated curves developed in the 1950s, RECALL could have developed, at that time, a much more accurate projection of GNEC and GNP growth up to 1980 and beyond.

The attention to this point has focused on the overall GNEC and GNP growths that could have been projected in the 1920s, 1930s, and 1950s. Clearly, RECALL could have forecast not only the timing of a subsequent growth bust and boom, but even the approximate average magnitudes. Those general observations could have been useful to a broad cross section of large industries, small businesses, government, and our parents. But, RECALL could also have offered some useful advice to specialized industries in the energy business. Let's now examine some of these energy-industry growth projections.

RECALL's Energy-Industry Forecasts— The Electricity Industry

What could RECALL have said about electricity growth projections in 1925? Remember, the electricity industry was only 40 years old and historical data on electricity consumption would have been particularly meager in 1925.

Difficult though it would have been, our knowledgeable RECALL company might still have estimated electricity growth for future years by examining the substitution logistic for energy used to generate electricity relative to total energy used in the United States. Since that fraction would have been less than 10 percent in 1925, the task would have been difficult. Some numerical tests of the procedure, based on historical data, suggest that the projected energy use for electricity generation in 1950 would probably have been over-estimated by as much as 50 percent; and the corresponding projected energy use in 1970 would have been even higher. In spite of those projection difficulties in 1925, the economic potential for electricity growth would still have been recognized decades ahead of time. And, a strong growth for new electricity applications would have become clear—a conclusion that would have been valuable for electric-appliance industry planners and their development laboratories in the 1930s.

By the 1950s, electricity growth could have been projected with much greater precision.

The percentage fraction of GNEC used for electricity generation had reached about 15 percent in the early 1950s—RECALL could by then have forecast that some 30 percent of GNEC would be used for electricity generation by about 1980.

Based on projections of (1) the substitution growth (energy used for electricity generation versus total energy), and (2) the GNEC growth itself, RECALL could also have forecast the absolute growth of energy use for electricity generation for the next 30 years. In fact, RECALL would have projected in 1950 that GNEC itself would more than double between 1950 and 1980. With the projection also of the two-fold increase in the fraction of GNEC used for electricity generation, RECALL would have forecast *more than a four-fold increase* in energy used for electricity generation in only 30 years (actually it was almost five times).

A growth forecast from 1950 to 1980, based only on the data available before 1950, is illustrated in Figure 9–4. The shaded band illustrates the uncertainty that would have been assigned to the forecast, including a 15 percent spread 35 years forward due to the long-term uncertainty in the secular growth and a 6 percent spread due to the uncertainty in the cyclic growth. The dots at five-year intervals following 1950 indicate actual growth data points from subsequent records.

In summary, RECALL could have projected:

- a slowdown of electricity growth in the 1925–1940 period on the basis of data available in 1925
- a very strong electricity growth in the 1950–1980 period on the basis of data available before 1950
- a potential overexpansion of capital equipment in the 1975 to 1985 period

Moreover, it is likely that regional growth data could have been used to project growth patterns in individual parts of the United States.

FIGURE 9–4
**Projection of Electricity Energy Growth (measured as input energy)
Projected by RECALL in 1950 for 1950–1980**

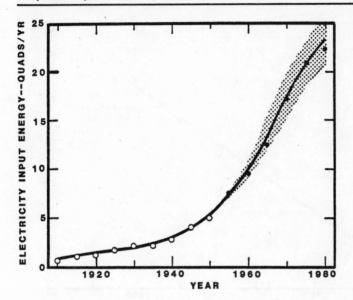

Surely all that information would have been welcomed by the electric utility and the electric-equipment-supply industries.

RECALL's Energy-Industry Forecasts—Fuel Resources

Could RECALL have been useful to other energy-related industries during the 1920–1950 period? For example, could RECALL have forecast probable business growths for specific energy-fuel industries? To examine this possibility, we'll review projections RECALL could have made on the growth pattern of fluid fuels (oil and natural gas) relative to coal fuel—although growths for the oil and natural-gas fuels could also have been forecast independently.

The substitution of fluid fuels for coal is illustrated in Figure 9–5, where the growth/ungrowth curve for fluid fuels is shown. In 1910, some 10 percent of the fossil fuels used in the United States consisted of oil and natural gas. By 1925, the fluid fuels accounted for 25 percent of the energy consumption, with coal reduced to 75 percent.

FIGURE 9–5
Logistic Extrapolation of Fluid-Fuel Use (F) Relative to Coal-Fuel Use (1 − F)

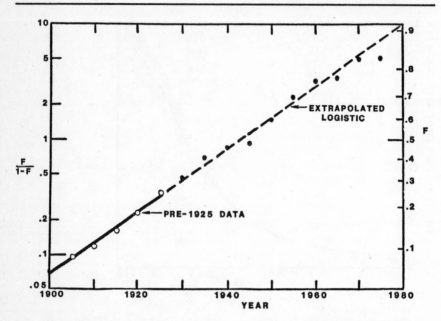

By using an extrapolation of the growth/ungrowth curve beyond 1925, RECALL could have informed the coal companies that by 1945 their share of the fuel market would drop below 50 percent, and by 1970 it would be a modest 20 percent.

That, of course, does not necessarily mean that a precipitous decline in coal use itself would occur between 1925 and 1970—only that coal use relative to oil use would decline. By using the overall GNEC (or fossil-fuel use) growth curve, RECALL would have known that overall energy use would grow about three-fold between 1925 and 1970. Since the fractional growth of coal was destined to fall by a factor of 3.75 (75 percent to 20 percent), and the overall GNEC growth would increase three times between 1925 and 1970, RECALL could have told the coal companies their business would decrease by about 20 percent. More happily, RECALL could have alerted the fluid-fuel companies that their share of the fuel market would grow from 25 percent in 1925 to about 80 percent in 1970.

By multiplying the fluid-fuel fractional growth by the expected GNEC growth itself, RECALL would have projected a 10-fold fluid-fuel growth between 1925 and 1970.

By estimating the cost of fluid fuels per unit energy content, it probably also would have noted that the top 10 of the Fortune 500 (had it been in existence in 1925) would be dominated by oil companies in the 1970s.

Summary

It appears that our mythical forecasting company, RECALL, could indeed have provided much useful information on GNEC growths as early as 1925—presuming it already had some rudimentary knowledge of logistic growth behavior and the long energy wave. Admittedly, RECALL would have been forced to acknowledge rather substantial uncertainties in its forecasts. Nevertheless, the projection of the GNEC growth slowdown between 1925 and 1940 would have been surprisingly good. Even more surprising, the projection of the GNEC growth boom between 1940 and 1970 would have been sound.

Presuming RECALL could have had some appreciation of the GNP relationship to GNEC in those earlier years, much could also have been foretold about the economy. The general timing and magnitude of the 1925–1940 GNP slowdown (as well as GNEC slowdown) could have been forecast—as well as the subsequent 1940–1970 GNP surge. A particularly significant observation from the long-wave growth is that the Great Depression should not be attributed to the Crash of '29 (a fact that has been emphasized by many economists). However, the seeds for both the Great Depression and the Crash of '29 were apparently being sown by a business growth stagnation and declining societal industry that was already beginning before the 1920s.

Primary attention has been given to the RECALL projections of GNEC growths and their implications on the economy. It has also been observed that RECALL could have supplied more specific growth forecasts to two important energy industries, the electricity-generating and fuel-resource industries. For example, it could have been estimated that:

- electricity use would grow some four to five times in only 30 years
- fluid-fuel use would increase some 10 times over the same period

It is easy to allow one's hindsight to underestimate the boldness of these mythical projections.

Perhaps a more significant observation is that similar projections in the 1980s should be on much firmer ground. Let's turn now to forecasts on industry growths that RECALL could also have offered in those earlier years.

CHAPTER 10

TESTING THE CREDIBILITY OF RECALL—TECHNOLOGY AND INDUSTRY GROWTHS

Even before the Crash of '29, RECALL could have projected rather accurately the average GNEC growth rates for the low-growth 1925–1940 and high-growth 1940–1970 periods. Those projections, although describing only the *results* of industrial-growth behaviors, could have proven useful for industry, business, and personal planning.

After the Crash of '29, and particularly during the depth of the Great Depression, RECALL might have offered even more useful advice—advice on probable directions of technology, industry, business, and workforce growths to be expected during a forthcoming long-wave surge.

Is it reasonable to expect that a forecaster or forecasting enterprise in the 1930s could recognize the important macroinnovation directions originating in that era? Could the actual business growth behaviors for the 1950–1980 period have been forecast in the early 1950s? At least some general observations on the *likelihood* of a wave of macroinnovations beginning around the 1930s should not be regarded as incredible.

In the 1930s, Schumpeter had published his two-volume book, Business Cycles, *indicating important technology innovations as sources of long-wave economic growth surges.*

If we presume RECALL had understood the principles of logistic growth (and especially the "substitution logistic" methodology) in the 1950s, our mythical forecasting enterprise could indeed have projected the takeover growths of various new industries that were destined to evolve in the subsequent 25 to 30 years. Remember that the Fisher and Pry method for calculating takeover growths was not really reported until about 1970. Since we are only interested in demonstrating the *applicability* of the growth principles, we will ignore that knowledge gap of 20 or 30 years. Let's examine what RECALL could and could not have said about technological and industrial growths in those earlier years.

After the Crash of '29—RECALL's Observations on New Technology and Business Directions

By the mid-1930s, RECALL would be even more confident of the existence and timing of the GNEC/GNP long wave. Furthermore, the causes and results of the long wave would generally be understood—especially the timing and growth of technology macroinnovations and their market implementations. Still, to establish its credentials with industry and business, we should expect RECALL to offer sound advice in the 1930s on at least three other significant points:

- when the macroinnovation surge of that era should be occurring
- when the market introduction of radically new products and services should subsequently begin
- how long those market growths should continue

Following the lead of Schumpeter, the RECALL forecasters would have already recognized that the strong economic growth between 1895 and 1925 depended largely on the cluster of macroinnovations having their origin in the 1870–1890 period. It would have been logical for RECALL to anticipate a new wave of macroinnovations some 55 years later.

As a first observation, RECALL would have concluded in the 1930s that the macroinnovation surge was already underway and would continue throughout the 1925–1945 period.

Such an observation in the depths of the Great Depression might have been rather startling to the many large industries buried in near-term problems and discouraged about the future. Still,

RECALL could have pointed to history showing (1) industrial winners of past growth waves were generally the venturists, and (2) the losers were those who stubbornly resisted change. RECALL could have urged bold new R&D, technology transfer, and entrepreneurial directions. Simultaneously, RECALL could have alerted universities, students, and career planners that career successes in the approaching years would depend more and more on strong technological training—in chemistry, in electronics, in engineering, and in associated business management.

How soon would RECALL have expected business growth surges resulting from the 1935 macroinnovations? Let's look again at the history of earlier business surges. Following the 1825 origin for the railroad macroinnovation, a significant growth of railroads began around 1840—about 15 years later. Following the 1880 origin for the electricity macroinnovation, significant home electrification began around 1895—again about 15 years later. And, following the 1885 origin for the automobile macroinnovation, a significant automobile industry began around 1900—once again about 15 years later.

As a second observation, RECALL would have projected strong business growths, resulting from the 1935 macroinnovation surge, to begin around 1950.

What time span would RECALL have anticipated for the new industries to grow from infancy to maturity? Remember, we already have defined a "characteristic growth time" as the time for a 10 to 90 percent adoption or substitution of a new technology. The characteristic growth times for home electrification, telephones, automobiles, coal-tar chemicals, and movie attendance were typically 15 to 35 years. Hence:

As a third observation, RECALL would have projected a typical 10 to 90 percent growth time of around 25 to 30 years.

Simply an indication of the macroinnovation and business-growth timing should have been of considerable interest to business planners of that era. Indeed, if you were a business leader of the late 1940s or early 1950s, you probably would have welcomed the advice that your company should be focusing on important new technology directions—not simply improvement innovations in obsolescent-prone businesses such as coal-burning furnaces, railroad travel, cellulosic (rayon-type) garments, or huge movie halls. How soon could RECALL have identified the various obsolescent-prone businesses? Or, when could the growth of the new business takeovers be projected?

One of the most valuable services of RECALL in the 1950s would have been the measurement and projection of new business growths at the early stages of a new product adoption or substitution.

New Technology and Business Growths—
The Probable Areas

RECALL's 1930s forecast of a 1945–1975 surge in energy use would certainly have hinted some new energy-consuming technologies might be forthcoming.

Based only on clues involving expected GNEC, electricity, and oil growths, RECALL might have inferred promising new opportunities in the development and manufacturing of new energy-consuming equipment.

Based on the likelihood of a new wave of technology innovations involving energy-use equipment, RECALL probably could have projected resurgences in industries such as electrical appliances, automobiles, air travel, electronics and chemical products. Just what those innovations might be would have to wait for the appearance of the new products, sponsored by a few of the more enterprising companies.

By the early 1950s, it would become clear that a few of the most important new growth industries would include:

- polymer-chemistry products (such as polyesters, plastics, etc.)
- air travel (including jet travel)
- home appliances
- television
- power-assisted automobile equipment

What, more specifically, could RECALL have told us or our parents about these emerging new industries in the 1950s? For the answers, let's examine each of the growth industries individually.

RECALL and the Polymer-Chemicals Industry

One of the most important new industries of the last 100 years has been the chemical industry. The growth potential of chemicals was recognized in this country early in the 1900s, as is borne out by the large number of U.S. chemical companies that had their origin around the turn of the century.

Organic chemicals, based on the use of by-product coal tars from the coke industry, offered a particularly fertile area for new businesses in the early 1900s. Could RECALL have foreseen, in the 1930 to 1950 period, any new industry that might compare to the earlier coal-tar chemical industry? In Chapter 9, it was noted that the fraction of fluid-fuel use relative to coal use had increased from 10 percent in 1905 to a little over 20 percent in 1925 (Figure 9–4). On the basis of that substitution growth, we saw that RECALL could already have projected in 1925 that the fluid-fuel contribution to U.S. energy use would grow from only 20 percent in 1925 to some 75 percent in 1975. We will also see that RECALL could have projected the enormous growth, by the early 1950s, of a new "petrochemical" industry—based on by-products of the gasoline-refining industry.

For good reasons, the growth potential of the *petrochemical* industry would not have been immediately obvious. The fraction of petroleum resources going into the petrochemical industry is relatively small even today. About 45 percent of our petroleum resources are used for gasoline production and another 45 percent for heating fuel. The remaining 10 percent of the resources are used for a variety of purposes (including lubricants).

Only about 5 percent of all the petroleum products are now used as feed materials or "feedstock" for chemical industries other than the oil, gasoline, and natural-gas industries.

Especially in the 1930s, the opportunity for petroleum by-product businesses would have been regarded as small. Yet, the projection of a 10-fold growth of oil use between 1930 and 1970 (see

Chapter 9) would have improved the prospects substantially. Moreover, these by-products, from the 5 percent of total petroleum use, could have been recognized as sources of potentially valuable chemicals, such as ethylene, propylene, benzene, toluene, xylene, and many others—some of which were already valuable in the 1930s. We now know that approximately one third of *all* the products of the chemical industry have their origin in petroleum (both oil and natural gas). Hence, even though 5 percent might still appear to be small today, the added value coming from these petrochemical products, and their related industries, is very substantial.

The historical growths of the petrochemical and related industries were discussed in Chapter 7, the Spawning of Business Megatrends. Here, we will confine ourselves to the projectability of those growths in, the 1950s. As a first example, we can look at RECALL's forecast for the growth of the petrochemical industry, relative to the coal-tar industry, by examining the takeover growth of important feed chemicals coming from the oil refining industry. Although many basic chemicals could be chosen for this examination, one very significant one is benzene.

In Figure 10–1, the growth/ungrowth curve is shown for benzene produced from petroleum relative to that not produced from petroleum (produced from coal tar). As already indicated (Chapter 7), about 10 percent of benzene came from the petrochemical industry in 1950, and 30 percent by 1955. From this growth behavior, RECALL could have concluded by 1955 that 90 percent of benzene would be coming from the petrochemical industry in 1965, only 10 years later. From this and other growth curves, RECALL could have projected not just the general trend, but the year-to-year growth magnitudes for petrochemical supplies to other industries.

While the growths of chemical feed materials supplied by the petrochemical industry is interesting, the growths of the numerous commercial products (textiles, plastics, rubber, and detergents) based on petrochemicals is even more fascinating. Dozens of product growths could be chosen to illustrate the surge in chemistry-based industries during the 1950 to 1980 period. However, only a few will be indicated here.

FIGURE 10–1
Substitution Growths of Petrochemical Benzene and Textile Fibers*

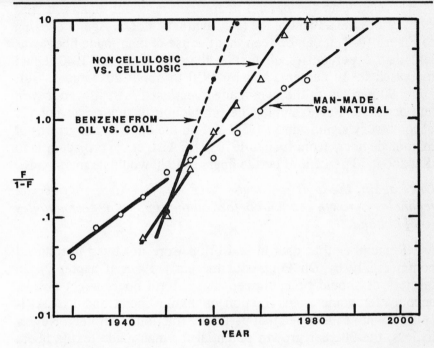

*Data prior to 1950, for example, could have been used to project man-made, textile-fiber growths beyond 1950.

The Polymer-Chemicals Textile Industry

One of the most important chemical industries, from an economic perspective, has been the textile industry. RECALL could already have discovered, by the 1940s, that the growth/ungrowth curve for the substitution of rayon for silk during the 1910 to 1940 period had conformed almost precisely to a logistic growth behavior—growing from a 10 percent takeover in 1912 to 90 percent in 1940. Rayon (and acetate) fibers are really reconstituted cellulosic (or wood-like) materials. They are generally included in the category of man-made textile fibers and not really regarded as synthetic fibers.

Somewhat surprisingly, RECALL could have learned much about the growth of all man-made textile fibers (including synthetic fibers) relative to the natural fibers (cotton, wool, flax, and silk) even before the advent of the truly synthetic fibers. Again referring to Figure 10–1, it can be seen that the use of man-made fibers was less than 5 percent of all textile fibers in 1930. By 1940 it had increased to 10 percent, and by 1950 to about 20 percent. But, about 90 percent of the man-made fibers used in 1950 were rayon and acetates. For example, the production of nylon had not yet become very significant in 1950. Yet on the basis of the growth of man-made fibers from 1930 to 1950, RECALL could project in 1950 that about 70 percent of textile fibers in 1980 would be man-made.

Once again, the logistic growth curve was forecasting an overall technology growth behavior before all the supporting technologies were in hand.

Remember that dacron and orlon were not even introduced commercially by Du Pont until the early 1950s (Chapter 7). In fairness, it should be cautioned that natural fibers might always account for some small fraction of textile fibers, and RECALL could not have identified that particular fraction accurately. Nevertheless, the 30-year growth potential for man-made textile fibers was already becoming clear by 1950.

Information in the 1950s on the growth of man-made fibers relative to natural fibers would surely have been useful to the textile industries, the chemical-engineering industries, and the farmers at that time. A more useful piece of information to the chemical-engineering industries would have been the growth of non-cellulosic (synthetic) textile fibers relative to the cellulosic (reconstituted-wood) fibers.

On the basis of information available between 1945 and 1955, RECALL could have foretold that at least 90 percent of man-made textile fibers would be coming from synthetic materials by 1980.

That would have been sobering information to the more traditional companies specializing in the production of rayon and acetate yarns. And it would have been comforting information to the more enterprising synthetic-fiber companies preparing to invest in new production facilities.

Other Polymer-Chemical Industries

In contrast to projections for textile growths, the projection of synthetic rubber growth might have been a rather confusing assignment for RECALL in the early 1950s. As was pointed out by Fisher and Pry (the inventors of the logistic substitution methodology), the substitution of synthetic for natural rubber showed an anomalous behavior during the years of World War II. At that time, U.S. access to the large rubber resources from Southeast Asia was interrupted. Because of the critical need for rubber, the U.S. government initiated a crash program around 1940 to manufacture synthetic rubber for meeting wartime needs. Toward the end of the war, about two thirds of all rubber was coming from these chemical-engineering plants.

After the end of World War II, the better characteristics of natural rubber again became important to our rubber manufacturing industries. Immediately following the war, synthetic rubber production dropped to about 35 percent of all rubber. However, by 1950, new technologies made synthetic rubber more competitive with the natural rubber. As a result, approximately 50 percent of rubber in the United States was coming from synthetic sources by 1950. That fraction increased to some 80 percent by 1980. The important conclusion from this example is that national emergencies, particularly during wartime, can distort normal growth behaviors significantly.

Detergents have had one of the most remarkable growths in the polymer-chemistry industry. RECALL could have recognized the relatively fast takeover for detergents by 1950, when over 10 percent of the available soap market had already been displaced. By 1955, almost 90 percent of the substitution had occurred— hardly enough time to alert interested clients.

Probably RECALL could also have recognized the phenomenal growth of plastics as they displaced more common industrial materials beginning in the 1950s. Substitution growths could have been developed for:

- plastic versus paper containers (e.g., polyethylene shopping bags)
- plastic versus wood veneers (e.g., formica for cabinets)

- plastic versus glass bottles (for a variety of special applications)
- plastic versus leather luggage (or upholstery)
- plastic versus metal (again for special applications)

The growth/ungrowth curves for these applications would have allowed RECALL to forecast after only a 10 percent takeover when a 90 percent takeover could have been expected. This information might have been relished by many businesses.

RECALL and the Air Travel Industry

What could RECALL have said about the future of air travel in 1940? Since the airplane industry was a late bloomer in the 1895 to 1925 industrial growth wave, civilian air travel was almost insignificant in the 1920s. Still, RECALL could draw on statistics in the 1930s and 1940s to develop a reasonably good forecast.

Assuming that RECALL was familiar with substitution growth methods by the 1940s, we can presume the forecasting company would have tested the methods on the important growth of automobiles in the 1900 to 1930 period. In a first test, the remarkable takeover growth of automobiles versus horse-drawn carriages might have been discovered. With that success, RECALL might then have tested its methods on the takeover growth of automobile passenger travel versus railroad passenger travel. That takeover growth curve is shown at the left side of Figure 10–2. Once again, it would have been seen that automobiles were displacing an older type of travel.

RECALL could have concluded that a reasonable projection of auto versus train travel takeover could have been developed as early as 1915—had the methodology been understood then.

With that background, RECALL might have mustered courage to apply its newly found talent to the projection of a takeover growth for air travel relative to the remaining rail travel business— mostly the business for long-distance travel. It will be presumed that the RECALL forecasters of the 1930s would have accepted the possibility of such a large air travel business in spite of some apparent constraints. The more conservative forecasters, for ex-

FIGURE 10–2
Logistic Substitution Curves for Auto versus Rail Travel and Air versus Rail Travel*

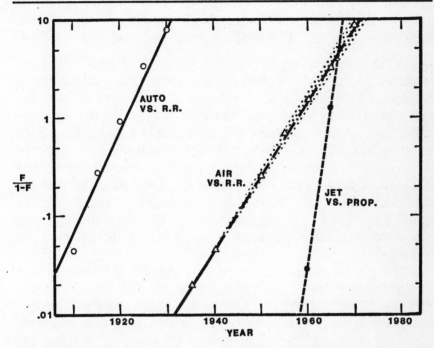

*The air versus rail growth curve illustrates how RECALL could have projected the subsequent takeover growth when only 5 percent of the growth had occurred. A dashed curve is also shown for the takeover of jet versus propeller commercial planes.

ample, would have worried about the enormous number of airplanes and the air congestion that could occur if airlines took over this market. In the 1930s, propeller airplanes were relatively small and slow.

On the basis of its knowledge from auto travel studies, RECALL would have learned that apparent growth constraints can frequently be overcome by technology advances. Just as electric self-starters, enclosed autos, and improved roads were responsible for the continuing uniform growth of automobile adoptions earlier, RECALL could have anticipated more convenient airplanes, faster travel, and better air-guidance systems that would remove potential bottlenecks in air travel. As indicated by the second line in

Figure 10–2, the data available up to 1940 would have suggested to RECALL the extrapolation shown by the shaded band.

By 1940, when the air travel accounted for only 5 percent of air and rail travel, RECALL could have projected that the passenger-miles of air travel would equal that of rail travel between 1955 and 1960.

A takeover percentage of 90 percent could also have been projected to occur between 1965 and 1975. One qualification is necessary, though. During World War II, from 1941 to 1945, the passenger travel on railroads was abnormally high due to troop movements. A correction for this effect could possibly have been made by RECALL (the 1945 point is omitted from the data shown in the figure). Still, this apparent anomaly might have shaken RECALL's faith in its 1940 projection. But, after the war the growth/ungrowth data returned to the growth line, as shown in the figure. The 10 to 90 percent takeover time for air versus rail travel was some 26 years compared to the 20 years for the auto/rail takeover.

The air travel growth curve also showed the same almost mystical properties as the curve for automobile projections discussed in Chapter 8. Why should we regard this straight-line curve as bordering on the mystical? Again, it presumes that important "growth-bottleneck" problems would be resolved to allow the projected growth. For example, the projection beyond 1940 would be made at a time when:

- less than 100 commercial airplanes were in service
- the propeller airplanes were relatively primitive and woefully small in carrying capacity
- jet airplanes had yet to be developed
- air-traffic control was almost non-existent (radar was not yet developed)

Once again, the technology takeover curves appear to have an internal sense for anticipating appropriate developments, thereby assuring a continuing growth consistent with a straight-line growth/ungrowth behavior.

This remarkably uniform growth behavior might seem to be too good to be true. Can we count on such a precise behavior for all new growths? Yes, as long as a clearly superior new technology is replacing an older inferior one. The behavior is controlled by the laws of nature (and free enterprise) already discussed in Part 1. However, at least two exceptions must again be emphasized. The dislocation of a large war can obviously distort a free-market growth. And, some fraction of the total market might not be available for a particular substitution or adoption, as was the case already indicated for the detergent takeover of the soap industry, which excluded some 15 percent of products used for facial and bath soaps. Or, as another example, household electrical equipment could not be expected to take over 100 percent of the homes at a time when less than 100 percent were electrified. With these and other obvious exceptions, the takeover curves are usually amazingly well-behaved.

One of the most important technology innovations of the air-travel industry was the jet airplane. We could not expect RECALL to forecast, in 1940, the actual development of jet engines. But, once jet aircraft were being adopted, RECALL could have projected the continuing rate of adoption by airlines. The substitution, in this case, was interesting because of the short takeover time involved.

The replacement of propeller airplanes by jet aircraft in the commercial air-travel industry was surprisingly fast—the takeover time from 10 to 90 percent substitution was only seven years.

This fast takeover was probably due at least partly to the experience with jet aircraft coming from military applications, but also due to some technology breakthroughs in the post-war period. The midpoint of this substitution did not occur until about 1965— 20 years after the end of World War II. Although the substitution growth again followed very closely an S-curve growth behavior, RECALL would have had little time, in this case, to alert the air-travel companies of the impending obsolescence of propeller airplanes.

RECALL and the Electricity Industry— Home Appliances

RECALL would probably have discovered in its 1930 to 1950 researches that the earlier electrification of urban areas had followed accurately a logistic growth curve—growing from 10 percent in 1906 to about 90 percent in 1935. As previously indicated, the primary motivation for this early electrification of homes was electric lighting. A few electrical appliances, such as electric irons, room heaters, vacuum sweepers, and refrigerators, were beginning to make an appearance even before the 1930s depression. Electric refrigerators, for example, were introduced in the 1920s and signaled the approaching demise of the local ice delivery business.

Between 1930 and 1938, when the number of homes with refrigerators grew from 20 percent to 50 percent—in spite of the depression—a takeover time of about 30 years was being indicated.

You may remember, from the previous chapter, that RECALL could have projected, in 1950, a five-fold increase in electricity use between 1950 and 1980. From that observation, the RECALL technologists might logically have been looking for other home appliances to appear around 1950, to account for part of this new growth surge for electricity.

In the late 1940s and 1950s, a whole new class of labor-saving home appliances was introduced. These included automatic clothes washers, clothes dryers, dishwashers, food-waste disposals, and food blenders. In addition, home owners were introduced to automatic furnaces, air conditioners, hot water heaters, and even electric blankets. The growth/ungrowth curves for these appliances again generally followed a uniform logistic growth (although a few have shown some modest irregularities). The adoption of the automatic dishwasher and food disposal, for example, could have been projected quite well in 1960 when about 10 percent of the growth had occurred. In 1965, RECALL could have verified that about 80 percent of the growth would still be available in the years between 1965 and 1995. Admittedly, it would not have been possible to define the percentage of candidate homes at that time (later data indicate it is about 50 percent of all households). But, even with that uncertainty, much could have been learned about the year-to-year volume of appliance business.

Another feature of appliance *sales* is significant:

Subsequent appliances sales can come from product replacements as well as the original adoptions, as new appliance designs can make older ones obsolete.

The overall market growth potential for new appliances (and other consumer items, such as automobiles, communications equipment, clothing, and food) depends on at least three factors:

- the original growth rate of household adoptions
- the growth rate of households themselves
- the product obsolescence time of earlier equipment—and, hence, replacement sales

In the early years of adoption, market growth depends primarily on the household adoption rate and, to some extent, on the household growth rate. If the product obsolescence time is short relative to the adoption rate (as is particularly the case for consumable products such as clothing), the market growth can soon be dominated by the product obsolescence time. This subsequently has become a factor in the appliance and automobile businesses.

In fact, replacement of appliance units might result from:

- technology obsolescence (newer refrigerators with freezer compartments)
- cosmetic obsolescence (newer units with more attractive colors)
- deterioration (units suffering from failures of motors, plumbing, etc.)

Clearly, the replacement of products due to deterioration or even cosmetic obsolescence does not generally enhance the popularity of the manufacturer in the eyes of the consumer public (food and clothing consumption are exceptions).

Technology obsolescence has been an especially important factor in the hi-tech equipment industries.

Technology obsolescence has been a useful expedient in marketing new electrical-appliances and automobiles. But, it has been an even more dramatic factor in the electronics industry. As might be imagined, the threat of early technology obsolescence puts great pressure on research and engineering for these industries. As a manufacturer, distributor, or consumer, we must all be aware of this threat. Let's examine its implications on the electronics and related industries.

RECALL and the Electronics Industries

We've seen that the 10 to 90 percent adoption times have generally been in the range of 20 to 40 years, with most cases being around 30 years. One clear exception was the household adoption of radios in electrified homes.

The household adoption of radios in electrified homes grew from 10 percent in 1923 to 90 percent in 1933—an adoption time of only 10 years.

Was the fast adoption time destined to be a characteristic of electronics technologies? And if so, when could RECALL have verified this characteristic?

Figure 10–3 shows three significant takeover growths for television products. The first curve (or straight line) on the left side indicates the initial household-adoption growth for black-and-white TV sets. The last curve on the right side shows the substitution growth of color TV sets for B&W sets. The intermediate dashed curve illustrates the estimated substitution growth of transistorized TV sets relative to sets using vacuum tubes. In each case the takeover time was approximately 10 years. An examination of other technology growths in the electronics industry, such as hi-fi equipment, stereo systems, LP records, and FM radio technology, shows not only a fast takeover time, but also a relatively short time between the basic innovation and the start of commercial growth.

Clearly, the electronics industry has been strongly affected by the short times both for innovation implementation and for takeover growth in the marketplace.

Even the relatively perspicacious RECALL organization could not have been expected to foresee the full potential of the electronics industry in 1950. Still, a few important observations might have been made then and certainly in subsequent years:

- Based on the historical 10-year growth period for radio adoption and the evolving adoption rate of TV in the 1950s (from 10 to 90 percent in only 10 years), there would be little room for newcomers in this industry unless a significant technology-obsolescence pattern should develop.

FIGURE 10–3
Household-Adoption Growth of Television Sets (left side) and
Substitution Growth of Color for Black-and-White TV (right side)*

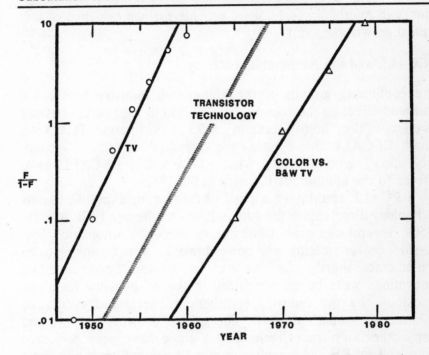

*The intermediate line represents the estimated substitution growth of transistor for vacuum-tube technology.

- Continuing events would have indicated that the frequency of technology innovations in the electronics industry would, indeed, show such a pattern, and assure a continuing strong growth potential.
- Companies hoping to retain a good business position in the manufacturing and marketing of electronics equipment would have to maintain a strong R&D program and/or technology-transfer capabilities.
- The continuing growth of TV technology might be expected to have an even larger economic impact on the service industries (in this case, the entertainment, education, and information industries) than on the TV manufacturing industry itself.

While major attention here has been focused on the TV, radio, and hi-fi industries, the computer industry has shown the same kind of rapid technology growth and obsolescence. Recent advances in microchip technology provide further evidence of this typical growth behavior.

RECALL and the Automobile Industry

The continuing growth of the automobile industry has had a profound effect on the economy in the 1950 to 1980 period beyond its effect in the "first-generation" 1895 to 1925 period. How soon could RECALL have seen the potential of this "second-generation" growth? And, what advice could RECALL have offered to the automobile industry in the 1950s?

RECALL could have applied its forecasting expertise to new technology directions in the auto industry by the late 1940s or early 1950s. Several significant basic innovations—the automatic transmission, power steering, and power brakes—were beginning to be implemented shortly after the war. In addition, important basic innovations were being introduced in the oil industry (catalytic cracking), the tire industry (synthetic rubber), and even road construction (superhighways). The general growths of these and many other auto-travel technologies could have been projected quite well by RECALL—after only a 10 percent growth in most cases.

The growth of automatic transmissions, power steering, and power brakes could have been forecast by observing the adoption fraction of factory-made cars using these mechanisms.

Based on the growth/ungrowth curves for these adoptions, the characteristic growth times would have been found to be 28 years for each of the new technologies, with growth midpoints at 1956, 1962, and 1969. As early as 1950, RECALL could have advised automobile manufacturers how rapidly they should imitate the technology leaders, and how promptly they should adopt the improved technologies as standard equipment in the lower-priced automobile lines. Had you been an automobile dealer in the early 1960s, for example, you could have used this information to show your clients just how rapidly their new cars would become obsolete without this auxiliary equipment.

Summary

Both the areas of energy use (electricity) and transportation (automobiles) were affected by important contributions from the 1880 innovation wave. These industries had a profound effect on the economy in the 1910 to 1930 period. Furthermore, it was probably clear to most farsighted people in the 1930s, that there was room for still more growth in these industries, in spite of the Great Depression.

Presuming that the experts of RECALL fully understood the long energy wave and the innovation/commercialization wave, they could have recognized that the Great Depression was simply a consequence of a long-wave stagnation period, albeit, a particularly severe one.

By examining substitution (or takeover) growths of electricity/ non-electricity energy, they would have seen there was no indication of a slowdown in the takeover ratio, even though significant slowdowns in overall growths would have been apparent in electricity and non-electricity separately. Hence, they would have surmised that electricity energy would continue to grow once the energy cycle itself began to grow again in the early 1940s.

By similar reasoning, RECALL would have concluded that the takeover of automobile versus railroad personal travel would continue. Growth in both the electricity and automobile industries could have been expected to continue in the next long economic cycle. Since the airplane and radio technologies also had shown some growth in the 1920s and 1930s, it would have been logical to expect further growth in these areas. Even without a knowledge, in the 1930s, of all the newer technologies that might arise from the 1935 innovation wave (such as TV equipment, computers, space flight, and antibiotics), RECALL could still have anticipated further growth in the industries already indicated.

However, RECALL could also have alerted industries that a new commercialization surge would be occurring between 1950 and 1980 which would include not only extensions of the electricity, communication, and transportation technologies that were already underway in the 1920s, but also many new technologies building on the expected innovation surge of the 1930s and 1940s.

What can we, as business people, investors, and consumers, learn from the RECALL observations? Beyond the timing of the long GNEC/GNP cycle, the RECALL experiences would suggest the following lessons:

- Innovation surges occur at roughly 55-year intervals and initiate new business growths beginning some 15 years after the peak of the innovation surge.
- A business swarming extends to many industrial sectors, even beyond the four or five major macroinnovations.
- The characteristic growth time for the 10 to 90 percent adoption of new industrial products is around 30 years for most industries, but as short as 10 years for the electronics industry.
- The very rapid technology obsolescence and business growth associated with new electronics products makes R&D, technology transfer, and technology training especially important for the electronics industries.

It is particularly important for us to realize that these business growth characteristics are not just lessons to be applied only to large manufacturing companies. The lessons are equally important to each and every one of us, whether our interests lie in engineering, marketing, distribution, services, or even consumption.

RECALL's forecasting talents, already applied to the last business growth wave, can now be applied with confidence to the next wave. Applications to the future growths of energy and the economy will be the subject of Chapter 11, while applications to future business growths will be reserved for Chapter 12.

CHAPTER 11

THE FUTURE ACCORDING TO RECALL—ENERGY AND THE ECONOMY

Like the Crash of '29, the Crash of '87 occurred approximately at the "autumnal equinox" of the long economic wave. As we will see from the year-to-year data in the 1980s, the average annual GNEC growth was falling to a below-average growth rate around 1985.

During the first few months following the Crash of '87, our political, financial, and economic leaders were divided in their opinions on the possible economic consequences of the crash. Did the crash signal the onset of a recession or a depression, and if so, how severe would it be? Could RECALL have offered any foresight on this possible economic adversity? Can it offer some foresight after the crash?

While RECALL can indeed offer a forecast on the GNEC/GNP growth trends for a low-growth period between 1988 and 1995, a more valuable projection might be its forecast for an ensuing high-growth period.

Remember that RECALL could already have inferred a long *GNEC* wave as early as the 1920s. But, much more information is now available on GNEC growth and the relationship of GNP to GNEC. With that added knowledge, we should expect more from RECALL in the 1980s.

In this chapter, we will examine what RECALL can now forecast about societal industry and economic prosperity. In addition, new trends in energy use will be identified. In the subsequent chapter, we will see what RECALL can say about future industry and business trends.

Before the Crash of '87—The Confusing Signals

As was the case in the 1920s, there was little in the 1980s to suggest the emergence of another catastrophic crash of the stock market. True, a few analysts had projected a market decline, but not of the magnitude that materialized. Reminiscent of President Hoover's reassurance following the Crash of '29, the White House issued a statement following Black Monday (1987): "the underlying economy remains sound." President Reagan added, "There is nothing wrong with the economy—all the indices are up."

Just as in 1929, a case could be made for those statements. The average GNP growth during the four-year period from 1982 to 1986 was over 4 percent per year. Even for the third quarter of 1987 (just prior to the Crash), the Commerce Department reported an annual GNP growth rate of more than 3.5 percent per year. While GNP growth could be described as favorable, the rise in the Dow Jones Industrial Average was sensational. In the five-year period between August 1982 and August 1987, the index increased more than 25 percent per year! Unemployment also declined, reaching a level of about 6 percent in October 1987, and inflation was modest. All the usual economic indicators suggested "go."

There were differences though. The federal budget deficit reached an all-time high of $220 billion in 1986, compared to a budget surplus in 1928. The foreign trade deficit was $170 billion in 1986. Computerized program trading on the market floor was frequently blamed for the Crash of '87.

Was the Crash of '87 more than an aberration? One school of thought simply dismissed the crash as a correction to an over-heated market, suggesting another assault on market highs would soon occur. Much of the loss on Black Monday was, in fact, recovered in the next few days. But that again followed a pattern similar to the Crash of '29. Only after the spring of 1930 did the stock indexes begin their more disastrous decline in that earlier history.

Although it can be argued that budget deficits, trade imbalances, high interest rates, program trading, or psychological factors created the Crash of '87, the position here will be more heretical. It will be asserted that GNEC growths, GNP growths, stock-market rises (or declines), and financial indicators, in general, are only results of a more fundamental behavior.

The Crash of '87 and other economic problems of the 1980s only reflected an industrial *growth stagnation as the macroinnovations of the 1930s finally ran their course.*

Assuming this Schumpeterian thesis is correct, the basic solutions will not involve just fiscal or monetary policies, but more significantly, industrial policies. A fascination with the financial maneuverings of Wall Street and Washington, for example, must be replaced by a greater attention on technological and industrial rejuvenation. Government (both federal and local) can contribute importantly to this rejuvenation, but not just by preoccupation with money supply, discount rates, federal budgets, or military strength. More discussion of appropriate government, industry, and personal-planning policies will be postponed until Part 4. Let's focus here only on recollecting the future. Could RECALL have projected credible GNEC and GNP growths before the Crash of '87? Would RECALL have expected a growth bust or boom in the years after 1985?

RECALL's Growth Projections— Before the Crash of '87

Since 1925, another 60 years of GNEC and GNP growth data were available to RECALL in 1985.

With over 130 years of GNEC growth data available, a "cycle-adjusted-logistic" (CAL) growth curve for U.S. total energy consumption could then be established with considerable assurance.

We should expect that RECALL could forecast, at that time, the growth of *energy* consumption for the next 35 years (from 1985 to 2020) within well-defined bands of uncertainties—bands that could still allow a very good glimpse of probable GNEC future growths. Moreover, some 80 years of data on the interrelationship of GNEC and GNP, should permit RECALL to project, with similar confidence, our country's *economic* future.

Figure 11–1 shows the history of GNEC and GNP growths from 1970 to 1986, with projections from 1987 to 2020. The shaded areas indicate both a 6 percent uncertainty band from 1970 to 1986—associated with historical year-to-year variations—and a 6 percent to 16 percent overall uncertainty band for the future years from 1987 to 2020—a band expected to include 50 percent of the data points. From those curves, RECALL could have been fully prepared to recollect the energy and economic futures—both for a near-term (10 years) period and for a longer range (from 10 to 35 years) period.

By now, you may be so familiar with the GNEC and GNP growth curves that you'll need very little help from RECALL to draw important conclusions.

FIGURE 11–1

Growth Projections for GNEC and GNP with Annual Data Points Shown for the 1970–1986 Period

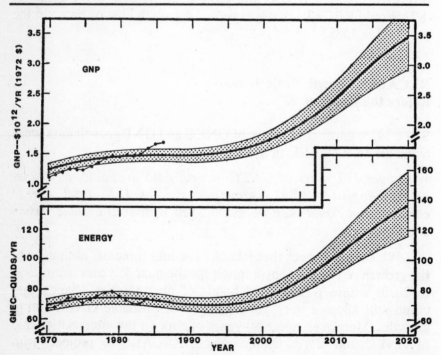

First, we can note that the GNEC peaked around 1979, as would be expected from the superposition of the GNEC long wave on its underlying steady growth.

The RECALL GNEC growth forecast shows a broad peak between 1975 and 1985. The actual GNEC data points show some bouncing around in this 10-year period, reflecting short-term variations—variations that do lie within the uncertainty band. The sharper-than-normal decline from 1979 to 1982 might have resulted partly from the higher oil prices at that time, which temporarily dampened our enthusiasm for energy use.

Second, we can see that the much-heralded economic growth of 1983 only moved the GNP level from a point slightly below to one slightly above the expected GNP growth curve.

The even more impressive growth in 1984 brought the GNP to a point about 8 percent above the median level, slightly more than the 6 percent band in which 50 percent of the actual points should fall. A few of the more euphoric economists projected (in 1983 and 1984) a continuing strong GNP growth of around 4 percent per year over the five-year period from 1984 to 1989. Such a growth would have increased the GNP by about 22 percent during that period—a growth that would have carried the GNP far above the uncertainty band.

Third, we can conclude that although temporary GNP increases of 5 percent or more per year (such as in 1984) could again occur, sustained growths of this magnitude should not be expected between 1985 and 1995.

Temporary GNP increases or decreases, as large as 5 percent over a single one-year period, generally reflect short-term business cycles and/or government manipulation of fiscal and monetary policies. In the first chapter, we suggested that government policies by any name (consumer-led or supply-side) might be expected to have short-range effects on the economy. Stimulative economic measures of this kind can only promote short-term improvements in the economy at some expense to subsequent corrections. It is difficult to see how a sustained large deficit-spending program, for example, could bring about any result other than disaster. Assuming that the long-cycle theory is valid, industry, not government, must be primarily responsible for new growth. Industrial activities, such as technological innovation initiatives or capital expansion or both must play the major roles in any renewed economic growth.

RECALL's Growth Projections— A 1980 to 2020 Overview

Based on the GNEC and GNP growth curves, as indicated in Figure 11–1, RECALL projections could be developed, even before the Crash of '87, for two interesting time intervals:

- a growth BUST: a near-term, low-growth period from 1980 to 1995
- a growth BOOM: a longer-range, high-growth period from 1995 to 2020

The upper and lower limits of the uncertainty bands could be used for GNEC in 1995 (15 years forward from 1980) and in 2020 (25 years forward from 1995) to develop optimistic and pessimistic growth projections for the two periods, 1980 to 1995 and 1995 to 2020.

The RECALL projections are illustrated in Figures 11–2 (for GNEC growth) and 11–3 (for GNP growth). In each case, the shaded area on the left shows the projected 1980–1995 growth, and on the right it shows the projected 1995–2020 growth. The corresponding forecasts (the dashed rectangles), indicate projections RECALL would have made in 1925 prior to the previous bust and boom cycle. Since the underlying secular growth curve describing our national economy is approaching closer and closer to an ultimate saturation, the GNEC and GNP *growth* estimates for the upcoming years are about 1 percent lower than those 55 years ago. This corresponds to the growth of a teenage boy whose weight increases at a less rapid rate in his 19th year than in his 14th year. Although the GNEC and GNP *growths* should be lower in these future periods, the per capita GNEC and GNP *levels* would be higher because our level of prosperity would be higher.

For a further perspective on national growths, the average growth rates for the entire 55-year period from 1925 to 1980 were:

FIGURE 11-2
GNEC Average Growth Rates for 1980–1995 and 1995–2020 as Estimated by RECALL in 1980

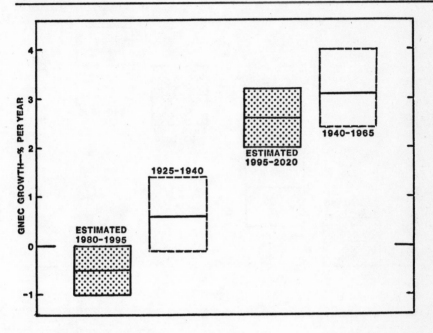

- 2.2 percent per year for GNEC
- 3.1 percent per year for GNP

With the projections for probable GNEC and GNP growths in the 1980–1995 and 1995–2020 periods, more can now be said about the implications. Let's examine these implications separately for the 1980–1995 low-growth period and the 1995–2020 high-growth period.

RECALL's Near-Term Projections—
After the Crash of '87

There was considerable optimism in the early months of 1930 that the Crash of '29 held little significance relative to the economy of the nation. It is not surprising that some forecasters should minimize the significance of the Crash of '87. In fact, it has already

FIGURE 11–3
GNP Average Growth Rates for 1980–1995 and 1995–2020 as Estimated by RECALL in 1980

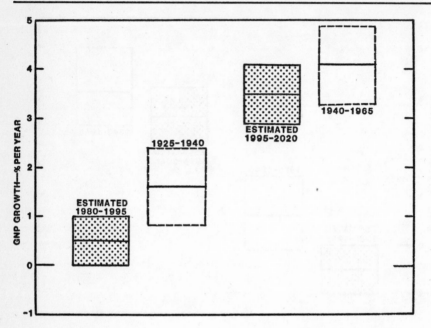

been noted that the Great Depression should not be regarded as a *result* of the Crash of '29.

It does seem clear, though, that the Crash of '29 and the Great Depression had a common cause—a business growth stagnation and a consequent declining societal industry.

After the Crash of '87, we can conclude that the growth decline already projected by RECALL before the crash is only more assured. Still, the severity of the crash should not approach that of the 1930s. After all, we do know much more about the effects of appropriate fiscal, monetary, and social policies.

RECALL would forecast an average GNP growth of only 0 to 1 percent, approximately, for the 15-year period 1980 to 1995, compared to the average GNP growth of about 3 percent for the last 55 years.

The difference between a 1 percent and a 3 percent growth might seem to be insignificant, but it is a decline of 67 percent. That two-thirds decline, or 2 percent difference translates into some $80 billion per year—an amount that would support four million jobs at $20,000 per person. If that dismal economic forecast is correct, it could have grim implications for all of us—both in our business and personal affairs. At least two questions are raised by the projection:

1. Is an economic growth bust inevitable?
2. If so, how severe could it be relative to the Great Depression?

Can we expect RECALL to answer these questions? RECALL probably *can* answer the first question, just as it could have done in 1925 for the 1930–1940 period (as discussed in Chapter 9). RECALL probably *cannot* answer the second question, just as it could not have forecast, in 1925, the depth of the depression to occur in the 1930s. Still other observations by RECALL on appropriate preparations for forthcoming GNEC/GNP growth changes will be discussed in Part 4.

Is an Economic Growth Bust Inevitable?

Is it possible that the upturn in GNP during the 1983–1987 period could suggest that a growth decline from 1988 to 1995 should *not* be expected? Is there a more direct way to identify where we currently are in the long wave? Perhaps the most pragmatic approach to our economic sleuthing is simply to examine how the year-to-year GNEC data points are now behaving relative to the underlying secular or logistic growth curve. This deviation curve, you will remember, was the one that showed a sinusoidal wave for the historical GNEC data. In contrast, the actual versus projected growths, in Figure 11–1, illustrated the year-to-date GNEC data points relative to the synthesized "cycle-adjusted-logistic" curve—the curve that *combined* the secular growth and the long-wave variation (not just the underlying secular growth itself). By subtracting the long-term secular growth from the actual year-to-year GNEC data points, we can see whether the deviation of the recent GNEC points (from the secular growth) is continuing to show evidence of the long-wave trend.

The deviations are shown in Figure 11–4 for specific years between 1970 and 1986, compared to the expected sinusoidal long wave. Data points are shown both for the year-to-year GNEC values and for five-year averages of those values.

There can be little doubt that the GNEC deviation is following very faithfully its historic long-wave pattern.

The data points are obviously following the expected trend line, although small oscillations around the smooth sinusoidal curve indicate the occurrence of shorter-term business cycles. The averaged points are continuing to show a downward trend, crossing the zero-deviation line between 1983 and 1985 in spite of the fact that those years were frequently touted as years beginning

FIGURE 11–4
Deviation of Total Energy from the Underlying Logistic-Growth Approximation*

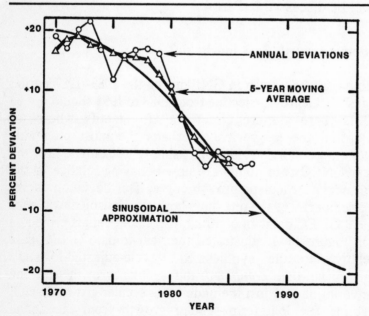

*Annual data points and 5-year averaged points since 1970.

a new boom period. From the individual GNEC points in 1985 and 1986, it now appears we have moved to annual data points *below* those suggested by the GNEC secular growth curve.

The GNEC growth decline was well underway in 1980 and was continuing in 1986.

How Severe Will the Growth Bust Be?

From Figures 11–2 and 11–3, it was already seen that RECALL would project average GNEC and GNP growths in the 1980–1995 period significantly lower than those for the 1925–1940 period. Moreover, the GNP growth from 1980 to 1987 was moderately strong (just as the 1925–1928 GNP growth was moderately strong) compared to the projected average of about 0.5 percent per year for the 1980–1995 period. Does this mean that the 1988–1995 period will be particularly severe (as was the case in 1930–1935)? That might be reading too much into projections over short periods of time. The depth of the depression in the 1930s was abnormally severe for a number of reasons that do not apply today. For example, federal deposit insurance of banks should prevent any future banking crisis as severe as that of the 1933 failures. Unemployment insurance, pensions, and our social security system should now ensure some degree of protection for individuals. A better knowledge of appropriate short-term economic policies should also help to prevent a decline as severe as that of the 1930s.

The decline of the GNEC deviation curve in the 1930s was significantly below the 6 percent error band associated with the expected GNEC curve. Even the RECALL forecasts would have been optimistic for the 1930–1935 period.

The recent GNEC data indicate we are following an expected 1980-to-1995 stagnation trend. The average GNP growth, when averaged over the 1980 through 1986 period, was little more than 2 percent per year—and could have been less without the stimulative tax reductions and heavy military spending. If the government succeeds in reducing deficit spending, that effect in itself will reduce the apparent GNP growth. If the Crash of '87 has a negative psychological effect on consumer spending, it also could result in some deterioration of our near-term economic growth. Finally, a default by some of the developing countries, with their large debt loads, could trigger further stresses throughout the world.

These conclusions may sound abysmally gloomy. But, before indulging in too much despair, let's look at the brighter side of the long wave—a period that will begin in less than 10 years from 1987.

RECALL's Longer-Range Projection— After the Crash of '87

Although it is important to recognize the consequences of an approaching growth bust, it might be even more important—at least in the long range—to recognize and understand the potential of the ensuing growth boom and the opportunities it will offer.

RECALL's median GNEC growth projection suggests a boom beginning around 1995 that will carry U.S. energy consumption in 2020 to about 1.9 times that in 1995, a 90 percent increase in 25 years.

If GNEC begins from the median point in 1995, but grows to the top of the uncertainty band as shown in Figure 11–1, the GNEC could be as large as 2.25 times that in 1995, an increase of 125 percent. Even if it grows only to the bottom of the uncertainty band, the increase would be 65 percent. Moreover, the corresponding median growth curve for GNP suggests the GNP level in 2020 will be 2.25 times that in 1995, a 125 percent increase in 25 years or 3.3 percent per year.

Two questions can again be asked:

- Is it absurd to think that energy consumption will increase some two-fold between 1995 and 2020, especially since society has apparently learned to conserve energy use in the 1979 to 1986 period?
- What factors would account for such a burst of energy growth?

Over the last decade, we have been energy-shocked, especially by oil shortages and price escalations. There has been a growing belief that a substantial consumption of energy in society is immoral or unpatriotic, since we are so dependent on foreign oil sources. Only now, according to energy critics, are we learning to curb our lust for energy use. Yet, there is a corresponding belief that a further strong increase in the gross national product is a morally appropriate objective. If energy is embodied in all of humanity's products (as was discussed in Chapter 5), it is hard to argue that a substantial GNP growth is admirable, but energy growth is not. Clearly, an overdependence on certain rapidly depleting energy resources is imprudent and, perhaps, immoral; but energy use itself should not be the target of zealous conservationists unless reduced growths in GNP and our standard of living are simultaneously attacked.

Since society will undoubtedly want a strong new GNP growth, consistent with the growth trends of earlier prosperous years, a 90 percent increase of GNEC in 25 years is not absurd—a growth that would compare to the 130 percent increase in the 1940 to 1965 period.

Turning to the second question, a large increase in energy use can be expected for two reasons already emphasized:

- A large resurgence of industrial growth, arising from an expected 1990 innovation surge, will require a new GNEC surge.
- A resurgence of capital equipment growth, both to replace the attrition of equipment from the prior growth cycle and to support the industries of a new cycle, will also contribute.

But, you might rebut: aren't there at least two possible offsetting arguments?

- Aren't we learning to use energy more efficiently?
- Won't the next long wave involve the less energy-intensive industries of the information technologies?

The answer, in each case, is: "Yes, with reservations." The trend to use energy more efficiently will undoubtedly continue, but that effect is already factored into the long-range secular growth. The second question might be more compelling. Still, it is likely that many of the energy-intensive industries will also continue to show a significant growth—particularly those associated with transportation, space activities, and new electricity applications.

Beyond those arguments, we can expect other factors to contribute to increased energy demands:

- a continuing modest population growth
- increased energy requirements to mine and process lower-grade ores
- an increasing need to give attention to environmental cleanup
- a continuing trend toward substituting energy (especially electricity) for manual labor

In summary, energy consumption will probably continue the growth pattern it has been following for almost 150 years.

The expectation of a new boom in GNEC and GNP growth beginning in only a few years should be exciting to all of us—both professionally and personally. How to prepare for this boom will be a subject of Part 4.

Just as the GNEC boom of the 1950–1980 period had some profound effects on energy-related industries of that era, we should expect the forthcoming boom to bring about some significant changes in those same industries. Let's ask RECALL: What can be foreseen about the future of electricity and non-electricity growths? What fuel resources will support those growths?

**RECALL's Energy-Industry Forecasts—
The Electricity Industry**

From decade to decade, our homes, offices, and factories have been finding new uses for electricity. It is no surprise that the electricity industry has been a growth industry through two long cycles. The RECALL growth curves indicate it will continue to be a growth industry in the 1995–2020 growth cycle. In fact, we can expect some surprising electricity versus non-electricity growth trends, as well as their consequences, to unfold before 2020.

Electricity growth data have a statistical history of 80 years—compared to 130 years for total energy consumption. The data base is still quite adequate to establish both an accurate substitution growth (electricity versus non-electricity takeover) and a cycle-adjusted-logistic growth curve for electricity itself. Figure 11–5

FIGURE 11–5
Cycle-Adjusted-Logistic Growth Curves for Input Energy to Electricity and Total Energy Input: 1970–2020

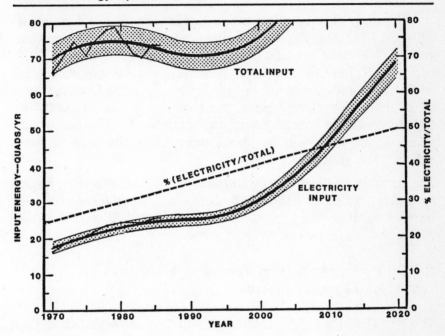

shows the RECALL growth curve for the input energy required by the electricity-generating industry during the period 1970 to 2020. Also shown for comparison is a portion of the RECALL curve for total energy (GNEC) reproduced from Figure 11–1.

In contrast to the GNEC growth curve, electricity use will continue to show a growth throughout the 1985 to 1995 period, albeit, an average growth only a little more than 1 percent per year.

Remember, 1995 represents the turnaround year for GNEC growth and is the beginning of the next GNEC boom period. We have already observed that RECALL would project GNEC to increase 1.9-fold during the 25-year period from 1995 to 2020. The RECALL forecast for *electricity* growth during this period is even more impressive.

RECALL would project a 2.6-fold increase in electricity use over the 25-year period between 1995 and 2020—an average growth rate of 3.8 percent per year.

Granted, this is more modest than the five-fold increase between 1940 and 1965—the equivalent of 6.4 percent per year growth. Nevertheless, the projected growth in the 1995 to 2020 period will require additional generating plants equivalent to almost two times the entire installed capacity in the United States as of 1985. Moreover, since most of the plants currently in operation will be retired during that period, the total number of plants to be built will be about three times the number now existing. Or, stated another way:

The number of generating plants to be built during the 25-year period, from 1995 to 2020, will be between two and three times the number of generating plants that have been built in the entire 100-year U.S. history of electricity energy.

RECALL's Energy-Industry Forecasts—Electricity versus Non-Electricity Growth

The growth of the electrical industry will have important effects on our economy, but not all of our energy comes through electricity. Let's examine the expected fate of non-electricity energy—energy used for transportation, industrial heat, and home heat that doesn't come primarily from electricity. Non-electricity energy growth can be measured simply by the difference between total energy use, GNEC, and the part of GNEC used for electricity generation. The RECALL growth projections for both non-electricity and electricity-generation uses are shown in Figure 11–6.

As might be expected, non-electricity-energy use will decline even more rapidly than total-energy use between 1985 and 1995. With the energy-consumption resurgence (beginning around 1995–2000) even non-electricity-energy use will increase, though not nearly so rapidly as electricity-energy use.

The energy consumption used for electricity generation will exceed the energy consumption for non-electricity use between 2015 and 2020—after 2020, the United States can truly be called an electricity-energy society.

FIGURE 11–6
RECALL'S Energy Growth Curves *

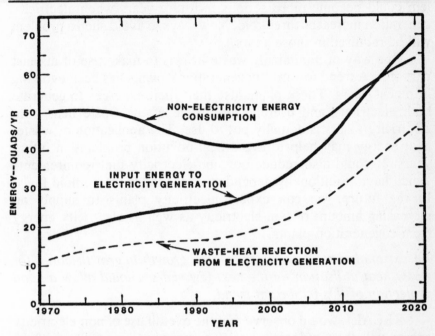

*Projected for non-electricity energy, electricity input energy, and electricity waste-heat rejection energy: 1970 to 2010.

An often overlooked aspect of non-electricity energy consumption is that some useful heat energy can also be generated from waste heat normally rejected by electricity-generation plants. The projected growth of this "waste heat" is illustrated by the dashed line in the lower part of the figure. On the average, electricity-generating plants convert less than 34 percent of the total input energy they consume into the electricity energy they produce. Hence, these plants are generally said to operate at a 34 percent efficiency. Higher efficiency plants are possible in principle, but they are not found to be economically optimum—at least with existing technologies. The other 66 percent of the input energy is rejected, and ends up in river or ocean waters, resulting in a modest temperature rise (perhaps as large as a few degrees). You may have read about this "heat pollution." The water is impartial to the source of the heat energy—the "pollution" can come from either coal-fired generating stations or nuclear stations. This problem could become more serious in future years when electricity generation increases three-fold. New ways to avoid such a problem will be required in those years.

One way of minimizing waste heat is to make use of at least part of it. A trend toward "cogeneration" plants has been evolving in recent years. These plants use their fuel resources to generate both electricity and useful heat—some of the waste heat from electricity plants is actually put to use. The application of waste-heat energy may help to avoid heat-pollution problems in future years. It could also reduce our non-electricity fuel requirements which have traditionally depended on the more scarce fluid fuels. In the future, we can expect electricity plants to supply an increasing amount of non-electricity as well as electricity energy from cogeneration plants.

An extrapolation of the year-to-year growth/ungrowth curve for waste-heat utilization, in the next few years, should allow a good projection of this important trend.

RECALL would observe that the overall use of non-electricity energy will show a decrease of 10 percent between 1985 and 2000 (in addition to a decrease of almost 10 percent that already occurred between 1980 and 1985). Since non-electricity-energy use in the last GNEC boom depended so heavily on fluid fuels, a decline in this energy use (caused partly by a preference for electricity even for heating) can be regarded as an opportunity to solve some of the dependency problems associated with the use of fluid fuels. RECALL would be quick to caution that less than 15 years are available before another surge in energy demands will put new pressure on oil and natural gas supplies.

A significant distinction between electricity and non-electricity energy use is the preference for type of fuel used for these two applications. Electricity generation depends predominantly on solid fuels, such as coal and nuclear resources. In contrast, non-electricity energy use has traditionally leaned more on the fluid-fuels, that is, oil and natural gas. RECALL can also forecast some striking new megatrends in fuel resource uses for the next few decades. Let's look at them.

RECALL's Energy-Industry Forecasts—Fuel Resources

With electricity consumption increasing and non-electricity-energy use declining for the next 15 years, a change in emphasis might occur between fluid-fuel use and solid-fuel use. The relative and absolute demands for these fuels in the next few years, and even more importantly after 2000 (during the energy-growth resurgence) should be of paramount concern to industry, government policy planners, and to all of us who depend on various energy resources. This is especially a concern for those resources that might be in short demand.

RECALL can shed considerable light on these questions, by applying the now-familiar logistic substitution methods to the relative competition between fuels—a competition already occurring. The RECALL methods can, in most cases, eliminate any arguments about the technological merits of a particular energy system. The RECALL approaches show what the energy-consuming public (as well as industry) is already selecting to be its technological or economic preferences. These selections are made independent of opinions by any pundits on the presumed merits of a system.

Obviously, substitution logistic curves should not be applied in blind faith. Fuel resource growths, in particular, have occasionally shown changes in trends after partial substitutions. Examples include:

- the change in wood-fuel growth brought about by the introduction of coal fuels in the early 1800s
- the change in coal-fuel growth brought about by the introduction of oil fuels in the early 1900s

These changes can usually be verified (or even anticipated) by an identification of reasons for the changes.

The vigorous fluid-fuel/solid-fuel substitution that occurred between 1900 and 1970 will be (and is being) reversed for at least two reasons:

- an escalation of fluid fuel prices (reflecting an over-demand and approaching resource-exhaustion)
- a growing importance of the electricity industry that uses solid fuels predominantly

Very approximately, the prices of oil and natural gas (when measured relative to their potential heat content) are double the price of coal.

How important is that price difference? With coal-fired generating plants, about half the cost of generating electricity (before distribution to customers) is associated with the cost of the coal fuel. If fuel costs doubled, your electricity bill would increase significantly.

The price of uranium fuel is even less than that of coal, although the higher price of a plant using nuclear fuel tends to offset at least part of the nuclear fuel price advantage. Still nuclear energy is competitive with coal-produced energy in many parts of the world and in some parts of the United States. At least for electricity generation, solid fuels (coal and uranium) will offer competitive advantages over fluid fuels, (oil and natural gas) in future years. The real distinction between solid and fluid fuels is price, not just the fact that one type is solid and the other fluid.

With the knowledge that solid fuels have a lower cost per unit of heat content and will continue to have a lower cost than will fluid fuels, let's ask RECALL what the relative growth rates of those two fuel types will be in the coming years.

The Growth of Solid Fuels (Coal and Uranium)

The curve (or straight line) in Figure 11–7 shows the substitution curve for solid fuels versus fluid fuels based on U.S. Department of Energy data from 1971 to 1986. Obviously the data base is small, just as the data base for forecasting fluid-fuel growth in the 1930–1970 period was small in the 1920s. But, as in that earlier example, the trend is clear.

The solid-fuel megatrend for the next 30 to 40 years is exactly opposite to the trend that occurred in the 1930 to 1970 period.

The time period for the solid-fuel substitution to grow one decade on the growth/ungrowth curve (i.e. for $F/(1 - F)$ to grow from 0.1 to 1.0 or 0.2 to 2.0) can be seen to be about 50 years. The corresponding one-decade growth time for the fluid-fuel substitution between 1930 and 1970 (see Figure 9–5) was about 40 years.

FIGURE 11–7
Projected Growth of Solid Fuels Relative to Fluid Fuels

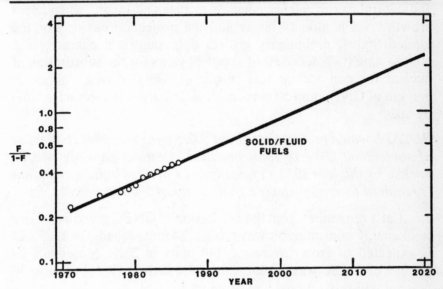

The one-decade growth time for coal substitution over wood fuel, between 1850 and 1900, was also about 40 years. Hence, the *two-decade* growth time, which is used as a "characteristic growth time" (because it measures the implied time for a 10 percent to 90 percent takeover) appears to be typically 80 to 100 years—a very long time for the takeover of any new energy system. That conclusion may be one of the most important observations of the logistic-growth studies on energy use.

From an extrapolation of the solid/fluid substitution growth, RECALL can now conclude that the use of solid fuels will surpass the use of fluid fuels, in the United States, between 2000 and 2005—only 15 to 20 years from 1985.

Many of the uses of oil and natural gas during the last 50 years will now be replaced by uses of coal and nuclear fuels—probably through the expedient of electricity. That subject will be discussed in the next chapter.

A substitution growth curve for nuclear versus non-nuclear fuel can also be developed, although the limited data base and the uncertainties of nuclear growth in the United States make such a projection more difficult. In countries where the costs of coal, oil, and natural gas are higher (such as France and Japan), the nuclear growth level is already larger and the projection easier. For the United States, preliminary growth data suggest a characteristic growth time (two decades) of about 80 years for the substitution of nuclear for non-nuclear fuel resources. On that basis, about 30 percent of GNEC and 50 percent of electricity will use nuclear fuel by 2020.

RECALL would project that about 800 gigwatts-electric (GWe) out of some 2000 GWe of total installed electrical capacity will be nuclear by the year 2020. (Typically, a 1 GWe or 1 million kwe plant is required to supply electricity to a city of 500,000 people).

Let's remember from the discussion of GNEC growth that our total energy consumption was around 74 units (quads) in 1985 and is expected to grow to around 140 units in 2020. Moreover, 29 percent of GNEC was produced by solid fuels in 1985, but some 70 percent will rely on coal and uranium in 2020.

The use of solid fuels will increase, then, almost five-fold in only 35 years (from about 21 units to 98 units).

If that growth should be supplied completely by coal fuels, the problems of coal mining, land reclamation, coal transportation, and even air quality would be enormous. Even assuming 800 GWe of nuclear plants by 2020, coal use would have to increase about three-fold—still a significant challenge for the coal production, transportation, and usage industries.

Under almost any circumstances, RECALL would foresee a strong resurgence of the coal industry in the next 35 years—a recollection that would seem to contradict most of the conventional wisdom.

As with electricity projections in the 1920s, still more precise forecasts of coal growth should be possible from growth/ungrowth curves during the next 10 years, even though GNEC itself will be declining. A continuing evaluation of coal growth should confirm the RECALL forecasts in the next few years.

Let's examine the potential role of solar energy in the future of fuel resources. The growth of solar energy in the last 10 years already allows RECALL to lend some perspective to this potential. The amount of heat energy produced by solar panels in the 1980s is less than 10 percent of that produced by nuclear energy. Again assuming an 80-year characteristic growth time, it is difficult to see how solar energy could contribute importantly to GNEC in the next 35 years.

It is unlikely that solar panels will contribute more than 10 percent to GNEC by 2020—although even that contribution will be significant.

On the basis of the foregoing observations, RECALL would reach the following conclusions:

- The fluid-fuel industries will cease to be growth industries in the 1985 to 2020 period (fluid-fuel use will decline almost 1 percent per year compared to the 5 percent per year increase between 1930 and 1970).
- Solid-fuel use will increase about five-fold during that period (an increase of almost 5 percent per year).
- Solar energy will not be a dominant contributor to GNEC in the next 35 years.

Summary

RECALL's primary interest in energy growth is its implications on societal industry as measured by GNEC and on economic prosperity as measured by GNP. RECALL's forecasts for both GNEC and GNP growths in the 35-year period from 1985 to 2020 have been divided into a near-term 10-year and a subsequent 25-year period.

Between 1985 and 1995, GNEC will remain constant and GNP will grow at only about 1 percent per year.

This 10-year period will mark the winter of a closing long wave. GNEC has already fallen slightly between 1980 and 1987, and GNP has grown at only about 2 percent per year. Various government and personal safety nets built into our system since 1930 should prevent a winter as painful as that of the 1930 to 1940 period—but that kind of judgment is beyond the capability of RECALL.

A new GNEC and GNP growth surge will begin around 1995.

RECALL can foresee, even at this time, more impressive GNEC and GNP growths for the 1995 to 2020 period—a GNEC growth at about 2.5 percent per year and a GNP growth between 3 and 3.5 percent per year. While those percentage growths might appear modest, at least relative to the 1945–1970 growths, the amount of energy use in 2020 will be almost twice that now used. Obviously, that amount of extra energy cannot come from oil or natural gas fuels.

Perhaps even more surprising, the total generating capacity of electricity in the United States will be about three times that now available—a formidable challenge to our electricity industry. Partly because of this huge growth of electricity, we will see an increasing reliance on coal and nuclear fuel resources for our energy needs. New technologies and, possibly, new institutional arrangements will also evolve to meet those demands.

An adoption-logistic projection as early as 1910 could have foreseen the enormous growth of automobiles destined for the 1910–1925 period. Yet it was not able to foresee in 1910 certain key innovations, such as the electric starter or the assembly line, that would assure the achievement of that growth. Likewise, RECALL cannot foresee at this time the new technologies and institutions that will assure the projected large electricity growth of the next 35 years. But, assuming no breakdown of our society, history indicates the necessary innovations will appear.

What will be the cause of such a huge energy growth in the 1995 to 2020 period? RECALL reminds us that a technology-innovation surge between 1980 and 2000 will fuel another swarming of new business growths beginning at the end of this century. What can RECALL tell us about the next industrial growth surge and our own business interests? Let's examine next the technological and industrial future according to RECALL.

CHAPTER 12

THE FUTURE ACCORDING TO RECALL—TECHNOLOGY AND INDUSTRY GROWTHS

RECALL could have projected an economic winter for the 1985–1995 period before the Crash of '87. More importantly, RECALL would now be emphasizing the forecast of a subsequent GNEC and GNP growth boom, with advice on how we should be preparing for it.

By recognizing and building on the wave of technology macroinnovations anticipated in the 1980–2000 period, businesses should be more likely to profit in the approaching 1995–2020 growth boom.

Can RECALL identify in 1990 the specific macroinnovations emerging in the 1980–2000 period? To lend some perspective to this question, let's reflect on earlier macroinnovation and business growth eras. Do you think that business pundits in 1880 would have fully appreciated the economic potential of electrification, automobiles, telephones, and organic chemicals? Surely, most would have scoffed at the idea that these possible technology macroinnovations would be destined to create giant industries in the 1900 to 1925 period—industries that would reshape the entire national economy. How many business leaders would have bet, in the midst of the Great Depression, that electrical home appliances, air travel, television, and synthetic textile fibers as macroinnovations would be largely responsible for another industrial growth boom between 1950 and 1975? Correspondingly, we should not expect RECALL to identify in 1990 all the *specific* macroinnovations that will evolve between 1980 and 2000.

Nevertheless, we might expect RECALL to indicate *general* technology areas where macroinnovations could be expected. In fact, some industries are already introducing a new generation of exciting basic innovations—the signs of macroinnovation incubation. We will begin by looking at probable areas for product swarming.

RECALL's Projections of New Technology and Business Directions

Drawing on the history of technology in the last 100 years, macroinnovations have consistently involved at least four general technology areas:

1. Electrification.
2. Communications.
3. Transportation.
4. New materials (such as chemistry products).

Table 12–1 summarizes the past macroinnovations—with speculations on our evolving new macroinnovation directions.

Other important macroinnovations of the past could have been included in the table, even a few that had their origins between the dominant surge periods. Two mid-cycle bloomers—radio (around 1910) and microchips (around 1970)—quickly flourished at the tail ends of business growth cycles. At least one, air travel (around 1910), waited until a succeeding business growth cycle for its large commercial growth.

Remember, RECALL's *technology*-forecasting talents are limited to two capabilities—recollections of:

- time periods when basic technology surges can be expected
- adoption or substitution takeovers of new products *after* some 5 to 10 percent of the growth has occurred.

The adoption of most new products arising from the 1980–2000 technology-innovation surge period is not expected to reach 5 to 10 percent until sometime after 2000. Therefore, you might conclude that "The Future According to RECALL" is a relatively sterile forecast of our technology and industry future. Not so! There is much that RECALL can already foresee.

TABLE 12–1
Technology Macroinnovations and Their Typical Directions

Macroinnovation	1870–1890	1925–1945	1980–2000
Electrification	Home electrification	Electric appliances	New applications
Communications	Telephone	Television	Digital communications
Transportation	Automobile	Air travel	Space travel
Materials	Coal-tar chemicals	Polymer chemicals	Biochemical products
Miscellaneous	Phonographs, photography, movies	Transistors, computers, satellites	Photonics, supercomputers, superconductivity, etc.

In this chapter we will examine what RECALL might already observe in four areas:

1. Electricity supply and use.
2. Communications trends.
3. Transportation possibilities.
4. Biotechnology trends.

Let's examine what RECALL can tell about electricity-supply innovations and electricity-use innovations.

Recall and Electricity-Supply Innovations

As was observed in the previous chapter: '

The capacity of U.S. electricity generating plants to be built in just 25 years (1995–2020) will be over twice the capacity of plants built during the entire 100-year U.S. history of electricity energy.

Such phenomenal growth brings with it profound consequences, for both the supply industries and consumers. Some effects on supply industries have already been indicated in the resurgence of the coal industry, further growth of nuclear energy, and possibly, a greater use of waste-heat energy. An examination of the electric utility industry will illustrate how industries—and we as consumers—can benefit during the upswing of a long wave, but be frustrated during the downswing.

You have probably been concerned (if not alarmed!) at the escalation of your electricity bills in recent years. Part of that escalation has resulted from additional ways you use electricity, such as air conditioners, microwave ovens, and hair dryers. Some of this increase has come from a general inflation in our economy. Still, the *unit* price of electricity in cents per kilowatt-hours consumed, has shown an even more dramatic change—a change in the very direction of the price trend.

Between 1940 and 1970, the unit price of electricity (when corrected for inflation) decreased some fourfold—an average reduction of about 5 percent per year. Between 1970 and 1985, it increased 1.5 times—an average increase of about 2.5 percent per year.

Part of the electricity price increase since 1970 has resulted from cost increases of oil, natural gas, and coal imposed on the utilities. However, a reversal in the electricity price trend was beginning around 1970—even before the first oil-price shock that erupted in 1974. Why did electricity prices decrease steadily from 1940 to 1970? And, why did a turnaround occur in 1970? Briefly, the years 1940 to 1970 saw some spectacular improvements in generating technologies. In contrast, the years between 1970 and 1985 were marked by an "improvement stagnation"—even a possible reversal in at least one improvement direction—the "economies of scale."

The Economies of Scale

The most significant contributor, both to the 1940–1970 price decline and the 1970–1985 price turnaround, has been the "economies-of-scale" effect. What does this mean?

The cost of construction for a power plant twice as large is not necessarily twice as great. In fact, the construction cost per unit of electricity generated was found, in the 1940–1970 era, to decrease substantially with the generating plant size—hence the name *economies of scale*. Moreover, the number of operators required for a larger plant is only slightly greater than the number for a smaller one. These economies of scale led utilities to build larger and larger plants between 1940 and 1970.

The typical size of a modern generating unit in 1940 was around 100 MW (100 megawatts or 100,000 kilowatts). In 1950, it was around 200 MW; in 1960, around 400 MW; and in 1970, around 800 MW.

By 1970, the vendors of *nuclear* plants were offering (and utilities were purchasing) power plants as large as 1300 MW—a size that could serve approximately a half million people. However, an unexpected change in the economies of scale became apparent, for several reasons. First, the construction time for these huge nuclear plants increased significantly because of more safety-related licensing requirements, the added complexity of larger plants, and the necessary quality control. Second, the financing costs for construction increased inordinately, due to higher interest rates on money and the long construction times. Third, the growth needs for new plants declined; the large unit sizes were riskier ventures in terms of matching growth to needs. Finally, it was found that the very large units tended to have more outage time—time when the plant was not operational.

The net effect was that the economies of scale had apparently reached a limit. This improvement trend had run out of steam (by about 1970).

Other factors contributed to the reversal of electricity price trends. Who can forget the sharp increases in oil prices that occurred in 1974 and again in 1979? Some utilities (especially on the West coast) that were dependent on clean-burning oil for fuel were severly penalized by the oil-price shock. Even coal-burning utilities in high-population regions were forced to use more expensive, low-sulfur coal or special equipment to remove pollutants as pollution became increasingly important with the large industrial growth of the last few decades.

The important conclusion is that our electricity-supply technologies (especially those associated with size) were beginning to reach their limits by 1970—a time marked by the turnaround in electricity price trends.

The Signs of Innovation

This kind of technology-growth stagnation and economic adversity has traditionally led to basic innovations. In the 1980s, RECALL would recognize several signs of potentially important technology innovations it would expect in the electricity-supply industry. Those signs include:

- the examination of smaller "modular" nuclear plants that can profit from factory assembly, rapid field construction, easy growth increments, and more fault-forgiving operational features.
- radical new coal-burning technologies that promise to reduce pollutant emissions more efficiently and economically.
- a developing interest in more efficient cogeneration plants.

- the recently discovered possibility of new "superconducting" materials that could allow efficient transmission over longer distances.

As these new technologies begin to be adopted in the marketplace, RECALL can measure their early adoption rate and project their future takeover growth.

At this time, RECALL can affirm that the stage is set for some exciting and promising basic technology innovations in electricity generation and its use—innovations that will participate in the next GNEC/GNP growth boom.

Recall and the Electricity-Use Innovations

RECALL has predicted that electricity consumption between 1995 and 2020 will triple. Electricity uses have been divided roughly equally among the domestic, commercial, and industrial consumption sectors of our economy. RECALL expects growths to continue in each of those three sectors. Let's look for possible new electricity uses in those sectors.

Since practically 100 percent of U.S. homes and buildings are now electrified, further electrification growth should not account for a three-fold growth in electricity usage. Moreover, more than 50 percent of our homes have relatively modern electrical appliances—refrigerators, hot-water heaters, washers, and dryers. Commercial institutions (stores, offices, theatres) are now generally equipped with modern illumination, air-conditioning, and commercial appliances. Manufacturing industries are already making generous use of electric motors, electric welding, and electrochemical processes (for making aluminum, tool-steel, and graphite). We should look for new technology directions to account for the expected strong growths of electricity use in these three sectors. This observation presents a challenge to all electrical-equipment entrepreneurs looking for new businesses.

What should we expect as potential emerging macroinnovations? Can RECALL help us in that prognosis? What impact might any new directions have on our domestic, commercial, or business planning?

Technology directions already underway suggest the possibility of two impressive macroinnovations—"climate control" and "robotics."

Let's examine the probable course of these macroinnovations in our domestic, commercial, and industrial sectors.

Electricity-Use Innovations—The Domestic Sector

The heat pump is not a recent technology innovation and is commonly used in many commercial buildings. It is now gaining popularity in modern homes and promises to become our most popular heating and cooling system.

Basically the heat pump is an integral heating and air-conditioning system that eliminates the use of natural gas, oil, or coal fuel. In principle, it is a small climate-control unit that operates like a *reversible* refrigerator. When your house is too warm, it can be used to pump heat from the inside to the outside of your house—just as a refrigerator mechanism pumps heat from inside to outside a storage chest. When your house is too cold, the heat pump can pump heat from the outside to the inside of your house. A recent trend has been to use heat pumps in conjunction with solar-heated water tanks. The main point is that heat pumps are more energy efficient than common electrical-resistance heaters, ("radiant heaters") and can be used for cooling as well as heating.

What can RECALL tell us about the probable growth of domestic heating by electricity—or about domestic climate control? As indicated in Figure 12–1, less than 1 percent of our U.S. homes were heated with electricity in 1950. The fractional adoption of electricity heating has faithfully followed a uniform growth/ungrowth behavior, as shown by the open circles in the figure. The error band for the individual points is only three years, and the takeover adoption time (for 10 percent to 90 percent adoption) is about 38 years. By 1985, some 25 percent of homes were heated by electricity.

An extrapolation of the growth/ungrowth curve indicates that 50 percent of U.S. homes will be heated by electricity, instead of gas or oil, in the early 1990s, and 90 percent between 2010 and 2015.

FIGURE 12–1
The Growth/Ungrowth Trend for Domestic Heat Pumps (circles) and Climate-Controlled Football Stadiums (triangles)*

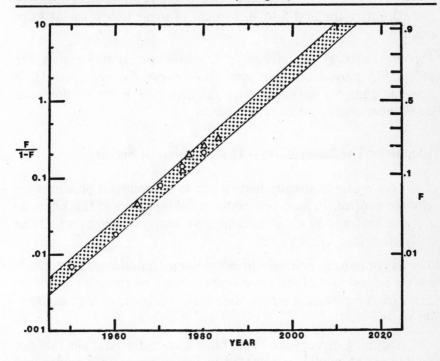

*The fractional growth scale is shown on the right side.

Not all our homes are candidates for electric climate-control systems, but statistics already show that 50 percent of *new* home construction does utilize such a system. This implies that these electrical climate control systems will continue to grow, at least for the next 10 years. From this RECALL exercise, you could conclude that your new home could have an obsolete heating system within 10 years if you do not adopt a heat-pump. RECALL can have its rewards even in your personal planning and investing.

Other new domestic applications of electricity will be found in the next business growth surge. By reflecting on these applications in the 1950–1975 period, we could speculate that the next surge of appliance innovations will involve computerized or robotized equipment—smart kitchen appliances, smart security systems, and smart household services. The important observation is that the home appliance industries, housing contractors, and home purchasers can all use the growth/ungrowth curves to project takeover growths once the first 5 to 10 percent of these new growths have occurred.

On the basis of experience with automatic appliances in the 1950–1975 period and the projection curve for heat pumps, it appears that the takeover time for any new wave of domestic appliances should be 20 to 40 years.

Electricity-Use Innovations—The Commercial Sector

The heat pump is already finding use in commercial buildings for climate control. In fact, few commercial buildings in the 1980s do not use heating and air-conditioning systems, whether partially or fully electric.

The use of climate control within commercial buildings is probably only a microcosm of the more extensive use of climate control we can expect both inside and outside these buildings in the next 30 to 40 years.

Shopping centers are being built with enclosed malls that are heated in the winter and cooled in the summer. In Toronto and Montreal, where the winters can be quite severe, sheltered shopping centers extend over multi-block areas of the city. Shoppers can park their automobiles in sheltered garages and walk into sheltered malls—malls that feature all kinds of commercial services including hotels, stores, banks, restaurants, and offices.

Similar shopping malls can be found in Hong Kong, where the heat is almost unbearable in the summertime. Visitors to the city can walk directly from their hotels to the shopping malls without leaving the climate-controlled area. Some malls are even equipped with people-mover walkways and escalators to move pedestrians from floor to floor.

This trend toward climate control is already occurring in several cities and suburban areas throughout the United States—for example in Palm Springs, California. Still we have seen only the beginning of a more extensive use of this technology. One way to recollect the future of climate control would be to examine the growth/ungrowth of total commercial floor area (including parking and walking areas) adopting climate control.

An interesting indication of the growth/ungrowth characteristic of commercial climate control is observed in the fractional adoption of this technology in football stadiums throughout the United States. The first application of stadium climate control was introduced in 1965 at the Astrodome facility in Houston, Texas. Figure 12–1 (which showed the domestic adoption growth of heat pumps) shows also the growth/ungrowth curve for climate control in U.S. football stadiums. By 1984, six of the National Football League teams were using domed stadiums, over 20 percent of the professional football stadiums.

The growth/ungrowth curve for climate control in football stadiums indicates that some 90 percent of the NFL teams will be using sheltered facilities between 2010 and 2015.

The coincidence of the growth curves for the adoptions of "astrodome" football stadiums (in the commercial sector) and home heat pumps (in the domestic sector) is only accidental. If baseball teams were used instead of football teams, the adoption rate would fall to about 10 percent. Nevertheless, it is likely that the growth/ungrowth curve for baseball adoption of climate control will have approximately the same slope. More importantly, the implication is that climate control for the entire commercial sector will show a takeover time of 35 to 40 years.

If it is assumed that some 5 percent of all commercial areas (including garages, malls, stores, and connected areas) used climate control in 1985, then RECALL would expect 50 percent of commercial areas to use climate control systems by about 2010; and 90 percent before 2030.

Electricity-Use Innovations—The Industrial Sector

So far, we have been talking primarily about *climate control* as a new electricity-use trend. A more substantial user of electricity in the industrial sector will undoubtedly be the industrial robot. Robots were already being tried, on a very limited basis, in the late

1960s and early 1970s. As is well-established history now, the Japanese industry has been especially aggressive in the application of robotics.

In the 1980s, industrial robots have found more and more uses—particularly in the automobile industry. Those uses include computer-controlled machining operations, welding, painting, material handling, and even some assembly operations. As the sophistication of robotic machinery improves—especially by visual and touch senses—we can expect still more blue-collar jobs to be replaced by industrial robots. The growth/ungrowth curve for the white-collar versus blue-collar work force provides some indication of how that trend will persist.

Blue-collar workers represented about 60 percent of the combined work force in 1950 and about 50 percent in 1970. A projection of that growth/ungrowth trend suggests 30 percent by 2000 and only about 20 percent by 2020.

Automation and robotics are upgrading the level of the work force—a subject that will get more attention in a later chapter. Of greater relevance here, the replacement of manual work by machinery and equipment will account for much of the increased electricity demands predicted by RECALL for the industrial sector.

Recall and Communications

Electronic appliances (radios, TVs, VCRs, and computers) depend on only small amounts of electricity to create, transmit, store, and reproduce audio, video, or information signals. In general, they do not consume as much electricity as electrical appliances (stoves, heaters, lighting, and motors). Another interesting characteristic distinguishes the electricity and electronic industries, at least from an economic perspective.

Electrical appliances typically have takeover growth times of 30 years compared to 10 years, or less, for electronic appliances. Thus, the electronic industry is more dynamic, exciting, and technology-demanding.

RECALL's prognosis of an emerging (or *erupting*) "information revolution" should come as a surprise to no one. Even now, RECALL can identify growths associated with several new communications innovations. Three examples are:

1. The word processor.
2. The compact disc player.
3. The fiber-optics telephone system.

The adoption growth of the word processor is now largely history. The substitution growth of the CD over LP records is sufficiently advanced to measure its outcome with precision. And, the substitution growth of fiber-optics for copper-wire telephone communications is well underway. These three technology innovations represent only the tip of the iceberg.

More importantly, a whole new macroinnovation—the digital-communication macroinnovation—is being spawned.

The Word-Processor Takeover

The principle of the typewriter was relatively easy to understand, at least in retrospect. The touch of a key caused a particular letter or symbol to strike an inked ribbon, transferring its configuration to the paper. But, the word processor key initiates a much more complex sequence of events. First, it sends a signal to encode the letter, number or symbol into binary language—then to store it, next to process it (check spelling, correct or change previous text, vary spacing between words), and finally to signal the printer to reproduce it, frequently as both text and graphics. Practically all modern-day secretaries have learned—in various degrees of expertise—to use the word processor. RECALL could have projected the takeover time for offices to adopt this new technology when the takeover fraction was only 5 to 10 percent—yet another area where RECALL could have helped you improve your business efficiency a few years ago.

The growth of the word processor is already reaching the top of its S-curve—a takeover time of only about 10 years.

The Compact Disc Takeover

A more recent product of the digital-technology revolution is the compact-disc (or "CD") hi-fi audio recording system. Here, the sound is encoded as on-off binary digits in the CD tracks, in contrast to the analog waves molded in LP tracks. With analog-type records, the sound signals are read directly by the phonograph stylus, amplified, and then fed to the speakers. With the CD, the digital signals are read by a light detector that responds to laser-beam reflections off the CD tracks. The digital information must then be translated to analog signals, amplified, and fed to the speakers. An important advantage of the CD technology is that record noise due to dust, wear, abuse, and even manufacturing limitations can be essentially eliminated.

The compact disc was introduced in 1983, based on technology developed jointly by the Philips Company in The Netherlands and the Sony Corporation in Japan. In 1986, CD sales accounted for over 20 percent of the record (LP plus CD) business in the United States. This phenomenal growth is ample testimony to the acceptance of the CD audio technology—in spite of a CD price (and production cost) that is roughly twice that of the LP. Figure 12–2 shows the impressive growth/ungrowth curve for the CD in comparison to the LP.

The growth/ungrowth curve for compact discs (versus the LP) suggests that over 90 percent of record sales in 1990 will belong to the CD—its takeover time will be an extraordinarily short six years!

The CD technology is already significant in terms of its economic impact on the audio recording industry. But, its basic technology (especially its enormous information storage capabilities) suggest still other possibilities for its application. For perspective, a personal-computer floppy disk, almost the same size as the CD, can store the equivalent of about 200 pages of written text. The more imposing PC hard disk can store about 5,000 pages of information. In contrast:

The CD has the astounding storage capacity of more than 100,000 pages of text.

FIGURE 12–2
Growth/Ungrowth Curves for the CD versus LP Takeover and the Digital versus Analog Telephone-Communication Takeover.*

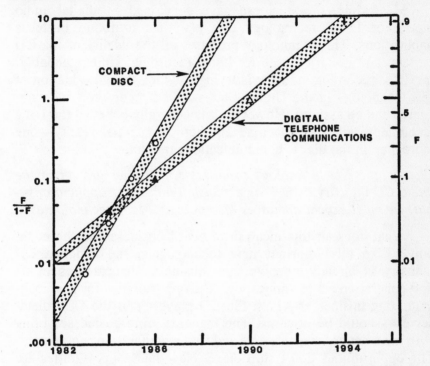

*The point shown for 1990 is estimated, based on planning forecasts by the various telephone companies.

The entire *Encyclopedia Americana,* for example, could be stored on a CD, with room left over for the *Encyclopedia Britannica,* and several dictionaries! This capacity has caught the eye of other industries, particularly the computer industry. It should be emphasized that the CD storage is limited to a "read-only-memory" (ROM) storage at this time. If and when it can be erased and reused, as can the floppy disk and the hard disk, it will usher in a new technological revolution.

Another candidate for a CD-technology takeover is the production of video records. Although video storage requires much more memory than audio storage, a 12-inch CD (instead of a 4.7-inch size) can allow the high-fidelity storage of a complete movie. Although the initial attempt at a video-disc industry was not successful, the progress in CD technology suggests video CD is more than just a possibility.

Meanwhile, the Japanese have developed a "digital audio tape" (or DAT) technology that also has profound business implications. This technology promises all the fidelity of the CD system, and it can be used for home recording. Understandably, the U.S. recording industry is trying to block the introduction of this technology in the United States unless record-copying safeguards can be assured. However, it is generally believed the DAT technology will soon become another commercial reality—one more step in the digital communications revolution.

Clearly, the CD technology promises still further growth in the audio CD industry as well as expansion into other applications— but, we must expect advances also in digital tape technologies.

What does all this mean in terms of business and the economy? Like all important new technologies, the fledgling CD industry is already opening new business opportunities in its first-generation audio application. The opportunities for new manufacturing businesses—both the CD players and the CDs themselves—should be obvious. The manufacturing businesses bring with them needs for new plants and new manufacturing equipment. The opportunities don't stop there. New sales opportunities are developing in the audio stores, and new service opportunities can be expected for properly trained technicians.

Audio CD technology represents only one application of CD technology. In fact, CD technology represents only one step in the digital communications megatrend suggested by RECALL. The fiber-optics technology represents yet another step.

The Fiber-Optics Takeover

The laser light source is a complementary technology used in retrieving digital information stored on the compact disc. Lasers are playing an equally important complementary role in the initiation and transmission of digitally-encoded light signals through glass (or "optical") fibers.

Telephone communications by fiber-optics technology consists of:

- the conversion of the sound (or other information) source from analog to digital signals
- the translation of these digital signals into intense (laser-induced) light pulses
- the transmission of these light-pulses in a glass fiber conduit
- the ultimate reconversion of the digitized light pulses back to sound (or the original information)

While fiber-optics communications have appropriately become recognized as another revolutionary technology of the 1980s, once again, it is the digital macroinnovation that is the more basic breakthrough.

By converting telephone sounds to digital signals, the signals can then be transmitted by a pulsed laser beam through a glass filament having a diameter roughly equivalent to that of a human hair. The light pulses can be turned on and off at a frequency of around one *billion* times per second. This means that the entire contents of a compact disc—already a staggering inventory of some four billion pulses—could be transmitted in only a few seconds.

Why is this enormous transmission rate so important? Telephone companies are anticipating a profound new revolution in information transfer as their lines are used more and more for computer "conversations" from office to office, from home to office, and from home to retail stores. In addition, this transmission technology is expected to open the way for more efficient cable TV transmission, video telephone systems, and possibly even the automatic translation of foreign languages.

Fiber-optics technology has still other advantages over copper-wire transmission. In addition to a hundred-fold increase in transmission capacity, digital communications have vastly superior fidelity, unaffected by electrical disturbances from adjacent power lines, or lightning. The optical fibers are more compact and more economically attractive than copper wires. Perhaps most important of all, "repeaters" (or booster amplifiers) are required at 20-to-30-mile spacings, compared to every mile for copper lines. Is it any wonder the telephone companies are excited about fiber-optics technology?

All of the independent telephone companies are racing to convert their systems to digital communications—particularly fiber-optics systems. While most of these digital systems use fiber-optics technology, which is the most efficient technology, fiber optics is not the only system capable of transmitting digital communications. Coaxial-cable and microwave transmissions, for example, are also making contributions to digital communications. Even a few of the satellite transmitters use this basic new communications technology. The growth/ungrowth curve for digital communications by telephone companies is indicated in Figure 12–2 (the same figure that illustrated CD growth). The takeover time appears to be eight years.

In 1986, 10 percent of our telephone communications were transmitted by digital technology; by 1994 it will be 90 percent.

Once again, we must conclude that word processors, compact discs, and fiber optics are only part of a much larger macroinnovation—the digital-communications macroinnovation. People in the 1890s probably marveled at the miracles of electricity, including electric lights, motors, and street cars, but the real growth of electrification must be assigned to the 1900–1925 period. Likewise, we are currently witnessing only the beginning of the digital-communications revolution. It will have a profound impact on our international commerce, domestic economy, businesses, careers, and lifestyles.

Recall and Transportation

Takeover times for communications technologies were observed to be typically 10 years or less, compared to some 30 years for electrical appliances. Takeover times for transportation technologies have resembled more closely those for electrical appliances.

In spite of the longer takeover times for transportation technologies, the future of transportation is destined to be exciting simply because of its greater departure from the familiar.

Again we should remind ourselves that recollecting the future is not the same as predicting the future. Although a few adoption trends are already becoming apparent, it is likely that the really spectacular transportation megatrends are yet to be defined. As a result, trend spotting can be more exciting at this stage than trend analysis. Even trend spotting has its merits relative to recollecting the future. Since our contemporary period is expected to be marked by a surge of basic innovations, trend spotting can help us identify likely candidates for new commercial growths.

Information on technology R&D abounds in various technical journals and books. The intent is not to duplicate that R&D literature here, but only to indicate a few of the transportation directions that might subsequently be amenable to growth/ ungrowth trend analyses. To bring some order to such an examination, let's classify the various transportation systems into five distinct travel categories:

1. Local (1 to 50 miles).
2. Interurban (100 to 500 miles).
3. Transcountry.
4. Transoceanic.
5. Outer space.

Today, *most* of our local travel depends on the automobile and the rest predominantly on airplanes—rail travel is relatively insignificant and space travel is not an option for us in the 1980s. It is becoming apparent that our transportation systems are suffering from three kinds of problems:

1. Traffic congestion.
2. An overdependence on oil.
3. Environmental pollution.

In view of these problems, what are the likely redirections we might expect for transportation technologies in the 2000–2025 period? Are there already technology trends that might help us recollect the future of transportation? Or, are there some technology innovations we should expect as the basis for upcoming trends? We'll begin by an examination of local travel.

Local Travel and Automobile Trends

Although some expansion of subway travel might occur in a number of large cities, it is likely that the automobile will continue to be the staple of local transportation. We can expect some continuation of automobile trends already underway.

Two continuing trends in automobile technology will be reductions in weight and increases in fuel efficiency.

The weight of automobiles decreased from about 4,000 to 3,000 pounds between 1970 and 1985. An extrapolation of that trend curve suggests another 1,000 pounds will be shed before 2015. Part of that decrease will probably come from the more efficient use of the non-passenger room—the engine space. Most of it will come from a greater use of improved plastics and fiber-reinforced plastics, or composites, in place of steel. The typical family automobile used only 10 pounds of plastic in 1950, compared to about 250 pounds in 1985. That incremental 240 pounds of plastic replaced at least 500 pounds of steel. A growth/ungrowth curve for this substitution indicates that some 50 percent of the steel in automobiles will be replaced by plastics shortly after 2000, and a 90 percent takeover can be expected before 2030. The 1985 automobile will seem as strange to the people of 2030 as the 1920 Tin Lizzy strikes us today.

The average gasoline mileage of U.S. cars increased from 13 miles per gallon (mpg) in 1973 to 18 mpg in 1985, and probably more nearly 25 mpg for the 1985 cars themselves. This suggests a mileage of around 50 mpg shortly after 2000.

Automobile fuel efficiency will improve partly because of the continuing weight decrease of automobiles, but also because of the greater use of computerized engine control.

Even now microprocessors are occasionally being used for ignition and carburetor control. Computerized brake equalizers and engine diagnostics have been introduced in some cars, and growth/ungrowth curves for their further adoption can probably be developed. Still other microprocessor innovations will undoubtedly appear in the next decade, and their adoption growths will quickly become apparent.

It is possible, of course, that more profound automobile innovations could occur in the next 10 to 15 years. For example, large weight reductions and improved electricity-storage technology could make electric automobiles more attractive, particularly for short-range travel purposes.

Long-Distance Travel and Related Technology Innovations

Currently, air travel accounts for most of our transportation for distances beyond 100 miles. However, air congestion, airport-to-city ground congestion, and economic factors could all change this preference for 100-to-500 mile trips. A spectacular technology innovation is already being tested in Japan and Germany. This technology combines some of the advantages of surface and air travel—and substitutes electricity for petroleum-based fuels as the motive power.

Magnetic levitation (maglev) is used to suspend trains above a "road bed," and electromagnetic induction is used to propel the trains at speeds of 250 to 320 mph.

Germany and Japan have been following different technology directions in their maglev systems. In the German maglev, the train is attracted upwards by train electromagnets that are wrapped around (and beneath) track magnets distributed along the train route. By careful control systems, a separation distance of about one inch is maintained between the attracting magnets in the coach and those on the track. A 10-mile section of track has been used to demonstrate the principle with passenger loads of 100 people traveling at up to 250 mph.

The Japanese maglev is lifted by repelling (instead of attracting) magnets, with the coach traveling on a U-shaped track several inches above the track magnets. Because a larger magnetic force is required in this case, the Japanese have been using liquid-helium-cooled superconducting magnets in the coaches. Not only is liquid-helium cooling expensive, but the helium storage and recovery system requires excessive space and weight. Newly reported breakthroughs with higher-temperature superconductors now promise the possibility of using liquid nitrogen, instead of liquid helium, which would simplify the technology considerably.

Both the Japanese and German maglevs use linear induction motors (separate from the levitation system) to propel the trains. This technology is no different than conventional electric motor technology, except that the induced motion is linear instead of rotational.

Studies in the United States have shown that the maglev technology would be more than competitive with air travel for distances up to a few hundred miles providing a train speed of around 250 mpg can be achieved.

The maglev technology is expected to be more attractive in Japan and European countries because of a heavier air travel congestion between their cities. Even in the United States, it could make economic sense for several busy traffic corridors in special parts of the country. At this time, maglev is only a basic innovation, not yet a commercial enterprise. If maglevs should subsequently follow the growth pattern of superhighways (in the last growth surge), we should expect a takeover growth, relative to short-range airline flights, that should be some 30 years. If a 1 percent growth should occur by 2000, a 50 percent takeover could be expected by about 2030.

Continental and transoceanic transportation will probably continue to be dominated by the airplane technology. However, important technology innovations should be expected in both these cases. Technology innovations on the drawing boards and technology substitutions already occurring suggest that the newer generation of airplanes will feature more efficient engines, the greater use of composites (fiber reinforced plastics), and the increased use of microprocessors, including computer control of airplanes that could approximate artificial intelligence. However, these developments are largely speculations, not recollections of the future.

It is quite likely that continental flights will use improved subsonic airplanes, while the longer transoceanic flights will be taken over by a new generation of supersonic or hypersonic aircraft.

Some of the trendspotters are already indicating that the higher-strength, lighter-weight, and higher-temperature materials now being developed for advanced military craft will soon find their way into civilian airplanes. Even at this time, engineers or business planners in both the supplier (materials) industries and the user (aircraft) industries could probably define, from takeover growth analyses, the probable future growth of these important applications.

Space Travel—The Next Frontier

In the 1880s, our grandparents wandered, on the average, some 100 miles per year by public transportation. In contrast, it is the unusual person in the 1980s who does not accumulate 10,000 miles of travel each year on his or her automobile—to say nothing of bus, rail, and air travel.

In another 100 years, our grandchildren will undoubtedly regard a vacation to a space habitat or perhaps the moon with no more anticipation than we view a vacation overseas.

What technology *innovations* might we expect in the next 10 or 20 years of space activities? What might we "recollect" about the future of space travel? As in other technologies, the future of *specific* space-technology innovations cannot be recollected—a prescription does not exist for that. However, our knowledge of basic innovation surges and subsequent implementation expansions can help us forecast the probable timing of new developments. As a basis for these recollections, we can reflect on some of our space-technology history.

The Russian launch of the Sputnik satellite in 1957 marked the beginning of actual space explorations. Manned space flights began in 1961 when the USSR, and shortly thereafter the United States, achieved successes. In 1961, President Kennedy declared, "it is time to take longer strides," by "landing a man on the moon and returning him safely to earth." That charge initiated a series of developments that increased the payload of space launches some 10-fold between 1961 and 1964, and another 10-fold between 1964 and 1967. With the Saturn V rockets, developed for the Apollo program, 150 tons of payload could be lifted into earth orbit and 45 tons into a lunar orbit. From that technology, six successful lunar landings were accomplished in a remarkable 5-year span (1968 to 1972).

The burst of progress in space technology between 1960 and 1970 coincided with the last growth cycle of other technology implementations—and the final upsurge of the GNEC growth cycle.

The 1960s were years of prosperity, for individuals, for industry, and even for the government; and our national enthusiasm for space activities also peaked during that time. But concerns about government spending were developing by the 1970s. When measured in inflation-adjusted dollars, the NASA civilian budget in the 1970s was reduced to only about half that in the 1960s; and in the 1980s, it fell even farther.

The development of an orbiting space station became an objective, in the 1970s, for both the United States and the USSR. In 1971, the USSR launched an 18-ton Salyut-1 space station temporarily into orbit. In 1973, it launched a 27-ton Salyut-2 with subsequent modules added in succeeding years. Those stations were used primarily for tests to gain information on the biological effects of living in space for several months at a time.

The U.S. space program in the 1970s initially focused on the combined development of an orbiting space station and a reusable space shuttle. In 1973, the huge 85-ton Skylab was lifted into orbit for physiological, scientific, and specialized-manufacturing studies. With only limited NASA funds and increasingly heavy funding demands for the concurrent space-shuttle development, Skylab was not fully utilized. One goal of the space-shuttle program was to use this launching system for all future space flights; consequently, the previously-developed Saturn space technology was abandoned. As delays developed in the space shuttle program, access to Skylab was limited, and finally it re-entered the earth's atmosphere and was lost in 1979.

An objective of the space shuttle program was to provide a reusable vehicle that could routinely lift scientific, military, and manufacturing equipment into orbit under reasonably economic conditions.

The maximum payload of the space shuttle was approximately 65,000 pounds—around 32 tons. A number of factors increased the payload *cost* for the shuttle more than 10-fold by the time it was deployed. The launching disaster in 1986 was yet another disheartening setback for the U.S. program.

While the average annual payloads launched by USSR space vehicles have steadily increased—about 10 percent per year—over the last 20 years, the annual payloads of U.S. launches peaked in the 1960s and have declined in subsequent years. The total weight lifted annually by U.S. rockets was around 100 tons in the 1960s, compared to about 25 tons per year for USSR launches. But, the U.S. average fell to about 20 tons per year in the 1970s, while the USSR average increased to over 100 tons annually. That trend appears to be continuing.

Rocket payloads have now reached a level sufficient to build fairly sophisticated space stations, suggesting that this technology will be commonplace by the time of the next GNEC growth surge.

RECALL and Materials Innovations

The polymer-chemistry innovations of the 1930s led to several economically dominant industries during the 1950–1975 economic growth surge. Included were the synthetic-textile, synthetic-rubber, plastics, and detergent industries. Synthetic textiles were largely responsible for a boom in practically all sectors of the clothing industry; plastics contributed to the furniture, cabinet, and container industries; and, among other accomplishments, detergents contributed to the success and welfare of the soap-opera industry.

Further contributions will undoubtedly come from a new generation of synthetic materials—particularly plastic materials.

A few of the chemical giants are already introducing another wave of plastics innovations—plastics with strength that makes them competitive with steel. Even more exciting is the development of fiber-reinforced composites (plastics or resins with glass, ceramic, or carbon-reinforcing fibers) that enhance the material strengths still more. As these materials find their ways into automobiles, aircraft, and perhaps building materials, RECALL will be able to anticipate when 90 percent of the metallic components in today's technology products will be taken over by these synthetic materials. Based on previous takeover behaviors of this kind, we should expect a characteristic substitution time of 20 to 40 years.

Important though those technology takeovers will be, it is a completely different kind of "materials" revolution that will replace polymer chemistry as the superstar of the next few decades—the *biotechnology* revolution. What can we say about the economic and sociological impact of that revolution?

The Biotechnology Macroinnovation

Basic innovations in genetic engineering were being featured in our newspapers and weekly magazines as early as the late 1970s. These innovations promise solutions to some of civilization's oldest problems, such as cancer, heart disease, hunger, and pestilence. Possibly of even greater immediate interest, genetic engineering may offer the only real hope for averting a disastrous AIDS (acquired immune deficiency syndrome) plague in the next 10 years.

Biotechnology research is currently focusing on three particular areas: medicine, agriculture, and energy resources.

About 60 percent of all biotechnology R&D is being expended on pharmaceutical products. This R&D is focused mainly on two broad classes of problems:

1. Hormone deficiencies.
2. Diseases.

Examples of genetically engineered hormone products are insulin (for diabetics) and growth hormones (for dwarfism). Examples of genetically engineered disease remedies include "interferons" (for viral diseases and possibly cancer), "interleukin-2" (a possible step toward an AIDS cure), and "plasminogen activators" (protein activators that produce a substance, plasminogen, which dissolves blood clots obstructing coronary arteries).

Genetically engineered insulin, which has already been developed and approved for normal use, is an excellent example of progress being made in the new recombinant DNA technology.

Insulin has been used by diabetics since the 1920s. However, until recently, insulin had been extracted from the pancreases of pigs and cattle. In 1978, human insulin was produced for the first time by genetic engineering. Scientists at the Genentech company, in San Francisco, were able to insert the insulin gene into a bacterial cell, thus allowing the insulin gene to be reproduced rapidly and efficiently along with the host bacterial cell.

The time from laboratory development to its market availability was a surprisingly short five years for genetically engineered insulin.

The development, testing, licensing, and marketing of other genetically engineered products have not fared as well. Nor is the process expected to be so rapid for future biotechnology products. A good example is the experience with interferon, the antiviral drug that was regarded as a very promising immune-system stimulator for fighting cancer cells.

Interferon was discovered as early as 1957, but the separation of interferon from blood proved to be an enormously difficult process. In 1980, the interferon gene was isolated, which allowed larger quantities to be synthesized by cloning techniques. At least three different kinds of interferon had been produced by 1984. Initial tests with interferon have been disappointing, but there is still considerable optimism for its ultimate usefulness.

Although some 60 percent of biotech R&D is supporting medical products, most of the remaining R&D is being directed toward agricultural applications. Already, work is underway to develop more disease-resistant, drought-resistant, and pest-resistant plants. Plants that produce their own nitrogen fertilizers are being pursued in the laboratories.

Clearly, the 1980s, and probably the 1990s will be marked as important years for a profusion of basic technology innovations contributing to a phenomenal biotech macroinnovation.

It is much too early to evaluate the commercial takeover behavior of genetically engineered products. First, and perhaps most importantly, the development and laboratory testing of new products require years of work and millions of dollars. Second, product qualification and government approval of new products will consume at least a few years. Nevertheless, once a new product reaches the marketplace, its growth can be expected to be very fast.

Based on experience with antibiotics in the 1940s and 1950s, as well as on the early experiences with genetically engineered insulin and growth hormones, we should expect growth times similar to or faster than the typical growth times for electronics products. And, like antibiotics in the prior growth surge, a succession of remarkable new biotech products will emerge.

The peak growth of the various commercial products from the biotechnology macroinnovation can probably be expected well after the turn of the century.

Summary

The average GNEC growth in the five-year period between 1980 and 1985 showed a decline of about 0.5 percent per year. During the same period, GNP showed a growth of only 2 percent per year, in spite of a temporary surge in 1984. Both of these growths were abnormally low. With the Crash of '87, we can expect an even slower GNP growth in the early 1990s.

During the 1990s, industries will be seeking more technologically advanced innovations to restimulate business growth in the coming decades.

A technology renaissance at this time would be consistent with a long-wave expectation that the 1980–2000 period should be marked by a surge of basic technology innovations. Attention in this chapter has been focused on possible technology redirections in four dominant industrial areas: electrification, communications, transportation, and new materials. Although it is too early to identify most of the basic innovations, growth characteristics for a few new technologies can already be discerned.

New electrification technologies, for both the supply industry and consumers, have typically shown takeover growth times (the time between a 10 and 90 percent adoption takeover) of 20 to 40 years. Transportation technologies have generally shown the same growth characteristics. This heavy-industry growth pattern should continue for the next few decades.

In contrast, the growths of emerging new communications technologies, such as microchips, fiber optics, and compact discs indicate a relatively short takeover time of five to ten years. This is consistent with the component growths of hi-fi, TV, color TV, and video recorders during the 1950–1975 growth period. Yet, the growth time for the *overall* television-industry macroinnovation was around 30 years.

It is likely that an overall digital-communications macroinnovation will also show a characteristic growth time of some 30 years.

The explosion of new technology innovations coming from the genetic-engineering macroinnovation promises to be at least equally as exciting as the microelectronics and optics innovations in the digital communications macroinnovation. Like the communications technologies, the growths of various individual biotech products have already indicated takeover times as short as five years. Still, it is likely that the overall growth of genetically engineered products will peak sometime in the early part of the next century.

As in prior economic growth surges, we should ultimately expect a commercial swarming that involves areas even beyond the four indicated. For example, a next-generation commercial swarming could extend to new technologies in our offices, stores, home construction, education, and medical care.

The technology innovation period we are already experiencing, as well as the commercial swarming of new products we should expect after 2000, will have profound effects on business, government, and individuals.

To examine the probable implications of these long-wave effects, and the impacts they will or should have on your own personal planning, Part 4 will discuss "The Lessons from RECALL."

PART 4

THE LESSONS FROM RECALL

CHAPTER 13

THE LESSONS FOR BUSINESS

GNEC growth was signaling the approach of an economic winter well ahead of the Crash of '87.

The winter of GNEC growth was beginning around 1985—the Crash of '87 only punctuated its onset.

For those seeking a silver lining to an economic cloud, perhaps the market crash can force us to prepare more effectively for the impending arrival of a low-growth phase of the long economic curve. But, can't RECALL tell us more—after the Crash of '87? Indeed it can! The lessons of RECALL can go far beyond the gloomy projection of a near-term economic slowdown. RECALL can advise businesses, large and small, on ways to benefit from:

- a surge of basic innovations between 1980 and 2000 that will create *completely new business directions* beginning around 1995—only eight years after the Crash of '87
- a phenomenal swarming of new business growths from 1995 to 2020, building on macroinnovations coming from the 1980–2000 period
- a huge growth of service industries that will account for 70 percent to 80 percent of all national income during the new business surge
- the "long-wave rules" of growth involving technology innovation, entrepreneurship, and work productivity

As some perspective for these longer-range recollections, let's first summarize what we already know about the 1970s and early 1980s.

The Economic Autumn

The period from 1970 to 1985 can be characterized as the autumn of the GNEC/GNP long wave. In 1970 the GNEC deviation curve (or long wave) reached its peak. Throughout the 1970s, GNEC was still above the level projected by its underlying secular growth curve, but a growth decline was beginning.

Beyond the sign of a GNEC decline, capital-equipment overexpansion was becoming apparent in the early 1970s, as was an overexpansion of office construction. Additions of electricity-generating plants were being curtailed at that time and industrial construction (measured in inflation-corrected dollars) had peaked in the early 1970s.

The long-wave signals of GNEC growth decline and capital-equipment overexpansion coincided around 1970–1975.

The economic autumn of 1970–1985 marked the end of a flourishing growth of businesses based on technology macroinnovations coming from the 1925–1945 innovation wave. Severe business competition was developing between companies and between nations in the 1970s and 1980s. True, new market growths were emerging in the autumn phase for a few late-blooming technologies, especially computers and some electronics equipment. But, weaknesses were developing in many of the traditional markets, such as agriculture, steel, and automobiles. More significantly, the earlier vigorous growths of industries based on such 1935 macroinnovations as synthetic textiles, commercial TV, air travel, and automatic home appliances were now saturating—they were no longer *growth* industries. These signs of economic stagnation were consistent with the events expected during an economic autumn.

One other sign of stagnation, particularly in the United States, deserves special attention—work productivity.

Work Productivity as an Economic Signal

Work productivity can be an especially interesting index, since it yields a different kind of insight into our industrial health.

Work-productivity growth is commonly used by economists to measure year-to-year industrial-efficiency improvements.

FIGURE 13–1
Factors Contributing to the Growth Decline in our National Productivity

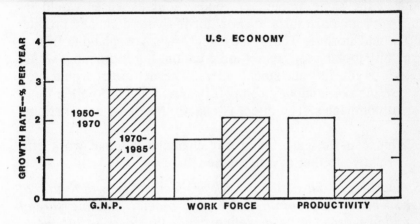

The simplest measure of productivity is the value of goods produced (corrected for inflation) divided by the number of work-force hours expended on production. A more sophisticated measure is the value of goods produced per labor-cost plus capital-cost invested. These measures might be applied to individual industries, to groups of industries, or to industry as a whole. For the cursory examination here, the broadest and simplest measure will be used.

Figure 13–1 illustrates averaged output and input factors contributing to productivity growth in the United States for two periods of time—the high-growth years 1950 to 1970, and the lower-growth years, 1970 to 1985. The unfortunate combination of both the recent GNP growth decline *and* the apparent work-force growth increase led to a particularly severe drop in productivity.* In fact, the well-advertised increase in our domestic work force may be double-edged. On one hand, job creation allows a larger number of income earners in our society. But, with an abnormally low GNP growth, a large job creation means our product output per unit of input, our work productivity, is being compromised.

---

*An excellent discussion of the U.S. work productivity decline and its implications can be found in a book review by L. C. Thurow (*Scientific American,* September 1986). This and other articles on work productivity are identified in the Reference section at the end of this book.

To illustrate this further, think how the principle might apply to your own company. If you hired a dozen more workers, but produced the same amount of goods, your expenses would increase with no extra sales to show for it—your company productivity would decline. That policy might win you plaudits from a community looking for greater job creation, but it probably would not endear you to your stockholders. The net effect would be a decrease in your company competitiveness relative to other more efficient companies. The effect is exactly the same on a national scale.

What can we learn about our changing national work efficiency relative to that of other nations?

A comparison of our national work-productivity growth to that of other successful industrialized countries provides one measure of our nation's growing or declining competitiveness in the world market.

The relative productivity growths of the United States, West Germany, and Japan, as illustrated in Figure 13–2, are especially interesting. Two conclusions are apparent. First, each of the three countries showed a decline in productivity from the high-growth to the low-growth periods. Second, the productivity growths in West Germany and Japan exceeded those in the United States. Part of

FIGURE 13–2
A Comparison of Productivity Growths for Three Industrialized Nations

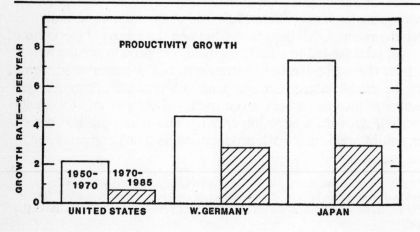

the difference results from an abnormally low level of productivity (and, therefore, an apparently high growth rate), for Germany and Japan, immediately after World War II. However, relative to the United States, these two countries still enjoyed some continuing significant growth of productivity in the 1970–1985 period. Although their GNP growths also declined somewhat, their work-force sizes did not increase so rapidly. As a consequence, their GNP output per work-force input did not decline quite so precipitously as that of the United States.

In summary, the growth declines of GNEC, GNP, and work productivity have all been consistent with long-wave expectations, but the U.S. productivity growth decline has been particularly severe.

The Long Wave—Government versus Industry Roles

Who is responsible for the long-wave behavior of our economy—government, industry, or individuals? Certainly, all three contribute. But, it has been a dominant thesis of this book—as early as Chapter 1—that industry is the primary source of long-range economic and sociological growth. Let's remember:

Technology innovations, capital investment, and the growth of new products and services—by industry—are generally responsible for the long-term growth of GNEC and GNP.

Think about the growths during the last long wave. Was it industry or government that developed and marketed television? Was it industry or government that developed and marketed home appliances? Was it industry or government that developed nylon, polyester, and acrylics? You might argue that our state and federal governments played a significant role in the innovations of super-highways, jet aircraft, and radar. True. But, even here it was not government economic policies, it was technology policies—a subject that will receive more attention in the next chapter.

It has been the entrepreneurial growth and competition throughout industry that has been the fundamental source of long-term GNEC and GNP growths. As workers in these industries, you and I can be the movers and shakers of our economy.

By looking at what we have learned from history, for both service-producing and goods-producing industries, we should now be able to apply the lessons of growth to our own businesses. Let's start by looking at growth trends in our service- versus goods-producing industries.

Service-Producing versus Goods-Producing Industries

Most of us work in private industries, either in the service-producing or goods-producing sector. Which of these industrial sectors will be mostly responsible for any future growth in our national income? Historical growth data, again, can allow us to recollect the future.

Although less than half the national income came from service industries in 1950, it was an astounding two thirds in 1985 and is likely to be three fourths by 2020.

The growing importance of the service-industry sector as a contributor to our national income is illustrated in Figure

FIGURE 13–3

The Growing Importance of Service-Producing Industries in our National Income

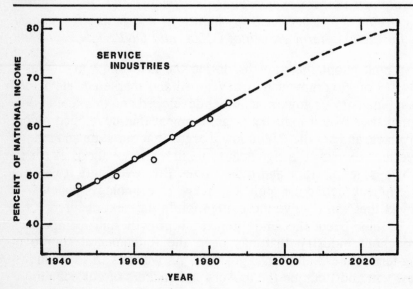

13–3. Compared to less than 50 percent in 1950, the service-industry contribution in 1960 was 53 percent, in 1980 it was 63 percent, and in 2000 it will be over 70 percent. Should that trend worry us?

It is common to hear concerns about the fractional decline of goods-producing industries in the United States. That fractional decline *in itself* should not be an overriding cause for concern; the same trend is probably occurring in all highly industrialized countries. Remember also, a similar fractional decline in our agricultural industry occurred in earlier years. That decline reflected two important changes. First, farm work productivity was being improved substantially due to the mechanization of farming equipment. Second, a much larger growth was occurring in the manufacturing industries. Very few people would argue today that that trend led to any weakness in our economy.

We should not be apprehensive about a similar fractional decline in our goods-producing sector (including both manufacturing and agriculture). We are only seeing yet another new industrial growth surge—this time in our service-producing sector. Our service-producing industries include some of the industrial giants in our country—electric utilities, telephone communications, television, movies, airlines, railroads, health services, financial services, and retail sales.

A shift from a predominantly goods-producing to a service-producing society is not a cause for alarm—but other factors certainly should be:

- *the technology content of our industry products and services*
- *the efficiency of our technology innovation and transfer*
- *our work productivity*

Does this mean that our goods-producing industry will become unimportant? Not at all. But, our service-producing industries must be as alert as our goods-producing industries toward technology content, technology innovation, technology transfer, and work productivity. This applies to all service industries, but particularly those involved in our electricity supply, communications, transportation, financial operations, and health care.

Technology Content—The Growth of High-Tech Industries

The appearance of industrial research laboratories in the early 1900s profoundly changed the technological character of products and services coming from our industries. Indeed, most of the technology *macroinnovations* originating in the 1935 surge came from the R&D laboratories of our largest companies, such as nylon from Du Pont and TV from RCA.

The macroinnovations originating in the 1980s and 1990s will come primarily from dedicated and highly competitive industrial R&D organizations.

It is no accident that the eminently successful AT&T, General Electric, IBM, and Du Pont, with some of the world's most prestigious R&D laboratories, have been able to perpetuate and expand their sphere of business influence. AT&T has moved from telephone services to electronics, to telecommunications, and to computer technologies. GE has moved from electrical generating and distribution equipment, to automatic home appliances, to electronics, and to space technologies. Du Pont has moved from munitions, to paints, to synthetic textiles, and to high-strength plastics. Leadership in R&D has allowed them to continue as technology pioneers.

This R&D formula has also allowed many smaller, rapidly growing companies to carve out technological niches for themselves. These include niches involving computer chips, computer software, special materials, biotechnology, medical diagnostics, and a variety of technological services. New technology companies have also sprung up in Japan and Europe—usually as the result of strong R&D. Why is *high-tech* growth itself so important to us in the United States?

Technology macroinnovations are important because of the quantum jumps they offer in the marketplace—they allow their companies to *take over from* (not just compete with) other companies. But even more importantly, these newer technologies can allow our national industries to exploit high-tech products—products that are not likely to come from the less R&D-oriented countries.

The older-line manufacturing companies of the United States cannot compete easily with those of the somewhat less industrialized countries, where technologies can be duplicated and manufactured with cheaper labor. Even the Japanese and Europeans are realizing this. What is the answer then? Do we abdicate our role as a manufacturing giant in the world? The answer should be, "only selectively."

At the very high end of the technological spectrum, our research laboratories, our scientists, and our engineers still rank among the best in the world. Innovativeness in the highest of our high-tech industries is generally competitive with that in other leading industrialized nations. In fact, the United States is still a leader in many technologies, such as supercomputers, computer software, lasers, advanced materials, and aerospace technology.

It is in the knowledge-intensive industries where U.S. industry can and should seek its growth.

It is likely that the newly developing industrial countries will become the manufacturers of the older-generation technologies, especially those that are labor-intensive (such as wearing apparel). The United States and other advanced industrialized nations will be forced to become competitors in the newer technologies. This strongly implies that our economic future as a nation lies in technology innovations, not the continuing pursuit of stagnating technologies. History teaches us that this kind of transition should be expected predominantly in the winter and spring phases of the long economic wave.

The trend toward knowledge-intensive industries places crucial responsibilities on our society to ensure the appropriate technically trained people, and on our academic institutions to provide those people. Our resolve to ensure a continuing leadership in knowledge-intensive industries is not an easy one. For example, our literacy rate, our high-school completion rate, our college completion rate, and even our quality of education (at the lower levels) are sadly inferior to those of Japan and some of the European countries. Politically popular tax reductions and tax rebates are not the most promising long-range policies for ensuring good education, job retraining, superior R&D, and better career opportunities for all of us in the highly competitive international community. These government-related policies will receive greater attention in the next chapter.

Let's examine more closely, now, the long-wave lessons of RECALL involving:

- technology innovation
- technology transfer
- work productivity

What can RECALL tell us about the application of these principles to our own businesses?

Technology Innovation—The Lessons of RECALL

As in the 1870–1890 and 1925–1945 periods, we should expect the 1980–2000 period to bring about some major redirections—not just small changes. The Crash of '87 has marked, quite emphatically, the end of a long growth wave.

Businesses at all levels must now expect major new technology directions as our industrial society searches for ways to escape from an economic winter.

With a new GNEC growth surge—especially in electricity use—beginning only 10 years after the Crash of '87, new energy-related technologies can be expected. Likewise, we can look for new technologies in communications, transportation, biochemistry, and practically every other sector of our economy. In a chain-reaction effect, we should expect changes in our own businesses, whether large or small.

Remember that the electricity macroinnovation beginning around 1880 opened scores of new businesses, including large electric utility companies, moderately-large electrical-fixture manufacturers, and small electrical contractors. The movie macroinnovation brought new businesses, from large movie studios to small local theatres. The polymer-chemical macroinnovation (from the 1935 wave) created big new businesses in the manufacture of synthetic textiles and plastic materials, but also smaller businesses in apparels, plastic containers, and numerous other enterprises. Even the air-travel macroinnovation opened opportunities for large car-rental companies and express delivery companies, as well as for smaller travel agencies and resort communities.

Macroinnovations are important, not just because of the *primary* technologies introduced, but because of the many related opportunities that follow major new redirections. In the approaching new wave we can expect countless numbers of new businesses to emerge, and old ones to change directions. They will include both goods-producing and service-producing businesses, although mostly the latter. They will build on the macroinnovations coming from new electricity uses, digital communications, computer technologies, transportation directions, biotechnology, and possibly still other technology areas. It is impossible, even for RECALL, to identify the specific new directions at this time. But, the alert business entrepreneurs will watch for the various macroinnovation redirections, and will adjust their own businesses to build on those redirections.

Technology Transfer—The Lessons of RECALL

While basic innovations can be crucially important to the success of large industries, the efficiency of moving these top-level innovations from the laboratory through engineering to manufacturing can also be critical. Even the prompt transfer of subsequent *improvement* innovations from incubation to implementation can be important. Some 75 to 100 years ago it was common for the innovator (Bell, Edison, Eastman, or Ford) to shepherd the new product or process through all steps, from the laboratory to the production line. Too frequently, our modern industrial giants have been guilty of over-isolating R&D, engineering, manufacturing, and marketing through organizational compartmentalization. Think about your own company. Are your development technologists familiar with what your marketing experts recognize as client interests? Are your engineers familiar with the problems of the manufacturers? Are you fully aware of your competitors' products, processes, services, and changing business directions?

Especially in many of our high-tech industries, the efficiency of technology transfer—from department to department, and even company to company—can be as critically important as technology innovation itself.

Both goods-producing and service-producing businesses must be alert to new ideas, whether coming from their own organization or that of a competitor. Success can be ensured only when the products or services reach the marketplace.

Work Productivity—The Lessons of RECALL

During the 20-year period from 1965 to 1985, national income in U.S. manufacturing increased by about 2.5 percent per year (when corrected for inflation). During the same period, the blue-collar work force declined about 1.3 percent per year. This implies that the work productivity associated with our labor force improved significantly. However, much of that productivity improvement has been offset by a substantial *increase* in the number of our white-collar workers.

The improvements in manufacturing productivity have come from more efficient machine tools, computer-assisted manufacturing processes, automation, and robotics.

Why has the work productivity for white-collar workers declined? We might have expected the opposite with the advent of office computers, word processors, better reproduction equipment, and improved communication systems. Frequently, advanced office technologies are only encouraging more management studies, more detailed accounting, more personnel records and more memos—without compensating improvements in productivity. Is this true for your own business? Has your office productivity—measured by increase in output *and* decrease in white-collar labor force—improved, held constant, or deteriorated in the last five years?

Clearly, technology innovation, technology transfer, and work productivity are all important factors in our drive for company (as well as national) competitiveness. By implication, there is an especially significant overall business responsibility: good business management. Only through good business management can all aspects of business be kept in proper perspective. As we will see, the relative emphasis on the various aspects of business planning and operations might be quite different at different phases of the long wave.

How can we use our knowledge of the long wave to help us identify the best management policies and procedures?

The Long Wave and Management Planning

It may *not* be sufficient for a business to put equal management attention from time to time on, for example:

- capital expansion versus capital attrition
- product-development versus product-improvement R&D
- market analysis versus market promotion
- manufacturing retooling versus manufacturing acceleration
- personnel hiring versus personnel retraining

Our knowledge of the long wave can be particularly helpful in focusing properly on optimum business directions at particular times.

Perhaps one of the most obvious examples of using a knowledge of the long wave is that of planning electricity-supply capital expansion. Had the cycle-adjusted-logistic (CAL) growth behavior of electricity consumption been understood earlier, the typical utility planner could have foreseen, say in 1970, that system expansion should not be based on the 7.5 percent per year growth that had been occurring between 1950 and 1970; or on even the 7.0 percent per year growth between 1965 and 1970. Instead, a utility could have anticipated that the growth between 1970 and 1980 would be around 4 percent per year, and between 1980 and 1985 less than 2 percent per year—growth-rate projections that would have been correct.

But, our knowledge of the long wave (including the technology connection) can be put to much broader management use, even outside energy-related industries. For example, it might not be expedient for business management to focus primarily on radically new product developments early in a long-wave growth when a product already consistent with an emerging macroinnovation is just beginning to show a strong growth in the marketplace. Conversely, it would be less than prudent to focus solely on manufacturing and marketing at a time when a particular product line has reached the top of its growth curve.

It is this kind of reasoning that ties management strategy to the long wave. Hence:

Management's relative emphasis on various policies of R&D, engineering, manufacturing, and marketing should be appropriate for a particular phase of the long wave.

Management information systems (MIS) became especially fashionable during the 1970s. Business schools taught courses on how to develop them; consultants profited handsomely by showing how to use them; and up-to-date business executives exhorted their staffs to apply them. But, the items commonly covered in the monthly or quarterly MIS reports almost consistently reflected the same kinds of information—marketing activities, company sales, sales revenues, production costs, profits and losses, production statistics, material or component inventories, and personnel activities. Major attention was only given occasionally to measurements of research progress, laboratory-to-production technology transfers, patent applications (and their significance), and scientist and engineering expertise. The more traditional focus of attention on product output would be quite appropriate for a business during an early or mid-range growth phase of the S-growth curve. However, it could be woefully inadequate, even misleading, during a transition when existing product growth is beginning to reach its saturation, but new product lines are not yet implemented—especially in a high-tech company.

Most new business growths tend to follow the long economic wave. In such a business, it would seem advantageous for the management to focus on its business status relative to the phase of the GNEC/GNP wave—including the status of its technology, R&D, engineering, sales growth, and productivity. Is your company involved in this kind of strategic evaluation? Does your company make a distinction in policies for early-growth, peak-growth and growth-stagnation phases? Are carefully planned research, development, and engineering activities promising your company new competitive opportunities?

The appropriate weighing of management attention can be illustrated by the matrix shown in Table 13–1. In the table, organizational orientations are indicated for two types of long-wave periods, a peak technology innovation period (Phase A) and a peak commercial growth period (Phase B). For example, company planning should be innovation-oriented during Phase A but commercialization-oriented during Phase B. During Phase A, R&D activities should be focused on new technology development and technology transfer. These efforts should lean toward improvement innovations during Phase B. Likewise, marketing activities should support R&D by appropriate analytical studies, as should

TABLE 13-1
Organizational Orientations for a Peak Technology-Innovation Period (Phase A) and a Peak Commercialization Period (Phase B)

Organizational Orientation	Phase A	Phase B
Planning analysis	Innovation	Commercialization
Technology R&D	Transfer	Improvement
Marketing	Analysis	Promotion
Legal	Intelligence	Protection
Personnel	Selective	Expansive

legal groups, during Phase A. Yet, promotional activities would be preferable during Phase B. Even personnel departments should be focusing on the recruiting of innovative technologists during Phase A. But primary attention should be on marketing, project, and manufacturing personnel during Phase B. These orientations may appear to be ovbious once the significance of the long economic wave is appreciated. But, are you really following this kind of policy in your company, whether large or small? And if not, shouldn't you be?

Correct management policies can be especially difficult during periods of growth saturation and profit stagnation—during the economic autumn and winter. In those periods business managers will probably be subjected to enormous pressures by stockholders, large institutional investors, and bankers, who all will be pressing for more near-term profits. It is easy, especially for an insecure company management, to identify R&D and new product planning as the most expendable areas for reducing short-term costs. But, this weakness can allow a more far-sighted competitor to seize a strong position for the longer range. It is also a policy that encourages disenchanted technologists to leave large companies to start new enterprises.

Summary

Most businesses do respond, though sometimes belatedly, to the overall surge of economic growth at the beginning of a new GNEC growth cycle. Unfortunately, they frequently do not recognize the signs of stagnation at the end of the GNEC growth cycle—until a market crash jars them from complacency.

A knowledge of the long GNEC (and GNP) wave can allow businesses—both goods-producing and service-producing—to recognize and adjust strategies and policies appropriate for the times.

While government fiscal policies can help to correct a stagnating economy in the short range (over a few years), it is primarily industry initiatives that must be responsible for economic growth in the longer range. Important technology innovations (or macroinnovations) in the industrial sectors are the economic machines that shape the long-range future of our economy. It is the innovativeness of industries within particular nations that will determine the commercial leaders in the international community.

By recognizing the causes and effects of the long economic wave, alert company management can more wisely select appropriate goals, policies, and even information systems to ensure proper guidance. Obviously, these factors are crucially important to our largest industries. But, they can be equally important to smaller companies—both manufacturing and service companies.

The Crash of '87 makes it clear that the economy is entering the winter phase of the long GNEC cycle. With that recognition, companies might assign an even higher priority to the encouragement of technology innovation and its prompt implementation. Successes in those efforts should enhance the competitiveness of the more dedicated companies, both nationally and internationally. Moreover, it should be increasingly apparent that our hope for industrial leadership as a nation will lie in the area of *knowledge-intensive* technology innovation, where the United States might by able to compete more effectively. We will see in the next chapter that appropriate government policies can be influential in this respect.

CHAPTER 14

THE LESSONS FOR GOVERNMENT

The years around 1776 were momentous ones for the English, not because they were losing the Revolutionary War with the Americans, but because they were winning a much more important war—the Industrial Revolution. The years from 1760 to 1780 were crucial because of the textile technology macroinnovation that would usher in a revolution changing England's, and ultimately the world's, industrial and sociological structure. Perhaps more than any other event, this macroinnovation made England the dominant world power during much of the 1800s.

A second wave of technology innovations again came largely from the English around the 1820s—the steam engine, the railroad, and the steamboat (to which Fulton in the United States contributed). As emphasized in an earlier chapter, the railroad macroinnovation actually had a larger impact on the United States economy than it did on the economy in the United Kingdom.

Very significantly, government policies—fiscal or otherwise—had little, if any, effect on either the macroinnovations or their industrial consequences in those first two growth waves.

True, the United Kingdom had an impressively large number of scientists, engineers, and craftsmen in the late 1700s and early 1800s, and this fact might be related to some government policies such as embryonic educational policies. But, there was no extensive public education, no government R&D, and no subsidized implementation of new technologies in England, nor elsewhere, in those years. Technology macroinnovations and subsequent industrial growths flourished almost independent of government policies prior to 1850.

The third important wave of technology innovations in the 1880s, including electrification, automobiles, telephones, and coal-tar chemicals, came from the United States, Germany, and France as well as the United Kingdom. The subsequent commercialization of these macroinnovations made the United States a dominant world power in the 1920s. Clearly, World War I cost the Europeans much of their former leadership. In particular, Germany's burgeoning chemical industry was devastated. Still, government policies in all the industrialized countries began to have more significant consequences in the early part of the 1900s. It was not fiscal policies that were important. Primarily, it was educational policies, preparing more scientists, more engineers, more business leaders, and more educators to multiply the impact of this effect.

It should not be surprising that a burst of more sophisticated technology macroinnovations came from the large industrial laboratories of the United States and Europe in the 1920s and 1930s.

This fourth wave of technology macroinnovations, originating in the 1930s, included the polymer chemicals, television, jet-air travel, and the sociologically important automatic home appliances. Although those macroinnovations came from both the United States and Europe, they were destined to make the United States an industrial leader in the world. For the first time, it can be claimed that government policies, involving education, national laboratories, computers, and space technology, played a distinct role in a strong industrial growth, the growth between 1950 and 1975. The important conclusion is:

Long-term industrial growth—while primarily a consequence of industry practices—can be affected by government policies of education, R&D, and new technology implementations (such as superhighways, space development, and air control).

While government fiscal policies are not a critical factor in long-term economic growth, they undoubtedly can contribute to shorter-term effects. It is possible that short-term government fiscal policies might actually impair the more industrially significant, long-term government policies. For that reason, we will look at some of the government fiscal policies of the 1980s.

Are Government Budget Policies Helping Us?

How did our federal spending priorities change between 1980 and 1986? Has "discretionary spending" been reckless? What are the likely consequences of the ongoing trend? Who is responsible? Let's begin with the last question.

Contrary to popular concepts, our elected government officials respond to what we want. It is not a We-versus-They problem. If we want tax reductions, the government usually responds. If we want tax rebates instead of increased educational spending, our national or local government usually obliges. We cannot blame "the government" for enormous budget deficits. They are only the results of what our government perceives we want.

"But," you might object, "I want only wasteful spending to be stopped." To place this seemingly logical complaint into a proper context, we can look at some simple arithmetic. Figure 14–1 illustrates the percent of overall government spending, in 1980 and 1986 (estimated), used for the following purposes:

FIGURE 14–1
The Declining Fraction of Discretionary Funding, 1980–1986*

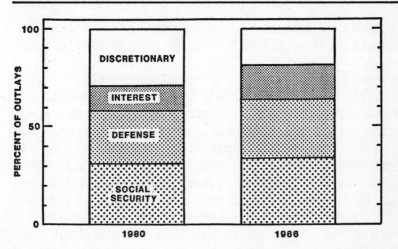

*As affected by spending increases for social security, defense, and interest charges on the national debt.

1. Social services (Social Security, Medicare, and civil service pensions).
2. Defense (including Veteran's Administration services).
3. Interest on the national debt.
4. "Discretionary funding."

Let's assume that the first three categories are untouchable—as we are frequently told. The remainder is the amount used for running the government (supporting the Departments of State, Commerce, Agriculture, Health, Education, Energy, and Transportation). This remainder does cover much more than salaries and wages of government services; it includes assistance to education, support of national health studies, construction and maintenance of national highways, control of the air traffic, support of the NASA program, and contributions to energy R&D.

In 1980, 31 percent of the budget went to the social programs (which are supported separately by your funding of social security), about 27 percent for defense (including 3 percent for Veterans Administration), and 13 percent for interest on the national debt. This left almost 30 percent for the so-called discretionary spending. In 1986, the social program outlay had increased to about 32 percent, defense to 32 percent, and interest to about 18 percent, for a discretionary increment less than 20 percent.

Even if all the discretionary budget had been eliminated in 1986, our federal budget would still have shown a deficit for that year.

In spite of these facts, you and I (or at least most of the public) prefer not to increase taxes. Our senior citizen population is growing, medicare expenses are increasing, and the social security budget will need to grow slightly as a fraction of the entire national budget. We seem unwilling to reduce the fractional allocation to military spending. And, if the deficit continues at an average of only $150 billion per year, with interest rates remaining constant, the accumulated deficit will increase by about one third in only five more years. This will cause the fraction of the budget required for interest charges to rise even more. Without a tax increase, the fractional funding for discretionary spending will grow even smaller.

From the perspective of government influence on long-term economic growth, the main conclusion is there will be little flexibility for federal policies supporting discretionary funding of programs involving better education, energy R&D, space programs, and highway improvement.

Severe limits on discretionary funding will probably weaken still further any government influence on long-term economic growth.

A government with no financial resources to plow into education, research, and technology is a government obsessed with status quo, not future progress. Is this what we want?

What National Resources Fuel Economic Growth?

Economic growth thrives best in a free enterprise system. It is doubtful that a state-controlled economy could have offered sufficient incentives to match the rapid electrification that occurred in the United States, the United Kingdom, and Europe in the 1890-to-1920 period. The assembly-line production of automobiles would not have flourished in the early 1900s without the entrepreneurship and industrial competition of the Olds, Ford, Willys, and General Motors companies. It is questionable whether nylon, polyester, and acrylics would have shown the remarkable takeover growths from silk, cotton, and wool without the stimulus of a free marketplace.

A primary national resource for economic growth appears to be the availability of a competitive and potentially rewarding free enterprise system.

Does this fundamental resource suggest that government has no role in long-term economic growth? Does it indicate that government can serve the economy best simply by "getting off the back of industry?" That does not seem to be the right answer. The world abounds with countries that are passive toward industries, yet where industrialization is almost non-existent. Is it possible that the abundance of natural resources—minerals, fuels, food, water, and climate—is the prime requirement? Again, this is apparently not the answer, as is amply demonstrated by the success of Japan.

There are at least four important national resources (beyond a free enterprise system) that appear to be essential for the emergence and continuing growth of a strong industrial economy:

1. Broad education and training.
2. Effective technology R&D.
3. Adequate GNEC (and electricity) growth capability.
4. Adequate transportation facilities.

Just how important are government policies—including federal, state, and local—in ensuring adequate strengths in these four resource areas? And if the policies are important, how can our government ensure continuing strengths in these areas? Before examining answers to those questions, and particularly before looking at a "scorecard" showing our national resource standings, let's remind ourselves once again: the government (at least in a free democracy) is not some detached bureaucracy that independently controls our national policies affecting long-term economic growth.

The government only responds to our public interests—interests relative to military dominance, social welfare, education, and public works—and our willingness to support those interests through tax revenues or, perhaps more regrettably, through borrowing.

Our National Education and Training Resources

Probably more than any other national resource, a broad education and training system is essential for a high-technology industrial society. RECALL would remind us that we as a nation have come far, in that respect, since 1900. In 1900, less than 10 percent of children in the United States finished high school. By 1940, the percentage was about 50 percent, and by 1965 it had increased to 75 percent. Unhappily, that percentage of school completion has remained at 75 percent for the 20 years since 1965.

College attendance has also shown a spectacular improvement since 1900. Only 2 percent of the U.S. population completed college in 1900, with the level rising to about 8 percent by 1940, and some 25 percent in the 1980s. How would RECALL judge these educational achievements relative to future needs?

The technological dominance of the United States in the 1950–1975 period depended largely on an educational system that supplied industry with an abundance of scientists and engineers— mechanical, aeronautical, electrical, electronics, and chemical engineers. Moreover, our educational system supplied industry and government with knowledgeable business strategists, managers, and supporting staffs. And, our vocational schools and work apprenticeships provided an even larger number of skilled laborers and technicians—office workers, lab technicians, draftsmen, machinists, mechanics, electricians, and electronics repairmen. The contributions of education and training programs were important at all levels of our industrial society. Those programs—mostly government-supported—have included:

- primary and secondary schools
- vocational schools
- colleges
- graduate schools

As the complexity of our technological society increases, both the breadth and depth of education in all categories will become still more critical.

Remember that airplanes, electrical appliances, electronics equipment, and polymer chemicals were among the growth leaders in the last long wave. And, our education system responded to needs in those areas. The next wave will involve digital communications (including advanced computers, computer software, fiber optics, lasers, and holography), genetic engineering (including pharmaceuticals, agricultural products, new energy-yielding processes), advanced transportation systems (including new ground travel modes, hypersonic aircraft, space vehicles), and probably still other relatively unfamiliar technologies. Is our education system sufficiently broad and deep to satisfy the coming needs for mathematicians, physicists, chemists, biologists, engineers, technologists, and industry leaders in these areas? Will it be able to supply the large cohort of skilled workers for job demands that will soon appear? Are we the government—meaning you and me—willing to pay the price for that technological leadership?

Just how does the U.S. level of education stand relative to other industrial societies?

At the elementary and secondary levels, the U.S. educational score is woefully poor relative to those of Japan and Europe; at the college level it is competitive; and at the graduate level it excels.

As a measure of educational breadth, less than 1 percent of the Japanese population is illiterate. In the United States, at least 20 percent of the population is functionally illiterate—a shocking indictment. In fact, U.S. welfare recipients have an illiteracy level that approaches 50 percent. About 90 percent of the Japanese children complete high school compared to less than 75 percent for the United States.

Beyond the attendance statistics, the qualities of our U.S. grade-school and high-school educations are inferior. Our school year is 180 days compared to 240 days for the Japanese schools. Little more than half of U.S. high-school students receive as much as one year of science classes. And, less than one third of our high schools are equipped to offer physics classes. Calculus is almost unheard of in U.S. high schools, but is commonly required in European, Russian, and Japanese high schools. International testing of grade-school and high-school students show that U.S. students score among the poorest. In fact, even on our own national scale, the scholastic aptitude test (SAT) scores for U.S. high-school students have declined almost steadily during the last 20 years.

Catch-up education in the United States begins in the college years—at least for the 25 percent that go on to college. This compares to 35 percent of the students in Japan attending college. For the 7 percent continuing into graduate studies (and the 2 percent receiving Ph.D. degrees), the U.S. graduate schools are the envy of the world. Our graduate schools are so respected that about 50 percent of our graduate students come from foreign countries. Perhaps one measure of the superiority of our advanced educational system is the dominance of U.S. scientists among all Nobel prize laureates.

Still, RECALL would remind us that our general lack of government dedication to a strong public school system does not bode well for our future technological society. Part of the problem stems from an educational complacency among parents, students, and the public at large—a complacency that is reflected by government policies. The result is an appalling school dropout rate and only a small fraction of our young population seeking (or being able to seek) advanced education, particularly in science and engineering.

The relatively small number of students entering college, and even smaller number entering graduate school, threatens to make the United States increasingly an elitist technological society.

If we truly want to offer equal opportunities for the next generation, we must find ways to provide college or vocational educations as easily as we now provide high-school educations. Moreover, these educations must allow future students to become broadly familiar with computers, robotics, lasers, bio-engineering, and the many other new technologies of the next growth wave. We must ask ourselves: Do we really want to pay the price for technological and economic leadership?

Perhaps RECALL would suggest another type of educational requirement that will become increasingly important, especially during the transition years between 1990 and 2010.

More and more of our work force will require either retraining or welfare as job opportunities shift from older technologies to newer ones—as well as from manufacturing to service activities.

Government support of job retraining has, all too frequently, suffered from government budget economies. Some states have experimented with "workfare" programs in place of welfare and these programs occasionally have included retraining. As the technological content of our work changes, retraining programs may become even more necessary. Indeed, retraining may become essential even for those of us already in responsible jobs.

Our National R&D Resources

RECALL would also remind us that the history of R&D growth has paralleled that of educational growth—probably not a surprising observation. As already indicated, Edison was an innovator of organized industrial R&D in the 1880s. A few of the pioneering industries of that period had established R&D organizations around 1900, but R&D as a fraction of GNP was negligibly small.

By the early 1950s, R&D expenditures (industry and government combined) had reached a level slightly less than 2 percent of the GNP. By 1965 it had increased still more, to almost 3 percent, but in 1984 it had declined slightly to 2.7 percent. The U.S. total expenditures for R&D, as a fraction of GNP, compare favorably with those of most European countries and Japan, but are somewhat lower than the 3.7 percent for the USSR.

While our expenditures for R&D, as a fraction GNP, are competitive with those of Japan and the European countries, a much larger fraction of R&D in the United States (and USSR) goes into military research.

Almost half of our R&D is supported by the federal government; and, almost one third of *all* U.S. R&D is related to defense activities. Hence, the fraction of GNP going only to civilian research is about two thirds that of Japan and West Germany. There is good reason to believe that this tilt toward military R&D spending—both in the United States and USSR—is offering the nonmilitary governments an even greater opportunity for improved competitiveness in the future.

It is more than possible that the significant international competition of the future will involve industrial supremacy, not military supremacy.

Sources of R&D funding in the United States are divided evenly between government and industry. Of the government-supported R&D, a little more than 10 percent goes to universities. Since our graduate schools are the greatest advantage of our educational system, let's look more closely at how government R&D spending affects university educational directions. In particular, how does our government R&D support to the universities prepare our future scientists and engineers?

Over 60 percent of university R&D funding comes from federal-government support. Even though only 10 percent of the federal R&D expenditures go to universities, this funding is the dominant source of university R&D and is vitally important in our advanced education. Actually, less than 20 percent of the federal funding for university R&D comes from the Department of Defense—an apparently modest amount. However, over 50 percent of R&D funding for mathematics, computer science, electrical engineering, and aeronautical engineering now come from the Department of Defense—a trend that has escalated substantially in just the last few years.

Much of the educational community has become deeply disturbed by this trend. First, there is a concern that defense R&D tends to be shrouded in secrecy and, therefore, cannot be shared for the benefit of the research community. But secondly, and perhaps more significantly, it suggests that more than 50 percent of our future scientists and engineers in these critical areas, are being trained for defense technologies, not civilian technologies.

Supporters of defense-oriented R&D claim that military technologists can ultimately have some spinoff to civilian applications. However, even this claim has been the source of much controversy.

Why is this subject important in recollecting the future? Again, remember that the successes or failures of our government's long-term policies depend on the guidance you and your neighbors supply it through normal democratic processes. We must be an informed part of decision-making, in national policy matters (including R&D), as well as in our commercial and industrial marketplace choices.

Our National Energy Resources

Perhaps next to education and R&D resources, a nation's capability for supplying economic and environmentally clean energy resources is of greatest importance. But, is this really a government responsibility?

If we are to remain a strong industrial society, the government (we, the people) must assume some responsibility for proper planning to ensure the availability of acceptable and desirable energy resources.

In 1970, about 70 percent of our U.S. GNEC depended on oil and natural-gas resources. We have become painfully aware that this dependence on fluid fuels is neither desirable nor acceptable as a national policy. What should we do about this overdependence?

With remarkable foresight (though not without objections), the government instituted an Energy Policy and Conservation Act (EPCA) in 1975 to enforce improved fuel efficiencies on new automobiles being produced between 1975 and 1985. This measure required downgrading automobile size, power, and comfort—to the annoyance of most manufacturers and luxury-loving Americans. Nevertheless, the policy proved to be a wise one, although one that is now being compromised due to temporary oil gluts and, perhaps, some political persuasions.

Transportation requirements account for about 30 percent of our GNEC in the United States, and more than 50 percent of fluid-fuel (oil and natural gas) consumption. Probably, transportation will continue to depend mostly on fluid fuels in the next 25 years. But, RECALL has reminded us (in Chapter 11) that electricity supply will be the most important energy growth industry of the 1985–2020 period. Electricity generation strongly favors the use of solid fuels (coal and nuclear). For this reason, RECALL has already alerted us to the large growth we can expect in the use of solid fuels.

Consumption of solid fuels in the United States will increase almost five-fold between 1985 and 2020.

With this enormous growth of coal and nuclear energy in only three decades, is our government putting appropriate attention on the energy problems that will arise? Remember our economic growth potential is directly related to our energy growth potential. Some examination of federal funding policies on energy R&D will reflect our government's attention on this important national resource.

From 1982 to 1987, federal support of nondefense energy R&D *decreased* approximately 10 percent per year. For perspective, note that during that same period, federal support of all defense activities *increased* about 10 percent per year. It is also significant that energy R&D accounts for less than 0.3 percent of the federal budget, compared to almost 30 percent for military spending. What energy R&D policies are being followed by the government? For an answer to that question, a recent report by the U.S. General Accounting Office is helpful.

The General Accounting Office (GAO) is an independent auditing committee reporting to Congress. As a result of questions by Congress, GAO looked at the appropriateness of the R&D directions being taken by the Department of Energy (DOE) in response to new Administration energy R&D policies established in 1981. In view of a reduced energy R&D budget, it was decided in 1981 that the intent of a reoriented R&D policy should be to emphasize "long-term, high-risk, high-payoff" technologies in their early stages of development.

In the report, issued February 1987, GAO concluded DOE had applied the long-term, high-risk, high-payoff criteria to most of the energy R&D technologies, but civilian nuclear reactor R&D had deviated from that general policy. For example, the report notes that funding for a "breeder reactor" *demonstration* plant was continued until 1984 in spite of conclusions by experts that the long-term payoff for this type of reactor was becoming increasingly questionable. Yet, *basic* R&D support for another type of advanced reactor, with high-temperature capability (and some significant safety advantages) was being curtailed in spite of its long-term payoff promise. GAO also concluded that the proposed funding for nuclear reactors changed radically in fiscal year 1987 to reflect a new DOE policy emphasizing military applications of nuclear energy relative to civilian R&D needs. In general, it was concluded that:

The reorientation of the 1987 DOE nuclear budget appears to have less to do with the long-term, high-risk, high-payoff criteria than with meeting defense-related objectives of the Administration.

What does all this mean? Like the previously discussed government policies toward education and R&D, our policies toward national nuclear energy resources are being tilted more and more toward military objectives. Limitations on discretionary funding in the national budget have compromised our longer-range civilian interests. Our laboratories, scientists, and engineers are being dedicated to a cause that threatens to decrease our attention on long-term civilian needs. With this policy, are we surrendering at least some of our future potential for international competitiveness? At best, the answer is not a reassuring one.

Our National Transportation Resources

RECALL has observed that much of our historical economic growth in the United States can be attributed to the enormous growth of the transportation industries.

Rail travel during the 1845–1870 growth wave, automobile travel during 1900–1925, and air travel during 1955–1980 each contributed importantly to GNEC/GNP surges during these periods.

Long-term government policies probably had little effect on the 1845–1870 rail-travel growth. But, government policies—primarily at the county and state levels—had a profound effect on the growth of automobile travel after 1910. And, government policies—primarily at the state and federal levels—have had a crucial effect on the 1955–1980 air-travel (and continuing auto-travel) growth.

Paved roads are not new. The Romans were responsible for some remarkable paved roads 2,000 years ago. Nevertheless, paved roads were still the exception only 75 years ago, when our grandparents traveled from their farms to the neighboring village. Even as late as 1920, only about 10 percent of U.S. roads were paved—and those were primarily in municipalities. Most of us are familiar with pictures showing an old Model T Ford struggling through a morass of mud, loosely defined as a roadway.

The planning of a more acceptable road system dates back to about 1915, at about the time that Ford was introducing assembly-line production of automobiles. It was not until 1920 that a tax was imposed on gasoline to help support state and local governments in their road construction programs. Between 1920 and 1930, the portion of paved roads increased from about 10 to 20 percent. And, by 1940, the portion had increased to 40 percent. Today, more than 90 percent of our public roads are paved.

It was largely initiatives of governments at the state and county levels that were responsible for the growth of paved highways.

Perhaps one of the most important highway innovations was the superhighway, introduced by Pennsylvania in the 1930s. This innovation—or really macroinnovation—was an extraordinarily significant one and it can be traced to government policies. For example, the mileage of divided highways, with four lanes or more, increased almost seven-fold over the 20-year period from 1955 to 1975. The federal government was an important participant in this highway growth. This growth surge coincided with the last long wave of economic growth.

The innovation of jet airplanes and radar control, again originating from government-sponsored R&D, ensured a huge growth of air travel in the 1955–1980 period. Contrary to the case for defense-related *energy* R&D, defense-related *aircraft* R&D has obviously had important spinoff benefits for the civilian sector.

It is likely that defense-related developments on high-temperature, lightweight materials, on advanced hypersonic aircraft design, and on space vehicles will offer still newer opportunities for future civilian technology applications.

One of our most serious problems in the 1980s has been the congestion of airplane (and to some extent, automobile) traffic—largely in short-range intercity commuting. It has already been observed that interesting innovations involving magnetically levitated train systems ("maglev trains") offer some hope of solving the air-traffic problem. Just how state- or federal-government policies might contribute to the commercialization of transportation systems for the 100-to-500 mile intercity corridor traffic remains to be seen. But, some of the more progressive state governments might play a role in such a development in the next long growth cycle.

Summary

It is increasingly apparent that government policies toward education, R&D, energy-supply availability, and transportation capability can all contribute importantly to long-range GNEC/GNP growth. But, these policies will only be pursued—in a democratic society—if the public shows a willingness to support them through taxation and dedication.

Especially in our elementary and secondary education systems, the U.S. public has recently been opting for lower taxes, less family involvement, and eased curricula, at least relative to Japan and most European countries.

We have been favoring the increasing expenditure of federal funding for military strength relative to long-range educational and industrial strengths. This trend appears to be contrary to directions RECALL would suggest. In the 1900s, the United States became a dominant industrial nation mostly because of the macroinnovations and their commercializations spawned by an aggressive civilian-oriented technological society. Even though these advances came primarily from the industrial sector, industrial growth was generally supported by far-sighted government policies related to education, civilian R&D, civilian nuclear energy, superhighway construction, air-traffic control, and even space exploration.

In a period of the long wave, when technology innovation has been of paramount importance, we must ask ourselves as a nation: Should we be opting for narrower education policies, less government support of civilian R&D, less encouragement for solid-fuel energy growth, less attention on new civilian transportation modes, and lower federal, state, and local taxes? Or, should we truly be preparing for the future—recognizing what it will cost us in terms of personal dedications to education, public dedications to government-supported civilian technology, and the additional taxation these dedications might entail?

As a final observation from recollecting the future, we might also ask what RECALL can tell us about our personal futures—a subject of the last chapter.

CHAPTER 15

THE LESSONS FOR YOU AND ME*

January 1, 2000 will mark a milestone in modern history—not only
the beginning of a new century, but the origin of a new millennium.
On that occasion we can expect a burst of media stories—stories
that will divide their attention between retrospectives of the 20th
century and perspectives of the 21st century.

What might we expect our mythical forecasting company,
RECALL, to project on that historic occasion? Perhaps the
following:

> *RECALL Release—January 1, 2000.* Having been conditioned by
> some 12 years of slow economic growth following the Crash of '87,
> we can easily overlook the dawning of a new golden age of
> technology and industry. This new growth surge promises to
> compare favorably with two remarkable economic surges of the last
> century—the golden ages of 1900–1925 and 1950–1975.
>
> How can RECALL be so confident of this new golden age?
> Following a growth decline of GNEC between 1980 and 1995 (as was
> projected by RECALL in the 1970s), our gross national energy
> consumption has already commenced a new growth between 1995
> and 2000. And, the growth of electricity consumption, which
> hovered around 1 percent per year between 1985 and 1995, has
> increased to about 2 percent per year in the 1995–2000 period. As
> was cautioned by RECALL come 15 years ago, our electric utilities
> will face the enormous task of more than doubling their entire
> generating capacity in only 25 years. The new growths of energy and

---

* This chapter was originally finished in September 1987—before the Crash of '87. It was
subsequently modified in organization, emphasis, and verb tense to reflect the occurrence of
the crash, which was anticipated in the earlier version.

electricity use during the next 20 years will reflect a dramatic resurgence of societal industry and economic prosperity—far beyond any level previously experienced.

What will be the source of this growth surge? RECALL reminds you that the burst of spectacular technology innovations in the 1980–2000 period is already being translated into new industrial products and services. The growth of new businesses based on macroinnovations in communications, electrification, transportation, bioengineering, and health care will fuel this explosion of new economic growth.

Even our federal and state governments are becoming involved in significant new projects. Having resolved some of the serious government budgetary problems of the 1980s, we are now directing more of our national income toward growth-oriented discretionary funding—including a more dedicated education effort and increased R&D programs for energy-supply, space-travel, microelectronics, and medicine technologies. These government trends provide yet another signal of the national growth rejuvenation.

RECALL is pleased that its forecasting methodologies are now being used successfully by a large cross section of industrial and government institutions to plan for this new era.

The RECALL Staff

This hypothetical press release presumes RECALL can still be offering advice to industry and government in the next century. RECALL lessons are, indeed, useful to businesses and government. But, can RECALL offer lessons to you and me directly—beyond vague generalities and inspiration? You bet!

RECALL can advise us on our economic future, including personal investment planning, as well as on career planning.

Remember that nature's and society's growth patterns provide the basis for recollecting the future, and therefore, preparing us for the future. These patterns indicated in the mid-1980s that we were entering the winter of the long GNEC wave. The Crash of '87 was only one more signal of this important transition period—a period with both economic and technological significance.

Unhappily, there are foreboding possibilities for each of us as our economy sinks into the low-growth winter. But more cheerfully, there are exciting new prospects in store for the ensuing spring. A new surge of technology macroinnovations is already emerging and probably will gain momentum in the 1990s. By the year 2000, the next long wave of business growths will begin, and by 2010 it will be well underway. Based on RECALL, you should expect once again a dramatic growth of new technological products and services as well as new career opportunities for you and your children.

Is it too early to worry about the events of 2000 or 2010? Absolutely not!

Some two thirds of all workers in 1985 will still be in the work force in 2010.

If you are between 30 and 40 years old in 1990, you will be only 40 to 50 in 2000, or 50 to 60 in 2010. College students arriving in business around 2000 or 2010 will be well trained in still newer technologies. These are the people with whom most of us working today will compete.

You're not worried about yourself? What about your school-age children? They'll barely be entering the work force in 2000 or 2010. What future shocks will they encounter? With the help of RECALL now, you can prepare them to be productive, successful, and happy adults in a highly technical and competitive future society.

In this final chapter, let's examine the lessons of RECALL as they apply to us individually; as earners, investors, consumers, career planners, and parents. What should we expect after the Crash of '87? What can be said about our investment opportunities? How should we plan our consumer spending? What can we learn about career planning?

THE INVESTMENT LESSONS

How Bad Will the Growth Bust Be?

We have already been forewarned by RECALL: We can expect a growth bust in the 1988–1995 period. Can the Crash of '87 be blamed for this growth bust? Why was the crash so sudden?

Did the signs and signals come out of nowhere? According to RECALL, at least one signal was already there.

The long GNEC growth period ended around 1970—a growth turnaround was becoming apparent even before the 1980s.

The reasons for the GNEC turnaround actually had little to do with the "noble" goal of energy conservation. Rather, it represented a decline in societal industry—for two reasons:

1. The long growth wave resulting from the 1935 macroinnovations had come to a close.
2. An overexpansion of capital-equipment growth became obvious with the resulting curtailment of large construction projects.

The Crash of '87 was just one more sign of growth stagnation. True, it was fed by a speculative fever, especially in the last part of the 1983–87 period, having little substance beyond superficial financial maneuvering in the stock market.

How severe will the growth bust be? That question was previously addressed in Chapter 11, where it was emphasized that RECALL's growth laws offer us only general limits on year-to-year GNP growth variations. Within those limits, history shows that GNEC and GNP growths can be predicted surprisingly well. Beyond the GNEC/GNP growth laws, intuition suggests the GNP growth decline will be aggravated by a national need to reduce both our government and our consumer debts.

At a minimum, we should expect the average GNEC growth from 1988 to 1995 to continue at a zero level or decline slightly, based on the projected GNEC growth curve already developed. What should we expect of GNP growth? Again at a minimum, we should expect GNP growth to decline from the relatively high 3 percent per year in the 1983–87 short-term period to a level of about 1 percent per year averaged over the 1988–1995 period. Just as the high growth from 1983 to 1987 was fed by government (and consumer) deficit spending, the following years can be expected to suffer from a born-again frugality of the government (and consumer).

Let's play the pessimist now and consider the worst-case scenario for the decline. Remember that the GNP data points in

1985 and 1986 were already abnormally high relative to the expected GNP curve. A correction of that trend could, by itself, add to the decline. As an even more pessimistic appraisal, we can look at the history of the GNP decline following the Crash of '29. In the three-year period between the end of 1929 and the end of 1932, GNP fell by over 30 percent—an average *decline* of about 10 percent per year! Not only was the nation's economy failing to grow its average 3 percent per year, it was falling at an abysmal rate. Such a decline was far more severe than might have been expected from the RECALL growth curve. For many reasons already discussed, such a decline following the Crash of '87 seems most unlikely.

The main conclusion is that we should fully expect a growth bust in the 1988–95 period, but it should not bring the suffering of the 1930s. Still we can expect a significant rise in unemployment and a decline in our prosperity.

Sometime after 1995, we can look for signs of a GNEC and GNP growth resurgence. The spring phase of the next growth wave will begin.

New investment opportunities will emerge in the years following 1995.

For a better perspective on personal investment opportunities, let's look at the history of significant bull markets in industrial stocks. When did the big bull markets occur and why?

A Perspective on Bull Markets

Unhappily, RECALL cannot render us overnight millionaires. Still, recollections of prior investment experiences and their relationships to the long wave can be useful. With this hindsight, we can find some guidance for future investments—investments that might include stocks, real estate, and savings.

In our free enterprise system, stock investments allow us to be partners in many of the nation's industries. We can even be selective—we can pick those companies we believe to have the best business oportunities. Choices are usually based on one of two general assessments:

- the growth potential of appropriate companies (usually over the long term)
- a speculative intuition (usually over shorter intervals)

As might be expected, the potential for *growth* returns tends to be greatest during the spring and summer phases of the long wave. After all, new industries are incubating, building, expanding, and prospering during the spring and summer phases. You should fully expect this period to be a profitable one for investments over 20 to 25 years.

What about speculative investments? Although *speculative* investment could, in principle, be sought at any time during the long wave, history indicates that for unexplainable reasons it becomes epidemic during the autumn phase. Still more can be learned about this distinction between the two types of market investments by looking at a history of stock values as measured by an appropriate stock index. In this context, much can also be learned about what to expect now following the Crash of '87.

Stock investments tend to be particularly appealing to the more venturesome investors since they can promise, in principle, relatively short-term gains.

It is not unusual to find two- or three-year periods where stock values have appreciated, on average, 15, 20, or even 25 percent per year.

Hindsight shows that these gains are most rewarding when stocks are bought at bottom dollar and sold at top dollar—a detail that escapes many of us. But, even ignoring that detail, more can be said about the potential for stock appreciations as measured, for example, by the Dow-Jones Industrial Average (DJIA). First, let's examine some long-term appreciations.

The 25-year period between 1945 and 1970 represented the spring and summer of the long wave. Had you invested in the DJIA beginning in the 1945–1950 period and held those stocks for 20 years, your average annual appreciation would have been 5 to 8 percent per year. That appreciation, together with profits from the dividends, would have compared favorably with practically any other kind of long-term investment. Your return during that period could have been even more rewarding had you selected companies heavily involved in the macroinnovations of the period. For example, had you invested in Du Pont, GE, RCA, CBS, IBM, GM, and American Airlines, your average appreciation over the 20-year period would have been well over 10 percent per year, exclusive of dividends (not all of these companies followed the general rule, though).

Now, what can be said about investments *over shorter periods* during this high growth era—assuming you were sufficiently clever or lucky to pick the correct buy and sell times? If you (or your parents) had invested in the DJIA stocks in mid-1953 and sold them in mid-1956, you would have earned a return of 25 percent per year—a very impressive profit. Between 1962 and 1965 you could have pocketed an average of 20 percent per year. Even over the relatively long period from 1949 to 1956, the average DJIA appreciation was 17 percent per year—not too bad a gain for a seven-year period. Just think, for every $1,000 you invested in 1949 you could have collected $3,000 in 1956.

In retrospect, we might logically have expected some brisk gains in the 1950s and 1960s, a period when short business cycle booms were frequently combined with the long-wave growth boom.

Are there other apparent periods of sustained DJIA growths *outside* the long-wave growth boom? Perhaps the most remarkable six-year bull-market period was from 1923 to the peak in 1929, a rather surprising time to expect a strong growth in stock values. This large growth came at the very end of the 1900–1925 business growth surge, when growths of the economically important businesses of that era were reaching a saturation level. Average appreciation for that period was more than 25 percent per year. In fact, from 1927 to 1929 the growth was an astounding 45 percent per year! The bad news is that the 1923–1929 bull market is better remembered for its 50 percent *per year* decline between 1929 and 1932. Why should the decline following that particular bull market have been so disastrous?

The 1923–1929 bull market was fed by speculative investing during a period associated with a downswing of the long wave—a downswing reflecting the last gasps of a long business growth.

Still one other bull market can be identified as an exceptional one for its philanthropy. The average DJIA for the five-year period between 1982 and 1987 grew over 20 percent per year before October 1987. The growth from mid-1985 to mid-1987 was a remarkable 40 percent per year.

Again, that sustained 1982–1987 bull market occurred during a period associated with a downswing of the long wave—a time marking the end of a long business growth cycle.

The similarity between the 1982–1987 and the 1923–1929 markets is striking—as is the similarity between their crashes. The economist and author, John Kenneth Galbraith, wrote a remarkably prophetic article in the January 1987 issue of *The Atlantic Monthly* on "The 1929 Parallel." Nine months before the Crash of '87, he warned of similarities between 1987 and 1929 that suggested the possibility of a market crash. Those similarities included:

- an abnormal speculative fever
- investment leveraging (by leveraged buyouts, junk bonds, etc.)
- the glorification of financial manipulating
- a tax relief for the affluent that was used primarily for nonproductive investments.

A market crash was being invited by the speculative abuses of the investment community, and the marketplace responded.

Professional arbitrageurs in the last years of the 1982–87 period, like those in the final years of the 1923–29 period, became preoccupied with the easy road to affluence. The quick profit became an end in itself. Instead of investments based on a potential for industrial growth, investments were more frequently based on takeover rumors, mergers, and inside trading. The yuppies who made headlines were the highly paid MBAs on Wall Street rather than the microchip engineers in Silicon Valley—the investment gurus rather than the technology gurus.

To complicate matters, the government (as well as the investment community) was pursuing policies in the 1980s that defied the laws of economic gravity. Why are these observations important to you and me? They simply emphasize the rough road we must follow on our journey back to reality.

After the Crash—The Journey Back

Even in the weeks following the Black Monday Crash of '87, a surprisingly large number of market analysts could be found suggesting: BUY! The basis for this wisdom was that the crash was only a temporary correction, and soon the market would resume its assault on a DJIA of 3500 or more. Indeed, a significant recovery did occur in the weeks following Black Monday, at least relative to the low value that was reached immediately following the crash.

What investment strategy should we pursue now? Can history provide any insight from the experiences following 1929? RECALL would be quick to caution us against short-term projections based on previous adversities, even assuming the stock market is a reasonable measure of GNP. Still, the stock market experience following the Crash of '29 does suggest other parallels and at least one possibility for future market trends.

Compared to the one-day DJIA decline of 23 percent in the Crash of '87, the two-day decline in the Crash of '29 was 22 percent.

In both 1929 and 1987, a decline of about 20 percent had already occurred over the month prior to the crashes. And, in each case, almost half of the decline during the crash itself was regained within two days.

Most surprisingly, the DJIA following the Crash of '29 increased almost consistently, though modestly from October 1929 until April 1930.

It was after April 1930 that the most resolute market decline began. In April 1930, the index was off about 25 percent from its *peak* in September 1929. By the end of 1930 the total decline was 50 percent. By the end of 1931, the overall loss reached 75 percent, and by the end of 1932 it was 85 percent. Had your parents or grandparents invested $1,000 in a cross section of stocks in September 1929, their portfolio would have had a value of $150 in 1932.

With the onset of an economic winter in 1988, it would not seem that heavy involvement in the stock market would be a promising investment opportunity. Even though the experience of the post-1929 market might not be repeated in every detail, other features of the long GNEC and GNP wave would suggest a cautionary note to would-be market investors. Probably some shorter business cycles in the 1990s will offer new profit opportunities to the more heroic investors—but at some risk.

However, by 1995 or 2000 the spring of a new GNEC/GNP long wave will begin.

In only 10 to 15 years after the Crash of '87, new industrial growths will emerge, bringing 20 to 25 years of strong investment opportunities such as those between 1945 and 1970.

As was the case in the 1945–1970 period, the growth appreciation of industrial stocks will be based on substantial business growths, not just speculative ventures. Shorter business cycles (of three to five years) will offer some speculative opportunities for the more venturesome, while the long-term appreciation should offer less risk for the conservative investor.

A careful selection of stocks, based on companies involved in the macroinnovations of that new growth era, should promise a return better than could be assured from a general cross section, such as the overall Dow-Jones composite of companies.

Other Investment Possibilities

Even though RECALL cannot provide us specific measures of imminent declines in our investments in a declining economy, can anything be said about the relative security of various other kinds of investments—real estate and savings? History can offer us a few hints, based on the downside period in the early 1930s.

Again we can refer to the history of the 1929–1932 period for a look at the possible downside exposure. Department of Commerce data indicate that the average value of single-family homes fell by about 30 percent in that three-year period. That happens to correspond to the fall in the overall consumer price index in the same period. However, the investment decline could have been much more severe for you, as a home owner, if 50 percent of your home had been owned by the bank through a mortgage. The bank would not have shared that loss with you, and your equity loss would have been twice as large.

"Aha," you might conclude, "I should not commit myself to a mortgage at these perilous times; I should keep my assets liquid."

In general, that might be a prudent conclusion. But, if our government should decide to increase money supply in a future adversity, it could lead to inflation with some benefit to those indebted (including the government).

Still, in the event of a catastrophe like that of the 1929–1932 period, the best investment would apparently be direct savings—presuming those savings were in federally insured accounts. The primary concern in this case would be the possibility of inflation. In general though, inflation should only become a threat as the result of an abrupt easing in money-supply policies by the federal government. Some forewarning should be available, allowing us adequate time for reinvestments.

These gloomy possibilities have been based on the assumption of a repetition of the Great Depression. You may have read the many opinions of respected economists and investment counselors who argue, quite logically, that such a severe disaster could not occur today because of the many safeguards we now have in our economy. But, you have probably also read the opinions of equally respected economists and investment counselors who point to the huge government deficit, the overextension of consumers, and the fragile international debt loans that could allow another economic disaster.

RECALL can only note that the years from 1985 to 1995 represent another winter of the long economic wave—a period when we should expect a significant slowdown in economic growth.

Although RECALL cannot identify the precise timing, extent, or side effects of the long-wave decline, it can caution us we are living in a sensitive period. Perhaps the most sound advice is that we should *not* be overextended at this time, either in stock or real estate investments.

THE CONSUMER LESSONS

What Should We Know about Consumption?

RECALL has already alerted us to the various kinds of technology growths we should expect.

- Electricity will continue to replace non-electricity energy in supplying our everyday energy needs.
- A surge of technology innovations can be expected in *major* equipment, including home appliances and automobiles; takeover growths for these major items will be approximately 30 years.
- A continuing surge of technology innovations can also be expected in the smaller electronics equipment; the much faster growths for this kind of equipment could render it obsolete within approximately 10 years.
- Because of the radical technology changes to be expected in the next 10–15 years, we must be especially cautious that our large investments do not become obsolete prematurely.

The growth of electricity use in homes for comfort heating, air conditioning and, possibly, robotic-type services could lead to the early obsolescence of a short-sighted home purchase, representing a substantial risk in that personal investment. The potential home purchaser should make a special effort to identify what technology directions that homes might be following.

While the lifetime of an automobile or a home appliance is less than that of a dwelling, the technology changes tend to be more rapid. For example, we can expect an increasingly large use of microcomputer technology in ignition, fuel-mixture, and braking control, as well as diagnostic instrumentation in new automobiles. And, we should expect more emphasis on "smart" home appliances.

Obsolescence will be fastest in the electronics industry—music reproduction, television, video reproduction, home security systems, and many other components. Here the consumer must be particularly wary.

Especially in a transition period, between stagnating old technologies and growing new ones, we as consumers must all be more conscientious in our investments.

THE CAREER-PLANNING LESSONS

Where Will the Job Opportunities Be?

Where is my future—what work classification, what industry, and what business? What should I be doing now to achieve my goals in life? Am I aiming toward an overcrowded or obsolete field of work? Once again, RECALL can help us by applying a fundamental growth law—the multivariate growth law. We have talked about several kinds of growth laws:

- adoption growths (of a single new technology, like home electrification)
- substitution or takeover growths (where a second technology displaces an older first one, like computers replacing typewriters)
- multivariate or successive takeover growths (where a third technology might displace a second one that already displaced a first one, for example, compact discs replacing L.P. records which replaced earlier phonograph records)

Historical and evolving growth trends of agricultural, blue-collar, and white-collar jobs can allow us to identify in which of these work classes future job opportunities will and will not occur.

Figure 15–1 indicates the growth trends for these three work classes as fractions of the total work force. In fact, our already-familiar procedure of plotting growth/ungrowth curves can help us again in describing these growth trends from 1900 to 2020. What do the curves tell us about the past? From them, what can we recollect about the future?

Disappearing Agricultural Work Opportunities

Although not shown explicitly on the graph, the work force of the 1800s was dominated by agricultural workers, perhaps including your own grandparents or great grandparents. As the Industrial (and Transportation) Revolution spread to the United States in the 1800s, the demand for industrial workers began to grow. People began to realize there were new job opportunities in the big cities. But yet another factor contributed to the blue-collar takeover.

FIGURE 15-1
Relative Fractional Growth Behaviors for Components of the Work Force

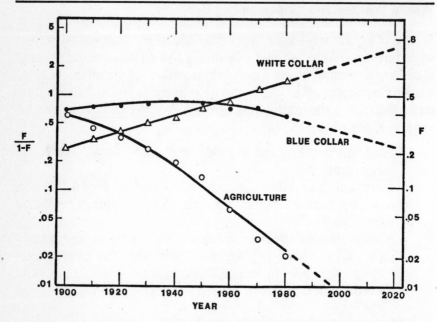

The late 1880s and early 1900s marked a period when farm equipment was becoming mechanized and more labor-efficient.

Gradually, farm machinery (with some significant farm-owner investments) replaced much of the grueling farm labor—labor that required large numbers of workers to accomplish what a single person can now do with a machine. This is not to imply that farm *enterprises* were disappearing, only job opportunities for farm laborers as a fraction of the work force. The number of these opportunities has decreased since 1900, and will continue to decline. As long ago as 1890, the blue-collar work force in industry began to exceed the farm workers in agriculture. But, who would have guessed in 1900 that agricultural labor as a fraction of the work force would decrease from some 40 percent to less than 4 percent in only 75 years? Who would have thought that high-tech labor would become so much more important than land-cultivation labor?

We must be careful to interpret this trend correctly. The curve for farm workers indicates the *fractional* contribution to the work force, which is a correct measure of job competition in the work force. For example, the fraction of farm workers decreased about two-fold between 1900 and 1930—from almost 40 percent to a little more than 20 percent. But, for this first 30 years, the *number* of farm workers remained nearly constant (it decreased less than 10 percent). During that 30-year period the total work force increased from about 30 million to almost 50 million workers. The incremental new workers were moving primarily into industry, not farming.

By 1970, even the number *of farm workers had decreased substantially over that of 1900.*

Over the full 70 years between 1900 and 1970, the number of farm workers showed a four-fold decrease, while the fractional number showed a 10-fold decrease from the 40 percent in 1900 to less than 4 percent in 1970. Work opportunities in the agricultural industry were rapidly disappearing due largely to an increase in work productivity (the output per worker). If young people in the 1930s had trained to follow their father's farming career in earlier years, or their grandfather's farming career in the late 1800s, many would have prepared incorrectly.

Diminishing Blue-Collar Work Opportunities

Between 1900 and 1930 large numbers of workers were moving into blue-collar labor jobs. Blue-collar workers as a fraction of the total civilian work force increased from 40 percent to 46 percent between 1900 and 1940. Since the total work force was also increasing, the actual number of blue-collar workers increased two-fold, from about 12 to 24 million workers. The trend curve (in Figure 15–1) indicates that the fraction of blue-collar workers reached a peak in the 1940s.

The fraction of blue-collar workers has subsequently decreased from the peak of 46 percent to some 38 percent in 1980, indicating another trend toward a smaller fraction of jobs for one of our labor classes.

What can RECALL tell us about blue-collar job opportunities of the future? The curve shows that the fraction of blue-collar jobs will continue its decrease from 40 percent in 1980 to only a little over 20 percent in 2020. Your children entering elementary schools today will be less than 40 years old in 2020. Should you assume they can be assured at that time of well-paying jobs as carpenters (in the construction sector), or assembly-line workers (in the manufacturing sector)?

The search for a blue-collar job in 2010 or 2020 might be surprisingly difficult, simply because the fraction of job opportunities in the classification will be so small. And, still another problem will arise.

Even the smaller number of blue-collar workers in 2010 to 2020 will be required to have a much more sophisticated knowledge of manufacturing and service-related equipment.

Advances in manufacturing and maintenance technologies will bring about radical changes in the workplace for blue-collar workers. Robotics, computer-assisted manufacturing (CAM), "smart" machines, and new quality-control equipment will require a new breed of blue-collar employees. A large fraction of the future blue-collar work force might be involved in the repair and maintenance of production or service equipment—equipment that will itself be doing the actual labor.

The outlook for blue-collar workers is not encouraging—especially for those with minimal technical expertise. The lesson is clear. Education and vocational training will no longer be luxuries. Even those expecting jobs in the smaller blue-collar market will be forced to acquire some special skills.

Growing White-Collar Work Opportunities

In which work classification will we find the best job opportunities of the future? RECALL clearly tells us those opportunities will be found in the white-collar class. White-collar workers accounted for only 20 percent of the total work force around 1900, a time when the work force was dominated by farm and blue-collar workers. Yet by 1965, half the entire work force was involved in white-collar work.

By the year 2020, more than three fourths of the U.S. work force will be white-collar workers.

With a literacy rate slightly over 75 percent today, this is an astounding projection for only 30 years forward. Where will all these white-collar workers be occupied? And, what skills will be required?

Remember, white-collar workers work in both manufacturing and service industries. RECALL concluded in Chapter 13 that service industries in the United States are accounting for an increasingly large share of our total national income and jobs. In 1985, the service sector (including government) already accounted for more than 60 percent of the work force, with this growth trend clearly continuing. A large fraction of the white-collar jobs will be found in the service-industry sector. But, what can RECALL tell us, more explicitly, about the *industries* where job openings will occur in the next 20 to 30 years? To answer this, let's examine in greater detail where the jobs were in 1985 and where they will be 25 years forward, in 2010.

Where Should We Look for Future Jobs?

The total U.S. work force in 1985 was approximately 105 million, with 30 million in goods-producing industries, 60 million in non-government service-producing industries and 15 million in government service activities.

What more specifically are the *goods*-producing jobs and who has them today? Those jobs belong to your friends and relatives in farm work, construction work, and various manufacturing enterprises. In fact, manufacturing accounts for about two thirds of all goods-producing jobs. These manufacturing jobs are divided almost evenly between manufacturing of durable goods (furniture, appliances, automobiles, and TV sets) and nondurable goods (clothes, food, soap, and newspapers).

Your family comes in contact with a much larger number of people in the *service*-producing enterprises than in manufacturing activities. Those contacts involve people in the retail and wholesale trades. But, they also include health-care workers (doctors, dentists, nurses), white-collar professionals (accountants, lawyers, computer programmers, private-school teachers), and workers in the transportation, utilities, and communications services. Government services account for almost 15 percent of all the work force. A little over three fourths of these government workers are involved in state and local government activities. They include our public-school teachers, police officers, and firefighters.

Why is all this relevant? This background provides a basis for understanding where our future job opportunities will evolve. Figure 15–2 illustrates the general distribution of jobs as they existed in 1985. The figure also indicates the distribution RECALL would project for 2010, based on long-term growth trends. Although the overall incremental increase in the work force will be an impressive 40 to 50 million jobs (a growth from 105 to 150 million),

FIGURE 15–2

Current and Projected Levels of Workers in the Goods-Producing and Services-Producing Sectors*

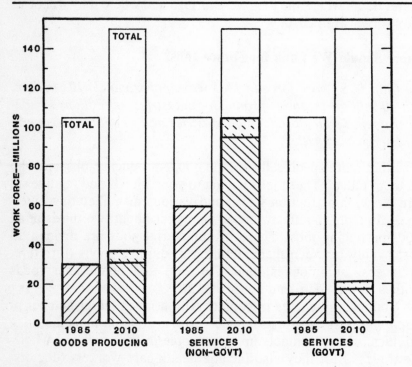

*Dashed blocks indicate estimated uncertainties.

about 80 percent of the increase will occur in nongovernment service-producing industries. Indeed, when government and non-government service jobs are combined, at least 90 percent of the increase will be in service activities.

Job Replacements and Creations

To identify the total number of job openings occurring between 1985 and 2010, we must add the incremental number of jobs being created and *the number of new workers replacing retirees.*

Because about one third of the present work force will retire before 2010, some 10 million jobs will open in the goods-producing sector just to replace attrition. And, about 25 million jobs will open in the service-producing sector. RECALL can project the total number of job openings in each of the three broad sectors (goods-producing, nongovernment service-producing, and government service-producing) by combining job creations with job replacements. This is done in Table 15–1.

Those who still might want careers in manufacturing can be cheered by the observation that job opportunities will not actually disappear in manufacturing. In fact, the growths in work force for some types of manufacturing are very impressive. For example, the work forces in electronic components and computer manufacturing are growing at a rate of some 3 percent per year. Those bright spots, are offset by the declining work forces in food production and apparel, automobile and furniture manufacturing.

Still, the prospects for jobs in the service-producing sector are much better than those for jobs in the manufacturing sector.

Including both job replacements and job creations, RECALL would conclude that more than 8 of every 10 jobs becoming available in the next 25 years will be in the service-producing sector.

This trend has little to do with foreign competition in manufacturing. Other industrialized countries are probably seeing the same trend. The trend is due largely to efficiencies that have been introduced in manufacturing—just as the similar trend in the agricultural work force reflected more efficient operations in that

TABLE 15-1
Relative Number of Job Opportunities Expected, 1985–2010*

| Sector | Job Level in 1985 (millions) | Job Growths (in millions), 1985–2010 | | | Percent Distribution of Opportunities |
		Job Creations	Job Replacements	Total Job Opportunities	
Goods producing	30	0–5	10	10–15	15
Non-government service	60	35–45	20	55–65	75
Government services	15	3–7	5	8–12	10

*Notes: (1) All numbers are rounded, and (2) job requirements are based on retirements of one third of workers in 1985.

sector. They include automated manufacturing processes, robotic operations, and computerized machinery.

Because of the better prospects for careers in the service-producing industries, this sector deserves special attention.

Where the Action Will Be

While most of the work-force growth in the future will occur in the service sector, not all service industries or businesses will offer good opportunities. Just as was the case for the broader sectors, opportunities in various segments of the service-producing industry will depend on the number of both:

- job replacements
- job creations

Job opportunities in any particular industry segment (of the broader service-producing sector) will depend on the current size (which affects job-replacement needs), and the growth rate of that segment (which affects job creations).

It will be the businesses having large growth rates that will offer the best job futures. For some perspective, just what is the norm for work-force growth? And, what growth rate should we look for, assuming we want a better-than-average prospect for a future career? Finally, which industries or businesses will promise that better-than-average prospect?

In order to define a norm for the work-force growth rate, let's refer to RECALL's projection of the overall growth rate—the growth rate for all jobs in our national economy. This projected overall growth rate, and various sector growth rates, are summarized in Table 15–2 for the 1985–2010 period. On the basis of a 1.5 percent per year average growth rate, RECALL can offer the following (somewhat arbitrary) definitions:

- Low growth   Less than 1.5 percent per year
- Moderate-growth   1.5 to 3 percent per year
- High-growth   Greater than 3 percent per year

With this perspective, let's look now at four subgroups of the service-producing sector (and the approximate percentage of jobs currently in those subgroups):

TABLE 15-2
Average Growths Projected for the Work Force, 1985-2010

Sector	Level (millions)		Growth (percent per year)
	1985	2010	
Total	105	150	1.4
Nongovernment	90	130	1.5
Goods-producing	30	30	0
Service-producing (nongovernment)	60	100	2.1

1. Retail and wholesale trade (40 percent).
2. Low-growth services (20 percent).
3. Moderate-growth services (20 percent).
4. High-growth services (20 percent).

Actually, retail and wholesale trade can (and will) be included in the low-growth industry group, but is separated here to illustrate its huge size. The other low-growth services include janitorial, cosmetic, fast-food, equipment-repair, and auto-maintenance services. The moderate-growth services include banking, investment, accounting, communications, and utility services. The high-growth services are, obviously, the most exciting. They include a large number of professional services and, as you might expect, health-care services.

The probable future job opportunities for these three groups of service industries are illustrated in Table 15-3, based on their typical growth rates during the last 10 to 30 years. The table suggests that about two thirds of the job openings will occur in the high- and moderate-growth segments, even though they account for only 40 percent of today's service-sector jobs.

One reason for using RECALL to identify where future jobs will occur is to indicate how you should prepare for the best opportunities. How much education or training will you need? Even though the simpler jobs (one third) will almost all require some basic reading, counting, and computer (e.g., computerized cash registers) literacy, lower-growth jobs will generally not re-

TABLE 15-3
Illustrative Work-Force Characteristics of Three Groups of
Nongovernment Service-Producing Industries*

Service Segment	Current Job Level, Percent	Approximate Growth, Percent Per Year	Job Openings, Percent of Total
Low-growth services*	3/5	1	1/3
Moderate-growth services†	1/5	3 ⎫	
High-growth services‡	1/5	5 ⎬	2/3

*Low-growth services include retail and wholesale trade as well as other common services.
†Moderate-growth services include investment, communications, and utility services.
‡High-growth services include health-care and other professional services.

quire special education or training beyond on-the-job training—assuming applicants have a reasonable high-school education.

But, the two thirds of the jobs associated with the higher-growth industries in the next 25 years will require an education or vocational training considerably beyond our normal high-school education.

To understand what this means to you and your children, let's look more closely at the high-growth service industries.

High-Growth Service Industries

Much has been written elsewhere about the high-growth industries in the United States. They are not necessarily high-tech industries at this time, but a large and growing fraction is involved in high technology. What are these businesses now, and what qualifications will be required to enter them?

Consider the health-care industry. Workers in this industry include the local doctor and dentist as well as the nurses and orderlies in your community hospital. But, that's only the beginning. It also includes the large number of professional people working in research laboratories, diagnostic clinics, blood banks, and health maintenance organizations across the country. As medical practice becomes more sophisticated, all of these businesses will grow more. In 1980, the jobs in health-care accounted for about half of the jobs in the high-growth businesses—about 10 percent of all service jobs.

By 2010, health-care jobs will account for over 20 percent of the service-producing jobs.

A large cross section of miscellaneous businesses and professional services (other than medical) has also been showing a spectacular growth rate in the last 10 to 15 years—a growth rate that is even larger than that of the health-care businesses. What are these businesses? Many of them are technology-consulting and technology-service companies, firms that supply consultants on management, employee training, equipment maintenance, quality control, toxic-waste management, information systems, and a host of other services. As you might guess, some of the fastest growing ones are supplying computer-related services—computer systems, software, programming, and operations. But, not all of the fast-growing businesses are in computer-related activities, nor are all of them involved in high-tech businesses.

Perhaps a more characteristic feature is that they tend to be small relative to the Fortune-500 corporations—typically employing fewer than 20 or 30 workers. So successful are these small, flexible, and efficient service companies that many of the large corporations are now depending on them for an increasingly large part of their needs.

The trends already indicate that the future will be particularly bright, both for entrepreneurs and workers in the fast-growing, high-tech service enterprises.

Career Preparation—The Race between Supply and Demand

For the 94 percent of workers in 1900 who had *not* completed high school, the possibility of learning a new job involving electrical, mechanical, or chemical engineering would probably have evoked sheer terror. Yet, the high-tech aspirants in the 1900–1925 period did learn to be electricians, machinists, mechanics, movie projectionists, and other kinds of technicians, as well as high-tech shop owners, sales people, and even engineers in some cases. Undoubtedly, many of those who chose to remain farm operators or farm laborers subsequently looked with envy on the ones who mastered a new trade through additional schooling, apprenticeships, or sheer doggedness.

In the early 1900s, dramatic progress was also being made in our public school systems and particularly our colleges—colleges that would prepare a new generation for more complicated business responsibilities.

Still, for the 85 percent of workers in 1955 who had not completed college, the prospects for professional advancement must have appeared grim. The GI Bill, providing college assistance to large numbers of veterans in the late 1940s and 1950s was a blessing not only for those who used it, but for our national future as well.

Why is it so important for us to understand these events of the past? Largely because we can fall into yet another trap, in the 1990s and early 2000s, if we ignore the lessons of RECALL.

In spite of the already-recognized trend toward a new wave of high technology, our high-school completion rates, science interests, and public apathy toward school support are all showing alarming trends in the United States. Possibly the only encouraging trend is one toward more graduate-school education. Table 15–4 reviews what RECALL can tell us about the population fractions completing our high school, college, and graduate-school curricula.

TABLE 15–4
Approximate Growth Characteristics of Educational Achievement among U.S. Citizens

	Percent Completion in 1980	Saturation Year	Peak Growth Year
High school	75	1960	1940
College	25	1970	1950
Post graduate	10	?	1965–1970

In 1980, approximately 75 percent of our teenagers were completing high school, 25 percent of our young adults were completing college and 10 percent were earning advanced degrees.

Quite logically, higher education has become increasingly popular over the years. The disappointing fact is that the fraction of U.S. children completing high school has apparently leveled off at around 75 percent. You will remember that this compares to a level of 90 percent in Japan, where the high-school curriculum is actually more rigorous. Also disappointing is the leveling off of college graduates at around 25 percent (compared to 35 percent in Japan). An encouraging observation is that the popularity of graduate schools in the United States is continuing to grow. How is that all related to job opportunities?

Remember (from Table 15–1) that 75 percent of the job opportunities in the next 25 years will arise in the nongovernment service sector, and (from Table 15–3) some 67 percent of the service jobs will occur in high-growth and moderate-growth services. This suggests about half of all job opportunities (75 percent of 67 percent will come in areas requiring a high content of education and skills.

With half of all the demand for workers coming in areas requiring high skills, but with only 25 percent of the candidates being college graduates, the competition for highly qualified people could be extraordinarily vigorous.

High demand and low supply, in a free market, typically leads to high price tags. Surely the prospect of a bidding war for specially educated people should offer an incentive to move into the path of progress. For those already past college age, adult education classes offer an opportunity for preparation. For those in high school and college, careful selections of classes associated with high-growth disciplines should promise handsome returns. And for those of you who are parents of school-age children, a rededication to the principles of education—as they were understood in the 1950s and 1960s—might be the most important legacy you can offer your children.

Summary

Perhaps somewhat surprisingly, RECALL's lessons for you and me as individuals can be at least as rewarding as the lessons for business and government. While the Crash of '87 has almost certainly had a sobering effect on stock speculators, there still are large numbers of investment brokers suggesting that the post-crash market offers impressive new opportunities for their clients. History suggests otherwise, at least based on the three-year period following the Crash of '29. Stock speculation during the winter of the long wave can always be expected to have a more-than-normal risk.

In contrast, the spring and summer seasons of the next long wave from 2000 to 2025 should offer excellent investment opportunities for those of us wanting to participate in the next solid business growth. In particular, investments in high-tech companies involved in the new surge of macroinnovations should offer special profit potentials.

Some of RECALL's best personal advice can come in the area of career planning.

From the simple growth laws of RECALL we can foresee and actually measure trends in white-collar versus blue-collar job opportunities, and in service-producing versus goods-producing industries. Just as the fraction of the work force in the agricultural sector has already diminished, the growth curves show the fraction of blue-collar jobs in general will now decrease—from about 40 percent in 1980 to little more than 20 percent in 2020. Even those who have resigned themselves to that lower-level of job classification will find increasingly heavy demands on higher levels of technical training.

The most surprising change might be the speed of the trend from job opportunities in goods-producing to those in service-producing industries. Even when job-replacement opportunities are included, more than 80 percent of the job openings between 1985 and 2010 will be in the service-producing sector. One third of those job openings will be in relatively low-level activities, particularly wholesale and retail sales, but about two thirds of the job openings will arise in the higher-growth, higher-technology service businesses—especially health care and other professional services. With over half of all job openings occurring in these relatively high-technology businesses, and with only 25 percent of all our population completing a college education, it is difficult to see how this demand will be met.

Clearly, the economic laws associated with supply and demand will offer some unusually lucrative opportunities for those willing to complete or extend their college and advanced vocational educations.

As a more general conclusion, it should be clear that the very simple growth laws developed and used throughout this book can be valuable to all of us in our business and personal lives. With an understanding of these principles, we can become better business managers, more alert technologists, more prudent investors, and more careful career planners.

Each and every one of us can become a RECALL veteran!

APPENDIXES

APPENDIX A

BACKGROUND ON GROWTH EQUATIONS

Purpose: This background on growth equations describes their mathematical derivations, and their applications. For those interested in using the growth methods, Section 2 of this appendix should be particularly useful.

An attempt has been made to keep the mathematics in Section 1 of this appendix relatively simple. Still, for those not interested in the mathematics, little will be lost by skipping this section (and the last). The second section, however, should be of redeeming value to *anyone* wishing to apply the principles and methods to his or her own business growth problems. The third section describes, in some mathematical detail, methods for developing less simple logistic growth equations.

The S-growth curve is frequently mentioned in business literature. Indeed, you probably have seen references to it in trade books, news magazines, or newspapers. Yet most of those discussions only refer to the S-curve as a general principle—they omit any description of how you can actually use the S-curve for your own *quantitative* business projections. That omission is unfortunate because the practical use of the growth curve is surprisingly simple—even for the nonmathematician. The step-by-step description in the middle section of this appendix should be particularly instructive and rewarding.

Background for the Mathematically Curious

Nature's most popular growth curve has the shape of a stretched-out S. A typical example is illustrated in Figure A–1. In the figure,

FIGURE A–1
**A Typical S-Growth Curve Used to Describe Biological, Population, or
Business Growth**

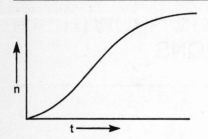

the growth size, n, is plotted against growth time, t. The growth
size might be pounds of weight, inches of stature, population of a
growing country, or number of offices adopting word-processing
equipment. The growth rate is measured by the change (repre-
sented by $\triangle$) in size per increment of time, $\triangle n/\triangle t$ (or dn/dt in
mathematical language). The growth rate (such as pounds gained
per year) begins slowly at the left side of the curve. It increases as
time progresses, until it reaches a maximum rate half way through
the growth cycle. The growth change per increment of time then
declines in the later years. Ultimately, the growth rate declines to
essentially a zero rate when the curve ceases to rise significantly
toward the end of the growth cycle.

Actually, mathematicians commonly study at least three kinds
of growth behavior: *linear, exponential,* and *logistic* growths. In
linear growth, the growth rate itself (dn/dt) is constant from time to
time (from year to year). The equation describing linear growth is,
simply:

$$\text{Growth rate} = \frac{dn}{dt} = C, \tag{1}$$

where C is a constant. The solution of this equation is:

$$n = C_0 + Ct. \tag{2}$$

C_o is the size of n at the time t = 0, the time at which we start
counting. For example, t = 0 is defined as 0 A.D. in our normal
calendar. If n is the population at that time (of American Indians
for the U.S. population), then n would become C_o in the year 0

A.D. In some growth problems, it is even conceivable that $n = 0$ at $t = 0$, in which case $C_0 = 0$. From any one year to another, then, n increases by the same amount, assuming a linear growth behavior.

More commonly, things grow by the exponential law. In this case, the *fractional* (or percentage) growth rate ($dn/n\ dt$) is constant from time to time. Our bank accounts, for example, increase by the same fractional value each year—by an amount, r (for rate) or i (for interest). The growth equation is:

$$\frac{1}{n}\ \frac{dn}{dt} = r \tag{3}$$

where dn/n is the fractional growth in n each interval of time, dt. The mathematicians know the solution to this equation is:

$$n = n_0\ e^{rt} \tag{4}$$

where n_0 is the value of n at the time chosen to be $t = 0$. The mathematician will recognize e as the base of the natural system of logarithms. For the nonmathematician, e is simply a constant, having the value 2.71828. . . . Mathematical handbooks commonly have tables of e^x for various values of x. The important point is that growths by constant *multiplication* rates, $(1 + r)$ each year are generally more common in our experiences than growths by constant *additions*.

Even exponential growth is not a popular kind of growth in nature. It suggests something can continue growing until it reaches an infinitely large size. Generally, growths are constrained by some upper limit. As the growth level approaches its final limit, n_f, the growth rate is diminished, depending on its proximity to the final growth level, that is, the growth rate is proportional to ($n_f - n$), which approaches zero as n approaches n_f. In this case, the growth equation is:

$$\frac{dn}{dt} = \alpha\ n(n_f - n) \tag{5}$$

This equation tells us that when n is very small relative to n_f, n_f predominates over n and the growth is essentially exponential, or,

$$\frac{1}{n}\ \frac{dn}{dt} = (\alpha n_f) = r_i$$

where r_i is the initial growth rate. But at very long times, when n approaches n_f, the $(n_f - n) = 0$ almost, so

$$\frac{1}{n} \frac{dn}{dt} \simeq 0$$

and

$$\frac{dn}{dt} \simeq 0$$

Hence, growth declines to zero, approximately.

Sometimes we are only interested in the fractional growth level of n, in other words, $F = n/n_f$, relative to its final, or "asymptotic," growth. For these cases, Equation (5) becomes:

$$\frac{dF}{dt} = \alpha F(1 - F) \tag{6}$$

which tells us that the growth rate of F is "jointly proportional" to F and $(1 - F)$. This equation describes the most common type of pure growth in nature, in businesses, and in our economy. It describes the principles of growth in mathematical terms exactly as they were described by nonmathematical terms in Chapter 2—growth is affected by the growth already acquired, and the amount yet to be acquired.

Equation (5) has the solution:

$$n = \frac{n_0}{1 + be^{-\alpha t}} \tag{7}$$

which is the general equation describing an S-growth curve. In the equation, b is a constant that allows us to select at what level of n we prefer to define $t = 0$. For example, if we choose $b = 1$, then at $t = 0$, $be^{-\alpha t} = 1$ and $n = 0.5n_0$. For this simple choice of b, the S-growth curve would reach half its final value at $t = 0$, or half the growth would occur for t values less than 0 (or negative t values), and half would occur for t greater than 0 (or positive t values). For other choices of b, we would choose n to be $0.1n_0$, $0.01n_0$, or any other value at $t = 0$.

Turning to the simpler Equation (6), its solution would be:

$$F = \frac{1}{1 + e^{-\alpha t}} \tag{8}$$

This equation can be abundantly useful to the business planner. In fact, the consequences of Equation (8) even make it easily usable by the nonmathematician. Why is this equation so usable?

With only a little mathematical manipulation, Equation (8) can be rewritten as:

$$\frac{F}{1 - F} = e^{\alpha t} \tag{9}$$

Remember that the ratio F is simply the fraction of growth that has already occurred. The ratio $(1 - F)$, or the remainder of F, is the fraction yet to grow. Hence, $F/(1 - F)$ is the fraction-grown divided by the fraction-ungrown, or what we have called the "growth/ungrowth" fraction throughout the book.

The fascinating point is that the growth/ungrowth fraction grows exponentially—like Equation (4) if n/n_0 is replaced by $F/(1 - F)$. If this ratio is plotted against time on a log-linear graph, the growth "curves" for $F/(1 - F)$ will be simple straight lines (as will be illustrated in Figure A–2). That characteristic can be profoundly interesting to a business analyst who wants to project future growth levels from past growth.

In their famous paper "A Simple Substitution Model of Technological Change," published in 1971 in the *Technological Forecasting and Social Change Journal*, Fisher and Pry showed how this simple relationship could be used for technology and business forecasting. They also defined a "takeover time" (or time interval) as the time for F to grow from $F = 0.1$ to $F = 0.9$, that is, for the market fraction, F, of a new product to grow from 10 to 90 percent substitution. This takeover time can be shown to be

$$\Delta t = t_{0.9} - t_{0.1} = \frac{4.4}{\alpha} \tag{10}$$

where α is the constant in Equations (6), (8), and (9). If we should prefer to define a "characteristic growth period," Δt_g, to be the time for $F/(1 - F)$ to grow from 0.1 to 10 (or F to grow from 0.091 to 0.91), then

$$\Delta t_g = \frac{4.6}{\alpha} \tag{11}$$

This characteristic growth period, Δt_g, is only about 5 percent greater than the takeover time, Δt. It is frequently more conve-

FIGURE A–2
Illustrative Substitution (takeover) and Adoption Growth Curves*

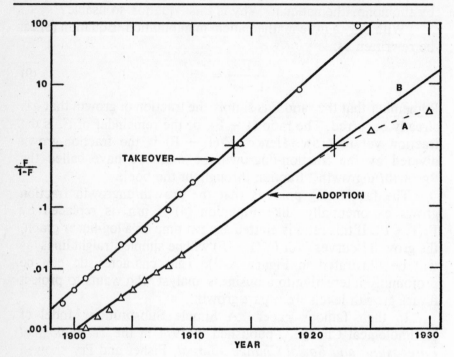

*The takeover curve shows how automobiles substituted for horse-drawn carriages in the U.S. The adoption curve shows the growth of automobiles among families in the U.S.

nient to read off the *characteristic growth time* from the graph showing the growth/ungrowth behavior for some technology takeover. That characteristic growth time is only 5 percent greater than the takeover time as defined by Fisher and Pry.

Using the Growth Curve

As a business planner, you might feel a bit uncomfortable with all this mathematics. The final mathematical result is Equation (9), and the practical *use* of the growth principle can be remarkably simple. Whether a mathematician or not, you can use these principles in your own business planning. To illustrate this, let's first examine two growth problems already discussed in Chapter 7, the automobile takeover growth from the horse and carriage, and the automobile adoption growth.

As a first step in any study of substitution growth, you will find it convenient to develop a table showing the following data in six columns:

- the year
- number of *new* products sold per year
- number of *old* products sold per year
- sum of the two (or total sales)
- fraction of sales, F, belonging to the new product
- growth/ungrowth fraction, $F/(1 - F)$

This is illustrated in Table A–1, where automobiles are the new products and carriages the old products. Data for this example are from the Department of Commerce *Historical Statistics of the United States—1970,* Volume 2. For simplicity, data are shown at five-year intervals.

The resulting $F/1 - F$) points are then plotted on a log-linear graph, which can be obtained from almost any office supply or college supply store. Usually, a "four-cycle" or "five-cycle" log scale will suffice. In the example here a five-cycle log-linear graph

TABLE A–1
Procedure for Calculating Takeover Growths, Automobiles versus Horse-drawn Carriages

	Annual Production, 10^3/yr			Fractions	
Year	$N_1{}^*$ (Autos)	$N_2\dagger$ (Carriages)	N (N_1+N_2)	F (N_1/N)	$\dfrac{F}{1 - F}$
1899	3	905	908	.0033	.0033
1904	22	937	959	.0230	.0235
1909	124	828	952	.130	.149
1914	548	538	1086	.505	1.02
1919	1652	216	1868	.884	7.62
1924	3186	30	3216	.990	99.0
1929	4455	4	4459	.999	999.

*U.S. Department of Commerce, *Historical Statistics of the United States—Colonial Times to 1970* (Washington, D.C.:Bureau of the Census, 1975), p. 176.
†Ibid., p.696.

has been used (to show how the data fit a straight line over such a large extrapolation).

Figure A–2 shows the results. Year-to-year data are shown from 1899 to 1910, although those data are not included in the table. The almost incredible conclusion is that a forecaster in 1905 could have projected, when only about 2 percent of the takeover had occurred, that automobiles would take over 50 percent of the sales sometime between 1912 and 1915—less than 10 years forward! Or, that some 90 percent of the market would be captured by automobiles between 1918 and 1920—only 15 years forward! Looking at a picture of a 1905 automobile, you would agree that such a projection would have been a bold one!

The point is that *quantitative* projections can be made using this procedure. The fraction of takeover, in the auto/carriage growth, could have been projected for any year after 1905 with surprisingly good results. And, the projection could have been made by anyone having the sales data—and a sheet of log-linear graph paper.

As a second example, the growth methods can also be applied to the fractional adoptions of a new product by households (or offices, factories, and stores). In this case you need to develop a table showing the following data in five columns:

- the year
- number of households adopting the new product that year
- total number of candidate households that year
- fraction, F, of adoptions
- growth/ungrowth fraction, $F/(1 - F)$.

This time the procedure is illustrated by Table A–2 for the household adoptions of automobiles. The results are, again, shown in Figure A–2. In this case, the curve suggests a forecaster in 1905 (when less than 1 percent of households had registered cars) could have projected that some 15 years later 50 percent of all households would own automobiles. The actual growth/ungrowth data points decline from the straight after 1920 (Curve A), indicating that not all families were candidates for automobiles. If 85 percent of the families had been assumed to be candidates, the adoption curve would follow the straight-line projection to 1930 (Curve B). The uncertainty in the fraction of candidate families would have had only a small effect on forecasts up to 50 percent adoption.

TABLE A–2
Example of Procedure for Calculating Adoption Growths of Automobiles per Household

Year	Numbers, 10^3		Fractions	
	N_1* (Auto Registrations)	N† (Households)	F	$\dfrac{F}{1-F}$
1900	8	16,000	.0005	.0005
1905	77	17,900	.0043	.0043
1910	460	20,200	.0227	.0232
1915	2,330	22,500	.104	.116
1920	8,130	24,500	.332	.50
1925	17,500	27,500	.636	1.74
1930	23,000	30,000	.767	3.30

* Historical Statistics of the United States, p. 716.
† Ibid., p. 43.

Clearly, both the substitution and adoption logistic-growth methods are powerful and useful for business planners.

More Complicated Growths

The growth/ungrowth curves for most technology (or new business) takeovers show a straight-line behavior over a remarkably large range, when plotted on a log-linear graph. That was the case for the auto/carriage substitution growth. This characteristic makes the F/ (1 − F) growth curve an unusually powerful tool for forecasting.

Unfortunately, nature is not quite so kind in many types of growth other than business takeovers. First, the F/(1 − F) curve might not show such a straight-line behavior for the more unruly kinds of growth. And, second, some growths in nature (and economics) have fluctuations superimposed on the underlying "secular" growth. Examples include human weight growth (as discussed in Chapter 2), various population growths, and our GNEC (as well as GNP) growths. Where a relatively long history is available, it is convenient to find a more empirical growth curve to represent the underlying secular growth. With such an empirical curve, it is easier to identify any systematic growth oscillations or growth waves.

The selection of an empirical growth curve (when the growth/ungrowth curve is not linear) can be difficult. Generally, three or four parameters must be selected to achieve an appropriate fit. Such a process is somewhat arbitrary, but the selection of the growth equation does not change the conclusion about the superimposed long wave (in GNEC growth, for example), as long as the secular growth covers several cycles. An inappropriate normalization of the wave can, obviously, make the superimposed wave appear to have higher peaks relative to the valleys or vice versa. But, the long wave, itself, cannot be eliminated or changed by the basic choice of the underlying secular curve.

The most common way to adjust the Equation (7) to approximate nonperfect growths (other than oscillatory effects) is to adopt a more generalized logistic equation, such as:

$$n = \frac{N}{(1 + ce^{-\alpha t})^\beta} \tag{12}$$

or

$$F = \frac{1}{(1 + ce^{-\alpha t})^\beta} \tag{13}$$

where c and β are additional constants to control the location (in time) and the shape of the curve. This type of equation has been used by Herman Kahn and others. (See the appendix of his book *World Economic Development,*(Morrow Quill Paperbacks; 1979).

By substituting

$$c = e^{\alpha t_0}$$

Equation (13) can be rewritten

$$F = \frac{1}{[1 + e^{-\alpha(t - t_n)}]^\beta} \tag{14}$$

which simply allows the time axis to be shifted by a time interval t_0. Although Equation (14), and the other forms of logistic equations, must utilize a time span from $t = -\infty$ to $t = +\infty$ to allow a complete growth from $F = 0$ to $F = 1$, in practice it is usually sufficient to allow a growth from $F = 0.001$ to $F = 0.999$, or even $F = 0.01$ to $F = 0.99$. Hence, it may be convenient to choose t_0 (and consquently c) such that $F = 0.001$ (or $F = 0.01$, or some other value) for $t = 0$.

In this case, the reference time is always t = 0 and negative time is eliminated. Actually, of course, the logistic equation would still permit growth from F = 0 to F = 0.001, but for all practical purposes that part of the growth can generally be ignored.

In fitting a logistic curve to U.S. population growth or GNEC growth, it is generally necessary to use Equation (13) or (14) with $\beta = 2$

$$F = \frac{1}{(1 + cd^{-\alpha t})^2} \qquad (15)$$

For electricity growth, a still larger value of β ($\beta = 4$) is required to describe the growth satisfactorily. Equation (13) is a solution of the differential equation

$$\frac{dF}{dt} = \alpha \beta F (1 - F^{1/\beta}) \qquad (16)$$

and, for $\beta = 2$, the solution is Equation (15). For increasing values of β (for $\beta > 1$), the fraction F tends to grow more abruptly and the inflection point of the growth curve occurs at somewhat lower values of F (F < 0.5).

The point of maximum growth rate, the inflection point, can be found by setting

$$\frac{d}{dt} \left(\frac{dF}{dt} \right) = 0$$

For Equation (13), this occurs at

$$F = \left(\frac{\beta}{\beta + 1} \right)^{\beta} \qquad (17)$$

For $\beta = 1$, the maximum growth (and the inflection point for the curvature) occurs at F = 0.5, and the growth curve can be shown to be symmetrical about F = 0.5. For $\beta = 2$, the inflection point occurs at F = 0.44; for $\beta = 3$, it occurs at F = 0.42. Hence, for these latter cases F grows predominantly during the period after reaching the inflection point. Quite obviously, the growth curve loses its symmetry for $\beta \neq 1$.

As discussed in Chapter 3 and Appendix B, these special forms of the growth law, especially to approximate the population or GNEC growths, are useful only for limited projections. They are not recommended for projections beyond 50 years.

APPENDIX B

POPULATION GROWTHS

Purpose: Appendix B describes how population growths in various nations have deviated from normal S-curve behaviors. It supplies some background for uncertainty estimates to be applied to projections of population-related growths, such as GNEC and GNP.

The mathematician would regard population growths of nations as unruly—though not as unruly as human weight growth. Human population growths do tend to show an S-growth behavior, but they almost always deviate from a pure logistic growth. Those deviations can be blamed on various disturbances in nature's wishes that are brought about by mankind—disturbances such as agricultural improvements, medical advances, birth-control practices, and warfare.

In his growth research earlier this century, the biologist R. Pearl (*The Biology of Population Growth*) measured alternative organic "population growths," such as yeast cells in a culture and fruit flies in a confined environment. His results for yeast-cell growth follow a growth/ungrowth straight line with excellent precision, from about 1 percent to 99 percent of full growth. Apparently yeast cells are not able to outsmart nature. Even the population growth of fruit flies appears well-behaved, although the measurements show a tendency for the growth to oscillate somewhat when the growth fraction reaches about 90 percent.

How unruly is the population growth of a nation? Actually, a surprisingly good growth/ungrowth curve can be fit to U.S. population growth from 1790 to 1980, if an asymptotic growth of about 300 million is chosen. For this choice, the growth/ungrowth curve is fairly good from about 1 percent in 1790 to approximately 75 percent in 1980. However, population growths for most other nations are not so well-behaved.

In spite of the frequent cases of population-growth anomalies, a study of them allows some estimate of the uncertainties typical in long-range growth projections. In particular, a good estimate can come from a comparison of population growths for various countries, as projected by Pearl and Reed in 1925, relative to actual data in 1950 and 1975. In *Energy in the Future,* Putnam reported such a comparison for 25-year population projections. We can now extend those comparisons for 50-year projections from 1925 to 1975.

Table B–1 summarizes the percentage errors associated with 25- and 50-year projections for seven industrialized countries or combinations of countries chosen for comparison here. In the table, Norway, Sweden, and Denmark have been combined into Scandinavia; England and Scotland into the United Kingdom; and East and West Germany into Germany. The numbers shown in the table indicate the percent deviations between the population projected by Pearl and Reed and the subsequent measured population. A plus number indicates that the projected population exceeded the actual one, and a minus number implies the converse.

TABLE B–1
Projected-Population/Actual-Population Expressed as a Percentage Error for Seven Industrialized Regions

	Percent Excess of Projected Actual	
	25 Years	50 Years
United States	− 1	−21
United Kingdom	+15	+11
Germany	+58	+48
France	− 2	−19
Italy	−11	−21
Scandinavia	− 5	−12
Japan	−13	−26
Mean deviation	15	23
Without Germany	8	18

The largest deviation for the 25-year projection was the one shown for Germany. There the projected population was almost 60 percent too high, an error that was almost four times that of any of the other deviations for a 25-year projection. Part of this error is due to the six million people exterminated during the Nazi regime and two million killed during World War 2. That death toll in itself could account for a population diminution in the 1930s and 1940s of more than 10 percent, while the selective removal of men normally approaching the age of parenthood must have had a further depressing effect on population growth.

The mean deviation for all seven cases is 15 percent for the 25-year projection. If the error for Germany is removed (based on its unusual conditions), the mean deviation is only 8 percent. The projection for U.S. population growth appears to be remarkably good.

The errors for the 50-year projection are, understandably, much larger, although the deviations are more uniform. The error for Germany is still about twice as large as the others, indicating that population recovery was not apparent even 30 years after the war. The mean deviation for the 50-year projection is 23 percent, but only 18 percent if Germany is excluded. It should be recognized that the projections would be much worse for developing and underdeveloped countries, where a population explosion occurred over the last few decades.

In summary, it appears that logistic growth projections of population growth for industrialized countries might typically show uncertainties of 12 percent (or less) for 25-year projections, and 24 percent (or less) for the longer 50-year projections. As discussed in Chapter 2, those uncertainties might be pessimistic for future projections of population growths in industrialized countries, especially the United States, where growths appear to be stabilizing.

How significant are the projection uncertainties relative to other factors affecting the GNEC and GNP growths? GNEC growth shows a cyclic behavior with a period of 50 to 60 years and an amplitude of 20 percent. Over a 25-year period, GNEC could grow from as little as 0.8 times to as much as 1.2 times its underlying logistic growth. Hence, the growth from the long-wave effect itself can be as large as 50 percent from minimum to maximum. In contrast, the uncertainty of less than 12 percent for the projection of the underlying secular growth of GNEC would be relatively insignificant.

However, the uncertainty associated with a 50-year projection could be quite large relative to the long-wave effect (which would cancel over a 50-year period). Largely for these reasons, projections in this book have been limited primarily to 35 years.

APPENDIX C

INNOVATION CLUSTERING

Purpose: Appendix C compares macroinnovation *clustering with the much larger data base for* basic innovation *clustering. Primary emphasis is placed on Mensch's studies of basic innovation frequencies.*

The primary intent of *Recollecting the Future* has been to review, explain, and illustrate for you, the general reader, some interesting and useful principles of technology innovation, business growths, the long economic wave, and their projectabilities. A secondary goal has been to stimulate in you sufficient interest to encourage further reading on the fundamental principles. A very large literature base exists on these and related subjects, and the bibliographies included in this book should be helpful in that respect.

Technology innovation and innovation clustering have been popular subjects in a variety of technical and nontechnical books and articles. The discussion of Chapter 6, Technology Macroinnovations as Sources of Economic Booms, presents some of the background on that subject, but generally follows a slightly different course than usually found. The hierarchy of technology innovations presented there includes:

- macroinnovations
- basic technology innovations
- improvement innovations
- pseudoinnovations (or cosmetic innovations)

With the possible exception of macroinnovations, the other classifications generally follow the convention of most literature on this subject.

Actually, it might be argued that the macroinnovations, as defined here, are similar to the major innovations discussed by Schumpeter in his two-volume book *Business Cycles* published in the 1930s. Mensch, in his more recent *Stalemate in Technology* has expanded on the Schumpeter long-wave theory by putting greater emphasis on the role of *basic* technology innovations. In addition to the book by Mensch, several other books have recently appeared on the subject. Two books, one by Van Duijn (*The Long Wave in Economic Life*) and one by Freeman, Clarke, and Soete (*Unemployment and Technical Innovation*), should be particularly useful for the more dedicated reader.

The definition, selection, and timing of *basic* technology innovations have received considerable attention in most discussions of the long economic wave. Mensch has identified "basic technology innovations" as those leading to entirely new industries, a definition that others generally follow. Still, as he and other authors point out, value judgments must be made in the selection of what innovations will be included, and when the initial implementation occurred. Those judgments vary somewhat from author to author, but there is a reassuring consistency in their selections.

In *Recollecting the Future* the macroinnovations have also been selected arbitrarily, although the emphasis is more on *systems* of technology innovations that have typically led to very important industries, relative to their economic and sociological impact. Macroinnovations, were chosen that were amenable to some measurement of industrial growth following their implementation. As a result of the broader nature of macroinnovations, several basic innovations frequently contribute to a single macroinnovation as defined here. For example, in the 1880 innovation wave, about 15 of Mensch's basic innovations, or 30 percent of his list, are associated with a single macroinnovation—electrification. Likewise, some 20 percent of the basic innovations in the 1935 surge belong to the single macroinnovation defined as polymer chemistry. In all, approximately 80 percent of Mensch's basic innovations in two waves can be associated with some 20 or so macroinnovations and 60 percent of them can be identified with the 10 macroinnovations selected here for detailed study.

In contrast, a few of the macroinnovations chosen in this book have little or no contributing basic technology innovations. For example, the movie industry was chosen as an economically (and socially) important macroinnovation associated with the 1880 innovation surge. Although Mensch does not indicate a related basic innovation, Van Duijn does include motion picture film (and the kinetoscope) among his basic technology innovations. A more obvious anomaly might be the inclusion of automatic home appliances as a macroinnovation. Presumably the mechanical or electrical equipment in an automatic laundry or kitchen appliance does not have sufficient technology content to justify a label of basic technology innovation for any of that equipment. Automatic home appliances as a group have been included as a macroinnovation because of their profound economic and sociological impacts.

Various authors writing on the long economic wave have generally accepted the principle that basic technology innovations tend to occur somewhat discontinuously in time. It also has been generally agreed that these innovations occur more frequently during the depression and recovery phases of the long cycle in contrast to the prosperity and stagnation phases. There are, however, disputes on the precise timing, the swarming principle, and the role of innovations (i.e., cause or effect) in the long economic wave. In spite of the points of disagreement, there appear to be more arguments drawing the various positions together than separating them.

Figure C–1 illustrates frequency distributions of innovations based on Mensch's and Van Duijn's tables of basic innovations. The curves represent averaged frequency distributions that were developed from five-point moving averages of the innovation dates. The results are quite similar, though the Van Duijn selection shows broader peaks and somewhat later peak times for the first and third waves. Probably one should not attach too much significance to the 1825–1840 data, both because of the meagerness of that data and the larger uncertainties. While the 1880 (or 1885) peak is quite consistent for the two sources, the Van Duijn data for the last wave imply an innovation peak somewhat later than that of Mensch—suggesting that basic innovations continued further into the economic spring. Largely on the basis of this timing, Van Duijn argues that new economic waves are initiated basically by other factors (for example, capital equipment replacement). Actually, if the innovation frequency already begins to rise during the depres-

FIGURE C–1
Illustration of Innovation Frequency Distributions*

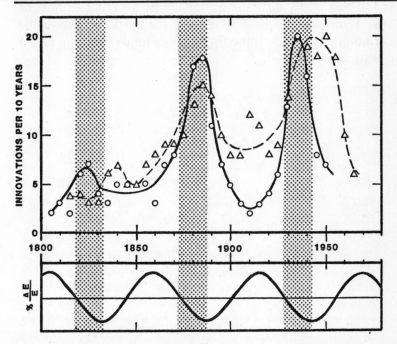

*Mensch is represented by circles and a solid curve. Van Duijn is represented by triangles and dashed curve data. Bottom figure shows energy deviation curve with bands to illustrate the depression quartiles.

sion phase, it is hard to deny that technology innovations might have some role in the recovery, even though the innovations may continue into the recovery period.

It has been argued by Freeman, Clarke, and Soete that the swarming effect described by Schumpeter is really a swarming of innovation implementations, not a swarming of innovations themselves. Certainly, the swarming of business growths resulting from basic technology innovations (or macroinnovations) is conspicuous from the various business growth curves indicated in Chapter 7. However, it would appear that some swarming of both the innovations and their implementations occurs, based on data presented here. Again, the arguments seem to be more a matter of degree than of existence.

In summary, it is clear that the choice of various candidates for identification as basic innovations and the choice of innovation dates tend to be slightly different as defined by different authors or evaluators. Even with these differences, there still appear to be significant nonuniformities in the time flow of innovations and their implementations.

APPENDIX D

BUSINESS GROWTH RELIABILITY AND GROWTH SWARMING

Purpose: Appendix D emphasizes two aspects of the growth/ ungrowth method: (1) potential factors that affect, or appear to affect, the precision of takeover growths, and (2) the large data base for growth swarming.

The use of the growth/ungrowth law for business projections was introduced in Chapter 3 and has been used extensively throughout the book. The potential value of that principle to business people can hardly be overstated. But, what can be said about the faithfulness of industrial growths?

Factors Affecting the Precision

It was observed in Chapter 3 that industrial growths might actually be expected to obey nature's growth laws even more religiously than organic growths. Whether we look at substitution, adoption, or imitation growths, they each follow the fundamental principle that the rate of growth of a growth fraction, F, is jointly proportional to the fraction already grown, and the fraction yet to grow. Mathematically, this is expressed:

$$\frac{dF}{dt} = \alpha\, F\, (1 - F)$$

That equation is exactly the same as the one identified as Equation (6) in Appendix A.

Potentially, the continuity of a new-technology substitution growth could be temporarily disturbed by a major social disaster, such as a major war or a boycott. For example, the steady takeover growth of air versus rail travel was interrupted during World War II when the railroads were pressed into service for abnormally large traffic involving troop movements. The takeover growth of synthetic versus natural rubber was actually accelerated during the same war when the East Indian supply of natural rubber became unavailable. These growths returned to their more traditional behavior after the war.

Some deviation of individual growth points from the growth/ungrowth line can be expected when the total population of data points is small—10 to 20 points. This can frequently be the case for imitation growths, where only a few large companies might be involved. These two reservations are unusual and should be apparent to a user when they are encountered.

A more subtle kind of frustration can come from another source—the appropriate choice of the eligible total population base for calculating the fraction F. This problem arises most frequently in adoption growths. Usually the eligible population base is 100 percent of families, 100 percent of dwellings, or perhaps, 100 percent of adults. For example, historical adoption curves have shown that 100 percent of dwellings have been candidates for appliances such as electric refrigerators, automatic washers, electric mixers, and TV sets. Some 85 percent of families were also candidates for automobiles in the 1900–1930 growth period. In contrast, only about 60 percent of dwellings have been candidates for dishwashers, disposals, and air conditioning. For electric clothes dryers and electric blankets, the fraction of eligible homes has been around 80 percent. Since that eligibility fraction cannot be ascertained until some 40 to 60 percent of the growth has occurred, this does impose one limitation on the projectability of adoption growths. Still, projections made at a time when only 5 or 10 percent of growth has occurred can be fairly reliable up to, perhaps, 40 or 50 percent even though the final growth fraction might only be 70 or 80 percent of the apparent market. Can the ultimate (or asymptotic) growth fraction be estimated at an early time, for example, when 5 percent has occurred? Perhaps it can in some cases. Alternatively, the business planner can examine various growth curves assuming, say, 100, 80, and 60 percent of families or dwellings as eligible candidates for ultimate adoption.

Another obvious point is that a continuing *replacement* market can exist for most home appliances (and automobiles) since they ultimately wear out or become obsolete. The adoption growth curve, then, is only useful for the first generation of a new product growth. If replacement (or displacement) becomes important because of obsolescence, a substitution growth can frequently be developed.

Substitution growths usually grow to a 100 percent takeover (instead of a partial takeover), but exceptions can occur. The substitution of detergents for soap illustrates this point. Fisher and Pry noted that the 15 percent of soap used as bath and facial soap was not a candidate for displacement by detergents. Hence, the eligible takeover fraction for detergents was 85 percent. Another example is the apparent takeover fraction of total energy use by energy for electricity generation. With electricity generation accounting for 36 percent of total energy in 1985, the growth/ungrowth curve for this substitution implies that about 70 percent of GNEC is eligible for ultimate takeover by the electricity-supply industry.

Two other interesting cases of partial takeovers are home electrification and home adoption of radios. Home electrification in the 1900–1930 period is found to obey the growth/ungrowth law quite faithfully if only *urban* homes are counted as eligible candidates. A second growth/ungrowth curve can be found for *rural* homes, extending from 1930 to 1950 approximately. This latter growth was motivated by government-subsidized rural-electrification programs during the depression years—a remarkably far-sighted government program during the low-growth phase of the economic long wave.

The household adoption of radios is equally interesting for somewhat related reasons. In this case, the adoption takeover is found to follow the usual growth/ungrowth behavior if only electrified homes are regarded as eligible candidates.

In summary, growth projections made when only 5 to 10 percent of growth has occurred can generally be quite accurate (for the remaining 90 to 95 percent of growth) if the adoption or substitution proceeds to a 100 percent takeover. If the ultimate takeover is expected to be less than 100 percent, the final takeover fraction generally cannot be ascertained until about 30 percent of the growth has occurred. Even without advance information on the ultimate eligible fraction, a growth/ungrowth projection can still be useful if alternative projections can be developed for several assumed ultimate takeover fractions. Generally, the projected growth behavior in the first 30 to 40 percent of takeovers will not be seriously affected by ultimate takeover fractions ranging for 70 to 100 percent.

Growth Swarming

It is quite clear from the commercial growths of new products during the 1900–1925 and 1955–1980 periods that a significant amount of growth *swarming* has occurred. This growth swarming of implementation can apparently be related to the growth clustering of technology innovations some 20 to 40 years earlier. However, there are exceptions, such as the case for air-travel versus rail-travel, where the commercial takeover waited until a subsequent long growth cycle.

The evaluation of commercial-growth swarming in Chapter 7 was based primarily on the Schumpeter thesis that economic growth leans heavily on the introduction of a few very important *macroinnovations*. These macroinnovations might be quite unrelated, but the resulting commercial growths seem to profit from the economic boost coming from the others. For example, there appears to be no obvious reason why electrification, automobiles, and coal-tar chemicals should show growth surges at the same time. Likewise, there is little reason why polymer chemicals, television, and automatic electric appliances should show common growths in the subsequent growth surge. Nevertheless, swarming did occur in each of those two periods, possibly because of the prior clustering of technology innovations or, perhaps, a more favorable business-growth climate for other reasons. Moreover, the swarming extended to new products in many other sectors of business, for example, food, home construction, news print, pharmaceuticals, and still other sectors.

While the Schumpeter thesis of macroinnovations was followed in this book, the alternative (and related) Mensch thesis of basic innovations could have been pursued. In the latter approach the much larger number of basic innovations would be examined and related to commercial growths resulting from those sources. If this latter course should be pursued, the choices of technology-innovation clusters and subsequent commercial growth swarming should be reasonably representative of the most important industries contributing to the overall economy. In this appendix, the latter approach is illustrated primarily to show that the results are similar to those already observed using the macroinnovation approach.

In this more detailed examination, some 40 commercial growths have been selected to be representative, not only of Mensch's basic technology innovations, but also of six important sectors of our economy:

- food
- clothing
- housing
- household appliances
- medical/personal-care items
- transportation
- communication/recreation

In addition a few growths have been added in a miscellaneous category largely because these technology substitutions contributed more generally—in some cases to several of the other sectors.

Table D–1 lists 15 new product commercializations with their year of peak growth and characteristic growth times. In a few of the cases, the peak years and growth times have been estimated, as indicated in the table. The average peak year for growth appears to be approximately 1910 and the average characteristic takeover time about 30 years. Growths for electric irons, fans, and such are indicated (for the household sector) without specific data simply to show that other items might be included.

Figure D–1 illustrates the growth/ungrowth behavior of technology innovations and their implementations associated with the 1880 innovation surge. First, a growth/ungrowth trend line is shown (at the left) for the growth surge of the basic technology innovations as reported by Mensch in *Stalemate in Technology*. The peak growth time for these innovations appears to be around 1880. The band of 15 growth/ungrowth lines at the right shows the general behavior of commercial implementations for the new

TABLE D–1
Background Growth Data on 15 Commercializations, 1900–1925 Period

Group	Item	Type*	Peak Year, T	ΔTg	T-1880
Food	Commercial versus home canning	S	1906	42	26
	Chemical fertilizer	A	1912†	50†	32
Clothing	Rayon versus silk	S	1927	26	47
Housing	Urban electrification	A	1921	29	41
Household	Electric irons, fans, etc.	–	–	–	–
Medical/ personal care	Aspirin	A	1910†	20†	30
Transportation	Automobiles versus carriages	S	1914	12	34
	Automobiles per household	A	1921	14	41
	Electric trolleys	A	1906	36	26
Communication/ recreation	Telephones per household	A	1910	30	30
	Snapshot photography	A	1912†	25†	32
	Movie attendance	G	1923	34	43
Miscellaneous	Open-hearth versus Bessemer steel	S	1907	42	27
	By-product coke ovens	S	1916	28	36
	By-product coke ovens	I	1908	28	28
	Linotype printing	A	1910†	20†	30
	Average		1914	29	34

* Type: S = Substitution.
    A = Adoption.
    I = Imitation.
    G = Growth (overall).
† Estimated.

FIGURE D-1

Logistic Growth Behavior of the 1880 Innovation Wave and 15 Product Substitutions/Adoptions Resulting from the Innovations

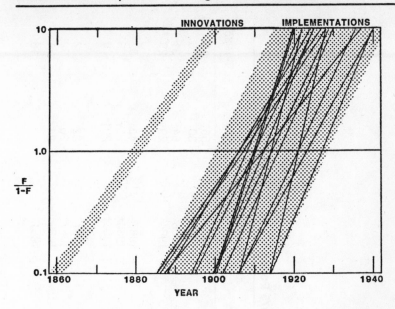

FIGURE D-2

Logistic Growth Behavior of the 1935 Innovation Wave and 25 Product Substitutions/Adoptions Resulting from the Innovations

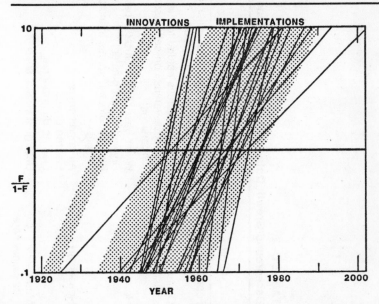

343

TABLE D–2
Background Growth Data on 25 Commercializations in the 1950–1975 Period

Group	Item	Type*	Peak Year, T	ΔTg	T-1935
Food	Margarine versus butter	S	1953	55	18
	Frozen versus canned food	S	1960	30	25
Clothing	Synthetic versus natural textiles	S	1966	54	31
	Cellulose versus non-cellulose fibers	S	1964	29	29
Housing	Water-base versus oil-base paint	S	1967	42	32
	Drywall versus plaster	S	1960†	25†	25
	Portable electric versus manual tools	S	1960†	20†	25
Household	Air conditioners	A	1967	22	32
	Electric dryers	A	1967	26	32
	Electric dishwashers	A	1969	24	34
Medical/ personal care	Detergent versus soap	S	1951	12	18

344

	Type*	Year		
Transportation				
Air versus railroad	S	1958	26	23
Jet versus piston aircraft	S	1965	7	30
Diesel versus steam locomotive	S	1951	12	16
Automatic transmission	A	1956	28	21
Power steering	A	1962	28	27
Power brakes	A	1969	28	34
Superhighways	S	1960†	30†	25
Communication/ recreation				
Television	A	1954	10	20
Color versus B&W television	S	1972	11	37
Color versus B&W photography	S	1960†	30†	25
Offset printing	S	1966	17	31
Miscellaneous				
BOP versus open-hearth steel	S	1968	11	33
Strip versus underground coal	S	1972	62	37
Oil versus coal for benzene	S	1957	23	22
Average		1962	27	30

* Type: S = Substitution
     A = Adoption
     G = Growth (overall).

† Estimated.

products identified in Table D–1. The peak growth times range from 1900 to 1925.

Table D–2 shows a similar list of 25 commercializations associated with the 1950–1975 growth period. Four cases have been estimated and a few others could have been indicated without specific data. In this case the year of peak growth is, on average, 1963, with the characteristic growth time 30 years.

Figure D–2 illustrates the growth/ungrowth behavior of technology innovations and their implementations associated with the 1935 innovation surge. Again, a growth/ungrowth trend line is shown at the left for the basic technology innovations, based on data as reported by Mensch. The band of 25 growth/ungrowth lines for commercial implementations is shown at the right, reflecting the data in Table D–2. The peak growth times range from about 1950 to 1975.

In summary, the conclusion regarding the periodic swarming of new businesses is the same whether looking at the commercialization of a relatively small number of macroinnovations or a larger number of basic innovations. Indeed, several of the growths resulting from basic innovations can contribute to the growth of a macroinnovation.

REFERENCES

References here have served as resources throughout the book and/or can be useful for further reading. They are divided into three groups:

A. General sources of statistical data,
B. General sources of information.
C. Specific sources (by chapter).

The order of presentation in categories A and B reflects approximately the frequency of use to this book. The order of presentation within individual chapters reflects the sequence in which they occurred in each chapter.

A. GENERAL SOURCES OF STATISTICAL DATA

Historical Statistics of the United States—Colonial Times to 1970. Bicentennial ed., Parts 1 and 2. Washington D.C.: U.S. Department of Commerce, Bureau of the Census, September 1975.

Statistical Abstract of the United States. Washington, D.C.: U.S. Department of Commerce. (Years from 1940 to 1985 have been used.)

1981 Annual Report to Congress. Vols. 1-3. Washington, D.C.: Energy Information Administration, DOE/EIA-0173-1,2,3, 1982. (Data from Volume 3 are most useful.)

Monthly Energy Review. Washington, D.C.: U.S. Department of Energy, DOE/EIA-0035, 1973–current.

EEI Pocketbook of Electric Utility Industry Statistics. 26th Edition. Washington, D.C.: Edison Electric Institute, 1980.

"New Generating Capacity:When, Where and by Whom?" *Power Engineering*. Published in April of each year.

Economic Almanac 1967–1968. National Industrial Conference Board. New York: Macmillan, 1969.

The World Almanac and Book of Facts. New York: Pharos Books, 1987.

Statistical Yearbook, 1981. 32nd Edition. New York: United Nations, 1983.

B. GENERAL SOURCES OF INFORMATION

Encyclopedias

Encyclopedia Americana. Danbury, Conn.: Grolier Inc., 1953.

Encyclopedia Americana. Danbury, Conn.: Grolier Inc., 1983.

Encyclopedia of Chemical Technology. 3rd Edition. New York: John Wiley & Sons, 1978.

McGraw-Hill Encyclopedia of Science and Technology. 3rd Edition. New York: McGraw-Hill, 1971.

Britannica Science and the Future Library. Volumes 1–3. Chicago: Encyclopaedia Britannica, 1982.

Books

Putnam, Palmer C. *Energy in the Future*. Princeton, New Jersey: D. Van Nostrand Company, 1953.

Mensch, Gerhard. *Stalemate in Technology*. Cambridge, Mass: Ballinger Publishing Company, 1979.

Schumpeter, J. A. *Business Cycles,* New York: McGraw-Hill, 1939.

Pearl, Raymond. *The Biology of Population Growth*. New York: Alfred A. Knopf Publishing Company, 1930.

Reports and Articles

Kondratieff, N. D., "The Long Wave in Economic Life." *The Review of Economic Statistics,* Vol. XVII, no. 6, November 1935, pp. 105–15.

Fisher, J. C. and R. H. Pry. "A Simple Substitution Model of Technological Change." *Technological Forecasting and Social Change* 3, 1971, pp. 75–88.

Mansfield, Edwin. "Technical Change and the Rate of Imitation." *Econometrica* 29, no. 4, October 1961, pp. 741–66.

Marchetti C., and N. Nakicenovic. "The Dynamics of Energy Systems and the Logistic Substitution Model." *International Institute for Applied Systems Analysis,* Austria, December 1979.

Forrester, J. W. "Growth Cycles." *De Economist* 125, NR, 1977, pp. 525–43.

C. SPECIFIC SOURCES (by chapter)

Chapter 1

Kondratieff, N. D. (See Reports and Articles.)
Schumpeter, J. A. (See Books.)

Chapter 2

Pearl, Raymond. (See Books.)
Putnam, Palmer C. (See Books.)

Chapter 3

Mansfield, Edwin. (See Reports and Articles.)
Encyclopedia Americana. "Coal." Volume 7, Danbury, Conn.: Grolier Inc., 1951, pp. 227–232.

Fisher, J. C. and R. H. Pry. (See Reports and Articles.)
Marchetti, C. and N. Nakicenovic. (See Reports and Articles.)
Marchetti, C. "Society as a Learning System: Discovery, Invention, and Innovation Cycles Revisited." *Technological Forecasting and Social Change* 18, 1980, pp. 267–82.

Marchetti, C. "On Energy Systems in Historical Perspective." 1980 Bernard Gregory Lecture at CERN, Geneva, Switzerland, 1980.

Marchetti, C. "Swings, Cycles, and the Global Economy." *New Scientist* 1454, May 2, 1985, pp. 12–15.

Marchetti, C. "Infrastructures for Energy." American Academy of Engineering Workshop on Infrastructures, Cape Cod, Mass., August 11–13, 1986.

Chapter 4

Kondratieff, N. D. (See Reports and Articles.)

Schurr, S. H. "Energy in America's Future—The Choices Before Us." A study by the staff of the RFF National Energy Strategies Project. Baltimore, Md.: Johns Hopkins University Press, 1979.

Jevons, W. S. "The Coal Question." *Reprints of Economic Classics.* New York: Augustus Kelley Publisher,1965.

Stewart, Hugh B. "Transitional Energy Policy, 1980–2030." New York: Pergamon Press, 1981.

Chapter 5

Costanza, Robert. "Embodied Energy and Economic Valuation." *Science* 240, December 12, 1980.

Chapter 6

Schumpeter, J. A. (See Books.)

Mensch, Gerhard. (See Books.)

Van Duijn, J. J. *The Long Wave in Economic Life.* London: George Allen and Unwin Publishers, 1983.

Forrester, J. W. (See Reports and Articles.)

Forrester, J. W., Nathaniel J. Mass, and Charles J. Ryan. "The System Dynamics National Model: Understanding Socio-Economic Behavior and Policy Alternatives." *Technological Forecasting and Social Change* 9, 1976, pp. 51–68.

Forrester, J. W. "Changing Economic Patterns." *Technology Review* 80, no. 8, August/September 1978.

David, Jr., Edward E. "Industrial Research in American: Challenge of a New Synthesis." *Science* 209, July 1980, pp. 133–39.

Chapter 8

Mensch, Gerhard. (See Books.)

Forrester, J. W. (See Chapter 6 references.)

Graham, A. K. and P. M. Senge. "A Long-Wave Hypothesis of Innovation." *Technological Forecasting and Social Change,* 17, 1980, pp. 283–311.

Van Duijn, J. J. (See Chapter 6 references.)

Freeman, C., J. Clark, and L. Soete. *Unemployment and Technical Innovation*. London: Frances Pinter Publisher, 1982.

Chapter 9

Kondratieff, N. D. (See Reports and Articles.)

Gailbraith, J. K. *The Great Crash*. Boston: Houghton Mifflin Company, 1961.

Chapter 10

Schumpeter, J. A. (See Books.)

Chapter 13

The Positive Sum Strategy: Harnessing Technology for Economic Growth. ed. Ralph Landau and Nathan Rosenberg. Washington, D.C.: National Academy Press, 1986.

Thurow, L. C. Book Review of *The Positive Sum Strategy: Harnessing Technology for Economic Growth*. *Scientific American,* September 1986, pp. 24–31.

Baily, M. N. "What Has Happened to Productivity Growth?" *Science,* October 24, 1986, pp. 443–50.

Quinn, J. B., J. J. Baruch, and P. C. Pacquette. "Technology in Services." *Scientific American* 257, no. 6, December 1987, pp. 50–58.

Thurow, L. C. "A Surge in Inequality." *Scientific American* 256, no. 5, May 1987, pp. 30–37.

Chapter 14

Kennedy, Paul. "The (Relative) Decline of America." *The Atlantic Monthly,* August 1987, pp. 29–38.

"Science in Japan: A Status Report." *Science* 233, no. 4761, July 18, 1986, p. 261 and succeeding pages.

Savage, D. G. "U.S. Students Top Only Third World in Math." *Los Angeles Times,* March 11, 1986,

Tharp, M. "High Schoolers in U.S. Lack Drive of Japan's But Show Spontaneity." *The Wall Street Journal,* March 10, 1987.

White, Merry. *The Japanese Educational Challenge: A Commitment to Children.* New York: Free Press, 1987.

Changes in Federal Funding Criteria and Industry Response. Washington, D.C.: United States General Accounting Office, GAO/RCED-87-26, February 1987.

Chapter 15

Karmin, M. W. "Jobs of the Future." *U.S. News and World Report,* December 23, 1985, pp. 40–44.

Appendix A

Fisher and Pry. (See Reports and Articles.)

Historical Statistics of the United States. (See catagory A references.)

Kahn, Herman. "World Economic Development—1979 and Beyond." New York: Morrow Quill Paperbacks, 1979, pp. 503–10.

Appendix B

Pearl, Raymond. (See Books.)

Pearl, R. and L. J. Reed. "The Growth of Human Population." *In Studies in Human Biology,* ed. R. Pearl. Baltimore, Md.: Williams and Wilkins Company, 1924.

Putnam, P. C. (See Books.)

Appendix C

Mensch, Gerhard. (See Books.)

Schumpeter, J. A. (See Books.)

Van Duijn (See Chapter 6 references.)

Freeman, Clarke and Soete (See Chapter 8 references.)

Appendix D

Fisher and Pry. (See Reports and Articles.)

Mensch. (See Books.)

INDEX